PHYSICAL AND MOTOR TESTS
IN THE
MEDFORD BOYS' GROWTH STUDY

INTERNATIONAL
RESEARCH MONOGRAPH SERIES
IN PHYSICAL EDUCATION

H. Harrison Clarke, Chairman of the Editorial Board

Physical and Motor Tests in the Medford Boy's Growth Study

H. HARRISON CLARKE

Research Professor
of Physical Education
University of Oregon

Prentice-Hall, Inc.

Englewood Cliffs, New Jersey

PHYSICAL AND MOTOR TESTS
IN THE
MEDFORD BOYS' GROWTH STUDY

H. Harrison Clarke

Library of Congress Catalog
Card Number: 71–140168

Printed in the United States of America
13–665596–3

Current printing (last digit):
10 9 8 7 6 5 4 3 2 1

PRENTICE-HALL INTERNATIONAL, INC., *London*
PRENTICE-HALL OF AUSTRALIA, PTY. LTD., *Sydney*
PRENTICE-HALL OF CANADA, LTD., *Toronto*
PRENTICE-HALL OF INDIA PRIVATE LIMITED, *New Delhi*
PRENTICE-HALL OF JAPAN, INC., *Tokyo*

To

*the Sixty-two Graduate Students
at the University of Oregon who
served as testers during the twelve years
of the Medford Boys' Growth Project*

Acknowledgments

The materials for this study are taken from the longitudinal Medford, Oregon, Boys' Growth Project. Annual testing of the boys for this project was conducted for twelve years, from 1956 to 1968 inclusive. Responsibility for the project rested with the Physical Education Research Laboratory, University of Oregon, and with the writer as Principal Investigator. Southern Orgeon College, Ashland, collaborated in the annual testing.

Many acknowledgments should be made for assistance rendered in the conduct of the Medford Boys' Growth Project. Among these are the following:

Supporting Agencies: Medford Public Schools, Southern Oregon College, Athletic Institute, Curriculum Development Fund of the Oregon State Department of Education, and the Office of Scientific and Scholarly Research and the School of Education's In-Service Program of the University of Oregon.

Medford Educators and Others: The late Dr. Leonard Mayfield, former Superintendent of Schools; Dr. Elliott Becken, Superintendent; Dr. Lee V. Ragsdale, Director of Physical Education; Louise Basford and Henry De Voss, Testing Service Directors; Wilson Slater, Clerk of the School District; Russell Acheson,

Ralph Mathews, and R. E. Wicks, physical plant officials; the principals and classroom teachers of the various Medford schools; the physical education staff; the boys who served as subjects and their parents.

Southern Oregon College: The late Dr. Theodore G. Schopf, Southern Oregon College, and his students who served as testers throughout the project.

University of Oregon: Dr. Arthur A. Esslinger, Dean, School of Health, Physical Education, and Recreation; Mrs. Ethel Cooper, Mrs. Betsy Lynch, and Mrs. Doris Maurer, secretaries; and Dr. Leona Tyler, Professor of Psychology and Dean of Graduate School, consultant.

Others: Mrs. Barbara Honeyman Heath, Monterey, California, somatotype consultant and assessor; Dr. Bhim Savara, Director, Child Study Clinic, University of Oregon Dental School, consultant; William C. Applegate, Chief Industrial Engineer, Oregon State Board of Health; Earl Lawson, M.D., Medford radiologist, for evaluating X-ray operation (skeletal age).

Research Instructors and Graduate Assistants, with present locations: Dr. Kay H. Petersen, University of Wisconsin, Madison; Dr. David H. Clarke, University of Maryland, College Park; Dr. Arne L. Olson, East Stroudsburg State College, Pennsylvania; Morgan E. Shelley, Grosmond College, California; Dr. Norman S. Watt, University of British Columbia, Canada; Dr. Etsuo Kurimoto, Juntendo University, Tokyo; Dr. James A. P. Day, Simon Fraser University, Canada; Dr. Robert B. Wilberg, University of Alberta, Canada; Dr. Jeffrey O. Miller, University of New South Wales, Australia; Dr. D. Allen Phillips, Colorado State College, Greeley, Dr. Richard A. Munroe, University of Arizona, Tuscon; Dr. Jan Broekhoff, University of Toledo, Ohio; Dr. L. Laine Santa Maria, University of Maryland, College Park; Dr. L. Richard Geser, University of Oregon, Eugene; and Dr. John Montgomery, Simon Fraser College, Canada. In addition, many graduate students from the United States and throughout the world served as testers during the twelve years of the project.

Contents

6/ Motor and
Athletic Abilities   **219**

7/ Summary and Implications   **272**

References   **292**

Other Medford Theses   **301**

PHYSICAL AND MOTOR TESTS
IN THE
MEDFORD BOYS' GROWTH STUDY

Chapter 1 / Medford Boys' Growth Study

Purpose of the Monograph

This monograph presents the significance of selected physical and motor tests in studying the growth of boys from 7 through 18 years of age. The presentation focuses on the physical and motor tests used in the Medford Boys' Growth Study, a twelve-year project conducted in the schools of Medford, Oregon. Chapter 1 provides an overall view of this growth project. Chapters 2 through 6 are devoted to representative tests used to evaluate maturity, physique type, body size, muscular strength and endurance, and motor and athletic ability. The final chapter, Chapter 7, presents a summary and conclusions and suggests some of the significant implications of this study for physical education.

The specific tests chosen for consideration were distinctive of the traits under scrutiny, were related significantly to other tests in the same category and other categories, and had relevancy for growth patterns and individual differences. For each test selected for the monograph, the following research data are given when applicable:

1

1. Description of the test as administered in the Medford project.
2. Origins of the test.
3. Modifications and better understanding of the test resulting from the Medford investigations.
4. Inter-age correlations.
5. Mean growth patterns and variability.
6. Relationships with other tests in the same category.
7. Relationships with tests in other categories.

Origins of the Medford Study

In 1955, because of troublesome problems arising from boys' interscholastic athletic competition in Oregon elementary schools, the Oregon Association of District Superintendents requested the State Joint Staff Committee, composed of representatives from the State Department of Public Health, State Education Department, and State System of Higher Education, to study whether current practices were harmful to the physical and emotional welfare of the participants. The Joint Staff Committee asked the School of Health, Physical Education, and Recreation, University of Oregon, to consider the matter, and in so doing to consult with appropriate personnel at the University of Oregon Medical School on a research plan designed to obtain answers to this problem. An elaborate ten-year research plan was developed. However, its cost was prohibitive. The Committee thus proposed that smaller phases of the problem be studied if the necessary financial support could be obtained.

Subsequently, the Physical Education Research Laboratory, University of Oregon, was able to raise a small amount to initiate a study involving certain nonmedical and nonphysiological aspects of the much more extensive plan proposed with the Medical School. The Athletic Institute, Chicago, Illinois, matched this amount, through the efforts of its president, the late Ted Bank; the Institute continued financial support for the twelve years of the project. This funding was sufficient to employ a graduate assistant, permit the administration of the selected tests, and establish a cumulative record system. The analysis of data was accomplished through theses conducted by graduate students who were members of testing teams. At the time of this writing, 76 such studies had been completed, including 52 doctoral dissertations and 24 master's theses. All of these studies have been published on Microcards and may be obtained from Microcard Publications in Health, Physical Education, and Recreation, Eugene: University of Oregon 97403.

The Medford school district was chosen for this growth study for three reasons: (1) Organized interschool athletic competition had been conducted in the fifth and sixth grades for many years, thus permitting the study of boys who participated in interscholastic athletics at this early level. (2) The Superintendent of Schools, Leonard A. Mayfield, and the Director of Physical Education, Lee V. Ragsdale, indicated strong enthusiasm and pledged financial support for the project (3) Through the interest and efforts of Theodore G. Schopf, Athletic Director, the nearby Oregon State College in Ashland volunteered testing and financial help.

Purposes of the Study

As indicated above, the initial motivation for the Medford Boys' Growth Study was to investigate problems pertaining to interschool competitive athletics among elementary school boys. The study of the elementary school athlete continued to be a concern of the project. As will be seen, however, the project became much more extensive and was planned as a comprehensive longitudinal growth study with numerous subsidiary investigations. The overall and long-range purposes were:

1. To construct physical and motor mean growth curves and growth acceleration curves, and to determine the variability of the tests used for boys 7 to 18 years of age for such traits as the following: body size, muscular strength, muscular endurance, muscular power, speed and agility, and reaction time.

2. To relate these physical and motor traits to physiological maturity, physique type, nutritional status, socio-personal adjustment, and scholastic aptitude and achievement.

3. To trace longitudinally the development of all traits mentioned above for boys who became athletes, honor-roll students, school and organization leaders, and the like.

4. To contrast all traits in the study for boys who make

and who do not make interscholastic athletic teams; to make similar contrasts for boys who score high and low on strength tests and batteries, agility and running speed, reaction time, and muscular power.

5. As concomitant studies, to revise and construct strength and other tests for boys of all ages; and to determine the interrelationships of the various traits included in the study at various ages.

Subjects

The number of subjects tested each year at the different ages is shown on the following chart. The diagonals starting at ages 7, 9, 12, and 15 represent the same boys tested annually. At some of these ages, additional subjects were included in 1959–60.

	7	8	9	10	11	12	13	14	15	16	17	18
1956–57	109		93	40	40	79	40	40	94			
1957–58		93		88			64			85		
1958–59			81		75				61		70	
1959–60				128		107				95		47
1960–61					108		83			84		
1961–62						104		78			77	
1962–63							93		69			56
1963–64								87		70		
1964–65									82		66	
1965–66										76		44
1966–67											69	
1967–68												42
TOTALS	109	93	174	256	223	290	280	266	340	315	282	189

In all instances, the Medford boys were tested within two months of their birthdays, in order to assure reasonable homogeneity as related to chronological age. No subject known to have a physical abnormality was included. The randomness of the samples is supported by the fact that all boys who met the requirement of being within two months of their birthdays were included during each test period.

The subjects' home community of Medford is located in an agricultural area at the southern end of the fertile Willamette valley of Oregon. In one socioeconomic analysis made, their parents were classified as: 42 percent professionals, proprietors, and executives; 54 percent, skilled labor, clerical, and sales; and 4 percent, unskilled labor.

In an analysis of 280 of the subjects by Irving (59), 48 (55 percent) of the 88 adult male somatotypes identified by Sheldon in his study of 40,000 males were found among the boys 9 through 15 years of age. By chi-square test, the distribution of the boys grouped into five somatotype categories did not differ significantly from the incidence of occurrence in Sheldon's monumental survey. The median inverse ponderal index (height-over-cube-root-of-weight) of the boys varied only slightly for the seven ages in this study. By extrapolating Sheldon's age distribution of these indexes to younger ages, the Medford boys fit his curve satisfactorily.

As will be seen in Chapter 5, the Medford boys were especially muscularly strong, since their mean Physical Fitness Indices ranged between 105 and 118 as contrasted with the normal expectation of 100. For all but two of the ages 7 through 18, the mean Physical Fitness Indices nearly reached, reached, or exceeded 115, the third quartile for the norms on this test. These high means are attributed to the presence of a strong physical education program in all grades of the Medford schools.

The Medford schools have consistently produced outstanding athletic teams. During the twelve years of the growth study, the high school teams were in constant contention for state championships; in one year, they won three state championships, in football, basketball, and baseball.

Although not germane to this monograph, it can be added that, academically, the school district has recorded average performances well above national norms on standard tests. Between 55 and 60 percent of its high school graduates go on to college or university. Moreover, some of the graduates enter universities with 30 to 40 hours of acceptable college credit.

Physical and Motor Tests

A listing of the physical and motor test items included in the Medford Boys' Growth Study follows.

Maturity: skeletal age and pubescent assessment.

Physique Type: somototype components of endomorphy, meso-morphy, and ectomorphy.

Body Size: standing and sitting heights, leg length, lung capac-ity, hip width, body weight, girths of arm, chest, abdomen, but-tocks, thigh, and calf, and skinfolds over triceps, apex of scapula, and lateral abdomen. Combinations of these measures were also used as indices.

Muscular Strength: right and left grip strengths, back and leg lifts, and eleven cable-tension strength tests of muscle groups throughout the body. The test batteries of Strength Index, Physical Fitness Index, and cable-tension strength average were formed from these tests and utilized.

Muscular Endurance: chinning, bar dips, and Rogers' arm strength score.

Motor Elements: standing broad jump, 60-yard shuttle run, and total-body and arm-hand reaction and movement times; athletic ability.

Descriptions of these tests will be found in the chapters where they are utilized as primary tests:

Chapter 2: maturity tests
Chapter 3: somatotype components
Chapter 4: anthropometric measures
Chapter 5: muscular strength and endurance tests
Chapter 6: motor ability elements and athletic ability

In the Medford study, measures of scholastic aptitude and achievement, personal-social status, and interests were also given annually to all subjects. These measures will not be described here since research results with these tests are not presented in this monograph.

Tester Competency

All physical and motor tests were administered by trained testers from the School of Health, Physical Education, and

Recreation, University of Oregon, and from Southern Oregon College. The testers underwent intensive training to prepare them for the proper administration of the tests. They were carefully instructed and supervised by qualified personnel.

The graduate students assigned the task of assessing skeletal age underwent initial training for X-ray assessment for several months. Initial instruction was provided by Bhim S. Savara, D.D., Director of the Child Study Clinic, University of Oregon Dental School, Portland. An objectivity coefficient of .96 was obtained from correlating independent skeletal age assessments of the same hand-wrist X rays by different testers, thus demonstrating a satisfactory degree of agreement between testers. Subsequently, assessors were trained on X rays from which proper skeletal age assessments had previously been made. When assessors obtained correlations over .90 on a sample of these X rays, they were considered competent for this purpose.

The somatotype pictures were taken by members of the testing team with special competency in that area. The assessment of the three somatotype components, endomorphy, mesomorphy, and ectomorphy, were made by Barbara Honeyman Heath of Monterey, California, who served as somatotype consultant for the Medford Boys' Growth Study, and is widely recognized as an expert in this work. For several years, she was associated with William H. Sheldon, as somatotype assessor. She has been engaged in somatotype research for more than twenty-five years.

For the anthropometric tests and all cable-tension strength tests, objectivity coefficients were obtained each year of the project. After instruction and practice, the testers were required to administer the tests independently to 30 subjects, and the scores recorded by two testers on the same subjects were correlated. If the resultant coefficient did not compare favorably with the standard established for each test, the testers continued to practice until the standard was achieved. For the cable-tension tests, the correlation coefficients ranged between .87 and .98. The objectivity coefficients for the anthropometric tests were in the high .90's.

The tests that comprise the Strength Index battery were administered by testers from Southern Oregon College. These testers were trained and supervised by Dr. Theodore G. Schopf at that institution, a highly competent and experienced tester in this area. Dr. Schopf participated in all testing sessions at Medford for the full twelve years of the project and personally administered nearly all leg lifts on the dynamometer. Comparably trained testers administered the motor tests included in the Medford project.

Growth Analyses

The Medford Boys' Growth Study was designed to permit four types of growth analysis; refer to the preceding chart of subjects to follow this explanation.

1. *Cross-sectional analysis* with different boys at each age. During the first year of testing, cross-sectional samples of 40 boys at each age 9 through 15 were tested.

2. *Longitudinal analysis* with the same boys at each age. During the first year, longitudinal samples of approximately 100 boys each were started at ages 7, 9, 12, and 15. Over the period of the project, these numbers increased, as the younger subjects overlapped the earlier ages of the older subjects. Thus, only one group of boys was tested from 7 to 9 years, but two groups were tested from 9 to 12 years, three groups from 12 to 15 years, and four groups from 15 to 18 years.

3. *Convergence analysis* at the end of four years of the project, utilizing the boys in the longitudinal phase at the overlapping years. Thus, the original 7-year-old boys overlapped the original 9's, the original 9's overlapped the original 12's, and the original 12's overlapped the original 15's. This type of analysis of growth data was proposed by Bell (3, 4) in order to approximate longitudinal results for many years with a number of short longitudinal series.

4. *Single-year analysis.* For many of the relationship studies, it was desirable to hold constant the effect of chronological age upon variables that change with age. This partialing effect was realized by taking subjects of the same age. As seen in the chart presented above, large numbers of subjects were accumulated at most of the ages by the end of the project.

General Supervision

During each of the twelve years of the Medford Boys' Growth Study, a graduate assistant was appointed to assist the Principal Investigator in its general supervision. This assistant was carefully selected for his testing competency, administrative ability, professional integrity, and personal reliability. In addition, the Supervisor of the Physical Education Research Laboratory assisted with the project in many ways.

Chapter **2** / **Maturity**

The major maturity measure used in the Medford Boys' Growth Study was skeletal age based on an X ray of the hand and wrist. Pubescent assessments were also made. This chapter is devoted to a consideration of these two tests in maturity evaluation. The chapter is devoted to a consideration of these two tests in maturity evaluation. The primary emphasis is on skeletal age, since it was found to be the more reliable and useful of the two measures.

Skeletal Age as a Maturity Indicator

The most commonly used indicator of physiological maturity in growth studies of boys and girls is skeletal age, the degree of development of the skeleton as shown by X rays. Each bone begins as a primary center of ossification and passes through various stages of enlargement and shaping of the ossified area; in some cases, an epiphysis is acquired. This process continues until the adult form is reached, when the epiphyses fuse with the main body of the bone. These changes can be easily seen in an X ray, which distinguishes the ossified areas from the areas of cartilage where ossification has not yet begun.

Skeletal maturity is judged from the number of ossified centers present and the stage of development of each. In theory, any or all parts of the skeleton could be used to provide an assessment of maturity. In practice, however, the hand-wrist area is the most convenient and commonly used part. This practice has been found acceptable, since several investigators have shown that the ossification pattern of the hand-wrist area closely approximates the degree of ossification of the skeleton as a whole.

The first report of the roentgenographic method of studying physical growth based upon X rays of skeletal development was published in 1905 by Pryor (81), ten years after the discovery of the roentgen ray. Since that time, various scientists have analyzed X rays of skeletal areas in terms of the extent or quality of ossification registered. A number of these investigators developed procedures for estimating anatomical or skeletal age.

Prior to 1907, four general processes were proposed to assess skeletal development, as follows: age of appearance of the carpal bones and epiphyses of the hand; stage and time of fusion of epiphyses and diaphyses; various schemes for determining the size of the carpal bones; and such ratios as sum of diameters of carpal bones to width of wrist, sum of least distance between carpal bones to width of wrist, and sum of greatest diameters of carpal bones to sum of least distance between them.

In 1937, Todd (102) published an atlas containing hand-wrist X-ray films separately for boys and girls. Age standards were provided for every three months during the first year and for every six months thereafter until maturity was reached (set at 19 years). In use, the X rays of children whose skeletal maturity was to be assessed were compared with those in the atlas in terms of degree of ossification of the bones, the contours of the ends and shafts of the bones, and the degree of fusion of the epiphyses. This evaluation provides a measure of the years and months of the child, as skeletal development in his progress toward maturity. Children whose skeletal ages are the same as their chronological ages are maturing normally; those whose skeletal ages are more or less than their chronological ages are, respectively, advanced or retarded in months of each boy's birthday.

In 1950 and again in 1959, Greulich and Pyle (49) revised this atlas, utilizing the original Todd X rays but also including additional data obtained during the intervening years. In the Medford Boys' Growth Study, the Greulich-Pyle atlas was used to assess skeletal age from hand-wrist X rays taken annually within two months of each boy's birthday.

Hand-Wrist X-Ray Procedures

The "Profexray" machine distributed by the Professional Equipment Company, Maywood, Illinois, was utilized to take the X-ray photographs. The current source for this machine is an ordinary electric outlet (115–120 volts, 60 cycles). An ample amount of power for penetration is supplied with the maximum rated capacity of 80 K.V.P. and 20 milliamperes. Constancy and accuracy of exposure are obtained through the incorporation of a ten-step voltage and variable milliamperage control unit which compensates for fluctuations in line voltage.

Maximum protection from radiation was provided for both the subjects and the operator. Adjustments were made by placement of a lead unit with an oblong opening in the aluminum cone of the X-ray machine, which restricted radiation to the area of the X-ray film only. Lead shields were incorporated into all sides and the bottom of a box into which the hand was placed through a slit, as shown in Fig. 2.1. Reports from inspections made by the Occupational Health Section, Oregon State Board of Public Health, and by Earl Lawson, M.D., radiologist, Medford, Oregon, indicated that the amount of X-ray radiation was slight and well within tolerance limits.

The following specifications were adopted for the production of satisfactory hand-wrist X rays with the X-ray machine described above:

1. Holder and film: no-screen cardboard holder for 8″ × 10″ X-ray film.

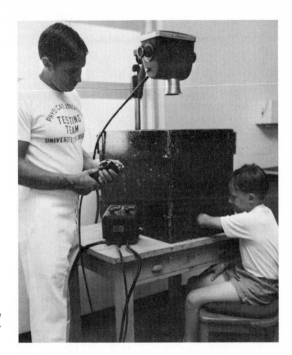

Fig. 2.1 X-Ray Machine and devices to protect subject and operator

2. Focal distance: lower edge of aluminum cone 30 inches directly above cardboard holder.
3. Amperage: 15 milliamperes.
4. Voltage: 110 kilovolts.
5. Exposure time: 1 second.

In taking the hand-wrist X ray, the left hand was placed palm down flat on the film holder with fingers slightly separated and the axis of the hand, wrist, and forearm in a straight line. The center of the X-ray tube was halfway between the tips of the fingers and the distal end of the radius. The resultant X ray included the complete fingers and wrist and at least 1½ inches of the radius bone.

Initially, each bone in the hand-wrist X-ray film was assessed for skeletal age by comparison with X-ray standards contained in the Greulich-Pyle atlas. The skeletal age of the entire wrist and hand was designated as the average of 30 bones, more or less depending on the boy's age, that were thus assessed. The reliability coefficient was established at .96; with trained assessors, objectivity coefficients were repeatedly obtained over .90.

Reduction of Bone Assessments

In the Medford Boys' Growth Project, Hayman (30, 53) investigated the possibility of reducing the total number of bone assessments needed in the overall determination of skeletal age. To do so would reduce the laborious, time-consuming procedure of making this assessment.

Procedures

The subjects were 273 boys from the Medford schools. Between 37 and 40 boys were randomly chosen at each age from 9 to 15 years inclusive. Complete skeletal age assessments were made on all boys following the Greulich-Pyle process and atlas.

The independent variables in this study were the skeletal ages of the individual bones of the wrist and hand; the dependent variable was the overall skeletal age of the hand. All independent variables were correlated with each other, and also with the dependent variable by means of the Pearson product-moment method. Multiple correlation coefficients between various combinations of independent variables and the dependent variable were computed by the Wherry-Doolittle method (23).

Results

ZERO-ORDER CORRELATION. The lowest intercorrelation among the skeletal age assessments of the hand and wrist bones was .9456 between the distal end of the ulna and the lunate bone. The highest such correlation between bones was .9986 each between metacarpals II and III, between proximal phalanges II and III, and between middle phalanges III and IV. The bones that generally correlated lowest with the other bones of the hand and wrist were the distal end of the ulna, the lunate bone, and the greater multangular bone; the range of the correlations with these bones was between .9456 and .9848.

In comparison with the intercorrelations of the individual bones of the wrist and hand, their correlations with the 30-bone skeletal age criterion covered a narrower range. The lowest correlation obtained with this criterion was .9718 with the distal end of the ulna; the highest correlation was .9960 with metacarpal IV. Thus, an adequate assessment of skeletal age could be obtained be obtained from metacarpal IV alone.

MULTIPLE CORRELATIONS. Due to the large number of bones included as variables in this study, it was considered desirable to divide them into four natural groupings for purposes of computing multiple correlations. In this way, a more comprehensive correlational analysis of the entire wrist and hand assessment was provided. The four groupings of wrist and hand bones were as follows: (1) distal ends of the radius and ulna and the carpal bones, (2) metacarpal bones, (3) proximal phalanges, and (4) middle and distal phalanges.

Multiple correlations were computed between the skeletal ages of the bones in each of the four groups, as independent variables, and the skeletal age of the entire wrist and hand, as the dependent variable. A fifth multiple correlation was computed between the skeletal ages of all bones appearing in the preceding multiple correlations and the skeletal age of the total wrist and hand. These multiple correlations were as follows.

1. Radius-ulna-carpals, .9943: capitate, distal end of ulna, distal end of radius, and triquetral.
2. Metacarpals, .9972: metacarpals IV, I, and V.
3. Proximal phalanges, .9958: proximal phalanges III and I.
4. Other phalanges, .9950: middle phalanx II and distal phalanx I.
5. All areas, .9993: metacarpal IV, distal phalanx I, triquetral, proximal phalanx I, distal end of radius, and middle phalanx II.

The six bones appearing in the highest multiple correlation (.9993) were not the easiest to assess. Also, while representing each of the areas of the wrist and hand, the bones were situated at varying distances from the longitudinal axis. These factors made assessments time-consuming. Consequently, a sixth multiple correlation was computed, in which the bones were selected as follows: A single bone was chosen from each of the four major areas of the wrist and hand; each bone was judged as being relatively easy to assess and was so situated in relation to the others as to reduce the time required for making the assessments. The bones thus selected were: capitate, metacarpal III, proximal phalanx III, and middle phalanx III. All of these bones lie directly above each other in the center of the hand. The resulting multiple correlation between the skeletal ages of these four bones and the skeletal age of the entire wrist and hand was .9989.

Skeletal Age Prediction. Multiple regression equations in score form were computed for the two multiple correlations to determine the best and easiest batteries. The equations, with standard errors of estimate, were as follows:

Best Battery. Skeletal Age = .28 (metacarpal IV) + .21 (distal phalanx I) + .13 (triquetral) + .14 (proximal phalanx I) + .11 (distal end of radius) + .14 (middle phalanx II) − 1.21. σ est. = 1.06 months.

Easiest Battery. Skeletal Age = .36 (metacarpal III) + .25 (middle phalanx III) + .21 (capitate) + .18 (proximal phalanx III) − .02. σ est. = 1.36 months.

In each instance, the mean skeletal age for all wrist-hand bones was compared to the means predicted by use of the regression equations. A random sample of 49 X-ray films, seven from each of the ages 9 to 15 years inclusive, was drawn for this purpose. The difference between the means by each method of assessment was tested for significance by application of the t test. The differences between the means for the assessed and predicted skeletal ages of the subjects were slight, .02 and .10 months; the t ratios were .00 and .02, indicating no significance in the differences between the means.

In the belief that the skeletal ages of the subjects could be predicted directly from the bones in the various multiple correlations without recourse to the regression equations, the average of the bones comprising each multiple battery was computed from the raw scores. These means were then compared with the mean obtained from assessing all bones in the wrist and hand. The differences between the means in this comparison were slightly greater than when the regression equations were used, although still very insignificant. The differences were .23 and .15 months, with t ratios of .04 and .03.

Summary

1. The skeletal ages of the individual bones of the hand and wrist are closely related to each other and the overall skeletal age of boys 9 through 15 years of age. No intercorrelation was less than .9456 and no correlation of a single bone with overall skeletal age was lower than .9718.

2. The hand-wrist skeletal ages of boys in the age range of the study can be determined with a satisfactory degree of accuracy from the skeletal age of metacarpal IV alone, since the correlation of this bone with the overall hand and wrist was .9960. Using the following four bones, the multiple correlation with the total hand-wrist was .9989: capitate, metacarpal III, proximal phalanx III, and middle phalanx III. The difference between the skeletal age means by assessment of the total hand-wrist and by assessment of the four bones was .15 month; the *t* ratio was .03.

Inter-Age Correlations

In three of the Medford boys' growth studies, inter-age correlations were determined. Inter-age correlations by Day (39) were for boys ages 7 to 12; correlations involving ages 7 and 8 were calculated for 46 boys, while those for the other ages were computed for 94 boys. Santa Maria (86) obtained inter-age correlations for 123 boys from 12 to 17 years of age. In an early Medford study, Kurimoto (66) presented inter-age correlations for boys between ages 15 and 18. The inter-age correlations reported by Day and Santa Maria appear in Table 2.1.

The inter-age correlations for the boys 7 to 12 years of age ranged from .749 between ages 7 and 12 and .926 between ages 10 and 11. For the older boys, the range of inter-age correlations was from .516 between ages 12 and 17 to .934 between ages 16 and 17.

The magnitude of the coefficients decreased with increases in time lapses between the two years correlated. With one-year lapses, the median inter-age correlation was .879 for the 7 to 12 boys and .915 for the 12 to 17 boys. For the other lapses, the respective median inter-age correlations for the two age groups were: two-

Table 2.1

INTER-AGE CORRELATIONS FOR SKELETAL AGE

	A. Boys 7 to 12 Years of Age				
Ages	*8*	*9*	*10*	*11*	*12*
7	.879	.810	.803	.758	.749
8		.817	.829	.774	.765
9			.846	.843	.763
10				.926	.867
11					.897
	B. Boys 12 to 17 Years of Age				
Ages	*13*	*14*	*15*	*16*	*17*
12	.893	.753	.656	.587	.516
13		.899	.816	.751	.683
14			.915	.854	.789
15				.915	.856
16					.934

year, .836 and .835; three-year, .774 and .751; four-year, .761 and .751. The single five-year lapses were .749 and .516 respectively.

Means and Variability

The skeletal age means and variability of the Medford boys from 7 to 18 years of age as determined from the maximum number of boys accumulated at each age appear in Table 2.2. The numbers of subjects at each age are given in the table.

At the ages of 7 and 8, when only one group and a smaller number of subjects were tested, the skeletal age means of the boys were retarded by 8.6 and 7.8 months respectively. For the ages 9 through 17, the skeletal age means corresponded reasonably well to the subjects' chronological age expectations. At age 18, the mean was 5.2 months advanced.

The standard deviations between ages 7 and 17 inclusive ranged from 11.9 to 15.1 months, despite the increase in means from 75.4 to 206.2 months. Thus, the individual differences in skeletal age of

Table 2.2
SKELETAL AGE MEANS AND VARIABILITY
(Months)

Age Years	Months	Number of Boys	Mean	Standard Deviation	Scores Low	High	Range
7	84	107	75.4	11.9	42	110	68
8	96	92	88.2	14.6	54	120	66
9	108	174	109.1	12.7	75	140	65
10	120	212	120.5	15.1	76	153	77
11	132	176	131.6	13.8	89	163	74
12	144	297	144.9	12.9	104	180	76
13	156	239	156.0	12.0	106	191	85
14	168	215	167.1	12.7	123	203	80
15	180	341	181.7	12.6	140	216	76
16	192	318	193.4	14.1	162	228	66
17	204	277	206.2	12.8	170	228	58
18	216	147	221.2	8.6	181	228	47

the boys at these ages, as shown by standard deviations, were approximately one year or more. At age 18, the standard deviation was only 8.6 months; this smaller amount was due to the truncation effect of many of the boys reaching maturity.

Although the range is an unreliable measure of variabiliay, since it is affected greatly by extreme scores, it does reveal the extremes in individual differences encountered at the various ages. For the boys in Table 2.2, the ranges varied from a low of 47 months at age 18 to a high of 85 months at age 13; the median range was 71 months, or 5.9 years. Truncation was observed beginning at age 16, as the highest skeletal ages reached the maximum of 228 months, the 19-year age in the Greulich-Pyle atlas.

Advanced and Retarded Maturity Groups

In longitudinal growth analyses by Day (39) and Santa Maria (86) with body size measures and by Jordan (61) and Bailey (1) with strength and motor tests, advanced and retarded maturity groups based on skeletal age were formed at age 9 by

Day and Jordan and at age 12 by Santa Maria and Bailey. Between 20 and 24 boys composed each group. The growth patterns of these groups were followed for four years, ages 9 through 12, in Day's and Jordan's studies, and for six years, ages 12 through 17, in Santa Maria's and Bailey's investigations. The differences between the means of these groups respectively for body size, strength, and motor tests were tested annually for significance by application of the *t* ratio.

For the advanced and retarded maturity groups formed by the four investigators, significant differences between skeletal age means continued for all ages in the respective studies. The *t* ratios ranged from 7.20 to 19.67, indicating pronounced significance. When the groups were formed at ages 9 and 12, the mean differences ranged from 31.46 to 36.0 months. The smallest difference between means at the ends of the longitudinal periods was 20.0 months in Santa Maria's six-year study.

With few exceptions, the differences between the means on the body size measures for the advanced and retarded maturity groups were significant at the .05 level and above at all ages in the Day and Santa Maria studies; the advanced groups in all instances had the higher means. The exceptions were hip width at 11, standing height at 17, and leg length at 16 and 17 years of age. The highest *t* ratios were 7.87 for weight and 7.31 for hip width at 13 and 7.64 for lung capacity at 14 years of age.

The advanced maturity groups had significantly higher means at all ages than the retarded groups on the strength batteries of cable-tension strength average and Strength Index; the *t* ratios ranged from 2.84 to 6.36. For individual cable-tension strength tests and left grip strength, the means of the advanced 12-year-old maturity group were significantly greater than the means of the retarded group at all ages. However, for the groups formed at age 9, significance between means was scattered among the ages and strength tests; only ankle plantar flexion and left grip strength showed significant mean differences at three of the four ages. Generally, the differences between the means of the maturity groups were not significant for Physical Fitness Index, bar push-ups, and motor ability tests.

Skeletal Age and Pubescent Development

Degutis (25, 40) compared the skeletal ages and the pubescent development of Medford boys 10, 13, and 16 years of age. These ages spanned the pubescent period in the following respects: at age 10, most boys are prepubescent, and their external sexual characteristics are mostly immature; at age 13, most boys are in early pubescence; at age 16, the pubescent development of the majority of boys is well advanced.

Procedures

1. Skeletal age was assessed in accordance with the hand-wrist X-ray procedures described earlier in this chapter.

2. The stage of pubescence was assessed in accordance with the development of secondary sex characteristics based on the criteria proposed by Greulich and others (50). By this method, pubescent status is described in terms of five categories which represent successive stages in the development of the genitals and the pubic hair. Group 1 represents the sexual development of prepubescent boys; group 5 has attained the external sexual characteristics of adults.

3. The hand-wrist X ray was taken and the pubescent assessment was made for each boy on the same day.

4. The subjects were 237 Medford boys. The numbers of boys at each age were: 86, 10 years; 65, 13 years; and 86, 16 years.

5. For the various pubescent groups found in this study, the means of the subjects were computed for various anthropometric, physique, strength, and motor measures. At each age, the differences between the means of the pubescent groups on these tests were tested for significance by application of the t ratio.

Distribution of Pubescent Groups

The age distributions of subjects by pubescent categories are shown in Table 2.3. At age 10, only two pubescent groups were found; 84 percent were in Group 1. Boys in all five pubescent groups were classified in all five pubescent groups at age 13; most of these subjects, however, were in Groups 2 and 3 (78 percent). For 16-year-old boys, two groups were again found, but these were in the upper pubescent categories; 74 boys, or 86 percent, were in Group 5.

Table 2.3

PUBESCENT DEVELOPMENT DISTRIBUTION OF BOYS
AGES 10, 13, AND 16

Age	Group 1	Group 2	Group 3	Group 4	Group 5	Total
10	72	14				86
13	2	25	26	8	4	65
16				12	74	86
						237

The pubescent ratings of the Medford boys were compared with comparable data from other studies. In general, there was a consistent uniformity in sex-character development as assessed in the various studies at ages 10 and 16. While boys at each of these two ages in all studies fell into two groups, a slightly greater proportion of boys in the present study was found in the more advanced maturity classification (Group 2 at 10 years and Group 5 at 16 years). At 13 years of age in all studies, only a small percentage of the distributions was found in Groups 1 and 5; in the present study, even fewer boys were found in Group 1. As compared with other studies, a greater percentage of 13-year-old boys was found in Group 2 and a smaller percentage was found in Group 4.

Contrast with Skeletal Age

CENTRAL TENDENCY. The differences between the mean skeletal ages of boys 10, 13, and 16 years of age in the different pubescent development groups appear in Table 2.4. This table is divided into two parts, as follows: Part A,—the skeletal age contrasts are made within each chronological age; Part B,—the skeletal age means of the same pubescent groups at different ages are compared.

At each chronological age studied, the mean skeletal age increased with advancing pubescence. The only difference which was not significant was between the means of Groups 1 and 2 at 10

Table 2.4

DIFFERENCES BETWEEN MEAN SKELETAL AGES (YEARS) OF BOYS 10, 13, AND 16 YEARS OF AGE CLASSIFIED INTO PUBESCENT DEVELOPMENT GROUPS

Ages	*Pubescent Development Groups*						df	D_m	σD_m	t
	1	*2*	*3*	*4*	*4 + 5*	*5*				
A. Contrasts within chronological ages										
10	9.926	10.138					84	.212	.292	.76
13		12.423	13.280				49	.857	.161	5.32
13		12.423			14.345		35	1.922	.163	11.79
13			13.280		14.345		36	1.065	.174	6.11
16				14.974		16.583	84	1.609	.227	7.10
B. Contrasts between chronological ages										
10		10.138					37	2.285	.265	8.60
13		12.423								
13					14.345		22	.629	.225	2.84
16				14.974						

years of age. All four of the other differences between these means were significant well beyond the .01 level; the *t* ratios ranged from 5.32 to 11.79.

At 13 years, the skeletal age mean of the Group 2 boys was below their chronological age by over a half-year; the Group 3 and Group 4 + 5 means were in advance of their chronological age by .280 and 1.345 years respectively. At 16 years, the skeletal age mean of Group 4 was approximately a year below their chronological age; the Group 5 mean was .583 years in advance of their chronological age.

In comparing the mean skeletal ages of boys in the same pubescent groups at different chronological ages, the two *t* ratios computed were significant beyond the .01 level; in each instance, the older boys chronologically had the highest skeletal age mean. The largest *t* ratio was 8.60, which resulted from the difference between the means of Group 2, at ages 10 and 13. However, some doubt is cast on the validity of the Group 2 assessments at 10 years of age. The comparison of the skeletal age means for the Group 4 boys at 16 years with the 4 + 5 boys at 13 years, provided some advantage to the 13-year-olds, due to the presence of some pubescent 5's in their sample.

VARIABILITY. The skeletal age variability for each of the pubescent groups, as indicated by the range, standard deviation, and coefficient of variation, is shown in Table 2.5. Generally, by these measures, variability was greatest at age 10, next greatest at age 16, and least at age 13. At age, 10, the three measures of variability for Group 1 exceeded those obtained for all other pubescent groups at the three different ages. They were: range, 5.85 years; standard deviation, 1.26 years; coefficient of variation, 12.68. For boys in Group 4 + 5 at 13 years, the measures of variability were lowest, as follows: range, 1.11 years; standard deviation, .41 years; coefficient of variation, 2.87.

Considerable overlapping was found for the skeletal age ranges of the different pubescent development groups within each chronological age. The greatest overlapping occurred at 10 years of age; the lower and upper limits of Group 1 exceeded the lower and upper limits of Group 2 by 19 and 24 percent respectively. Two pubescent categories, 4 and 5, occupied 56 percent of the combined skeletal age range for 16-year-old boys. At the age of 13, for Groups 2 and 3, 30 percent of their skeletal age was held in com-

Table 2.5

SKELETAL AGE (YEARS) VARIABILITY OF BOYS 10, 13, AND 16 YEARS OF AGE
CLASSIFIED INTO PUBESCENT DEVELOPMENT GROUPS

Age	Pubescent Development Group	Number of Cases	Low	High	Range	Standard Deviation	Coefficient of Variation
10	1	72	6.90	12.75	5.85	8.79	12.68
10	2	14	8.33	11.66	3.33	1.26	8.67
13	2	25	11.08	13.25	2.17	.52	4.17
13	3	26	12.25	14.44	2.19	.61	4.59
13	4 + 5	12	13.75	14.86	1.11	.41	2.87
16	4	12	14.08	16.90	2.82	.63	4.22
16	5	74	14.17	19.00	4.83	1.16	6.97

mon; 22 percent of the combined skeletal age range of Groups 3 and 4 + 5 was common to both of these pubescent groups. No overlapping of skeletal age ranges was found for Groups 2 and 4 + 5 at this age.

Physical and Motor Measures

For the various pubescent groups established in this study, the means of the subjects were computed for the following measures:

Physique type: somatotype components of endomorphy, mesomorphy, and ectomorphy.

Anthropometric: standing height, lung capacity, body weight, chest girth, hip width, arm girth, and calf girth.

Strength tests of muscle groups: left grip, back lift, leg lift, elbow flexion, shoulder flexion, and shoulder inward rotation.

Gross strength batteries: Rogers' Strength Index and cable-tension strength average (12 tests).

Relative strength battery: Rogers' Physical Fitness Index.

Motor elements: standing broad jump and 60-yard shuttle run (10-yard distance).

At each age, the differences between the means on the experimental variables of the pubescent grounps were tested for significance by application of the *t* ratio. With the exception of the somatotype components, the 13- and 16-year-old boys who were advanced in pubescent development nearly always had higher mean scores on the experimental tests; generally, the differences between the means were significant. At age 10, the only significant difference was between the means of the average of 12 cable-tension strength tests. The evidence supporting these conclusions follows.

The mean differences between all the tests, except the 60-yard shuttle run, for 13-year-old boys in Group 4 + 5 and Group 2 were significant, generally beyond the .01 level. For 13-year-old boys in Groups 3 and 2, the differences between the means in the following tests were significant: all anthropometric measures; two strength tests of muscle groups, grip and elbow flexion; and cable-tension strength average, a gross strength battery. The significant differences between the means of Groups 4 + 5 and 3 were as follows: standing height and lung capacity; all strength tests and batteries except the three cable-tension tests; and standing broad jump and 60-yard shuttle run.

At the age of 16, the following differences between means for Groups 5 and 4 were significant: all anthropometric measures except standing height and hip width; back lift, leg lift, and grip strength; and Strength Index and mean cable-tension strength.

In general, the most significant tests of each type, insofar as this was possible to judge, were standing height and body weight for anthropometric measures, grip strength for strength tests of individual muscle groups, and cable-tension strength average for gross strength. A further analysis revealed that the older boys chronologically, but with the same pubescent rating, generally had a significantly higher mean on the tests included in this study. This generalization did not hold true in the case of relative strength as determined by the Physical Fitness Index.

The only significant difference for the somatotype ratings was found at the age of 16, when a greater percentage of ectomorphy was found in Group 4 than in Group 5 (.05 level of significance).

In this study, too, 13-year-old boys who were advanced in pubescent assessment had superior athletic ability, as rated by their coaches, to that of boys of this age who were normal and retarded in pubescent development. A significantly greater percentage of boys at this age in the 4 + 5 group was rated as outstanding athletes than was the case for boys with pubescent ratings of 2 and 3. Conversely, a significantly smaller percentage of boys with pubescent ratings of 4 + 5 was found in the nonparticipant group. For other levels of athletic ability, this type of differentiation did not occur.

Summary

Of the three ages studied, physical maturation was differentiated most effectively by pubescent assessment at 13 years of age, although it was not as sensitive to maturational changes as skeletal age. At age 16, maturational differentiation by this means was much more limited; at 10 years of age, little or no value could be attributed to this method. With few exceptions, the 13- and 16-year-old boys who were advanced in pubescent development had higher mean scores on the body size, gross strength, and motor tests studied. Generally the differences between means were significant.

Correlations

In attempts to locate general maturity factors, four factor analysis studies were conducted in the Medford Boys' Growth Project. Single-age factor analysis studies were completed by Willee (113), Burt (10), and Torpey (104) at 9, 13, and 16 years, respectively; these ages were selected as representing prepubescent, early pubescent, and advanced pubescent boys (as shown above in Degutis' study). In a more comprehensive approach to this problem, Phillips (80) factor analyzed tests for the same boys at each age 9 through 16. In all instances, skeletal age was included as a maturity criterion; the independent variables were tests of physique type, body size, muscular strength and endurance, and motor ability. The numbers of subjects in these factor analyses were: Willee, 82; Burt, 62; Torpey, 194; and Phillips, 62.

Inasmuch as the initial computation in factor analysis is to intercorrelate the test scores for all variables to be analyzed, the zero-order correlations of skeletal age with the various independent variables were available. Many other studies in the Medford project have included correlations between skeletal age and various physical and motor tests. However, the correlations presented here are taken from the four factor analysis investigations; the significant correlations from these studies appear in Table 2.6. A summarization of the results follows.

SOMATOTYPE COMPONENTS. With the exception of age 9, mesomorphy correlated significantly with skeletal age; the correlations were positive but low, ranging from .27 to .45. For ages 9 through 13, endomorphy correlated positively and, for the same ages plus 16, ectomorphy correlated negatively with skeletal age. Again, the correlations were low, in the high .20's and low .30's.

STRUCTURE. The structural, or anthropometric, measures were tests of body bulk, linearity, and combinations in the form of indices.
1. *Bulk*. Without exception, the body bulk measures correlated significantly and positively with skeletal age. Generally, the magni-

Table 2.6

SIGNIFICANT CORRELATIONS BETWEEN SKELETAL AGE AND PHYSICAL VARIABLES FROM MEDFORD BOYS' GROWTH STUDY

Experimental Variable	Chronological Age										
	9a	10a	11a	12a	13a	14a	15a	16a	9b	13c	16d
Somatotype Components											
Endomorphy	.28	.34	.30	.29	.26	—	—	—	.30	X	—
Mesomorphy	—	.29	.30	.30	.27	.38	.37	.45	—	X	.32
Ectomorphy	—.26	—.37	—.33	—.33	—.27	—	—	—.31	—.28	X	—.25
Structure											
Weight	.51	.56	.56	.65	.74	.77	.69	.60	.59	.68	.43
Hip Width	.36	.45	.52	.57	.65	.65	.43	.33	.39	.59	X
Arm Girth	.49	.47	.52	.56	.68	.71	.63	.47	.48	.50	.48
Chest Girth	.49	.48	.55	.57	.72	.76	.71	.58	.51	.56	.44
Calf Girth	.47	.55	.57	.31	.67	.41	.53	.46	.52	.57	.27
Abdominal Girth	X	.51	.56	.35	.58	.52	.45	.41	.52	.31	.27
Buttock Girth	X	.56	.56	.60	.69	.55	.63	.54	.53	.62	.35
Thigh Girth	X	.50	.54	.55	.59	.61	.60	.54	.51	.35	.37
Lung Capacity	—	—	.36	.51	.67	.75	.59	.41	.35	.64	.40
Height	.39	.42	.46	.59	.72	.76	.66	.45	.46	.72	—
Sitting Height	.29	.34	.44	.59	.73	.77	.70	.64	.45	.73	.47
Leg Length	.37	.41	.39	.43	.61	.60	.47	—	.36	.59	X
Lung Capacity/Height	—	—	—	.38	.57	.68	.52	.35	—	.49	.39
Chest Girth × Height	.49	.50	.42	.65	.78	.81	.76	.63	.48	.67	.32
Weight/Height	.50	.56	—	.61	.68	.70	.62	.55	.56	X	.42
Chest Girth/Height	.31	.26	.25	.27	.30	.38	.37	.35	X	X	X
Weight/(Ht.)^2	.44	.52	—	.51	.54	.55	.47	.47	.48	X	.38
Ht./$\sqrt[3]{\text{Wt.}}$	—.34	—.45	—	—.34	—.29	—.25	—.26	—.36	X	X	X
Muscular Strength											
Arm Strength Score	—	—	—	—	.32	.43	.44	—	X	X	X

Right Grip	—	.30	.41	.68	.81	.66	.42	.29	.53
Left Grip	—	.37	.26	.61	.76	.61	.40	.44	.56
Leg Lift	—	.27	.28	.39	.59	.67	.47	.37	.54
Back Lift	—	—	.27	.50	.28	.61	—	.36	.45
Strength Index	—	.29	.34	.52	.68	.67	.42	X	X
Knee Flexion	—	—	.39	.40	.61	.53	.40	X	.29
Knee Extension	—	.25	.43	.36	.53	.63	.50	X	.36
Ankle Plantar Flexion	—	—	—	.37	.44	.50	.39	X	.39
Trunk Flexion	—	.27	.38	.38	.57	.29	.31	X	.43
Trunk Extension	—	.25	.28	.32	.49	.32	.26	X	.39
Hip Flexion	—	.32	.47	—	.63	.52	.36	X	.40
Hip Extension	—	—	—	.29	.65	.44	—	X	.45
Elbow Flexion	—	—	.27	.37	.44	.55	.35	X	.56
Shoulder Flexion	—	—	—	.42	.33	.52	.42	X	.32
Shoulder Inward Rotation	—	—	—	.30	.35	.54	—	X	.32
Cable Tension Average	.27	.34	.44	.52	.68	.64	.54	X	X
Motor Tests									
Standing Broad Jump	X	X	X	—	.39	.40	—	X	.25
Athletic Rating	X	X	.44	.26	.39	.44	—.36	X	.32

Code : X = variable not included in this study.
— = variable included but correlation not significant.
(Correlation of .25 needed to reach significance at .05 level.)

a Phillips' study.
b Willee's study.
c Burt's study.
d Torpey's study.

tude of these correlations increased from age 9 to ages 13 and 14 and then declined. The highest correlations at ages 13 and 14 were .74 and .77 for weight, .72 and .76 for chest girth, and .68 and .71 for arm girth. The main exceptions to this general correlational pattern were for abdominal and thigh girths, where the magnitude of the correlations remained fairly consistent for all ages.

2. *Linearity.* With the exception of lung capacity at ages 9 and 10, the linear measures correlated significantly and positively with skeletal age. As for the bulk measures, the magnitude of these correlations increased from age 9 to ages 13 and 14 and then declined. The correlations for the linear measures at ages 13 and 14 ranged between .60 and .77.

3. *Combination.* The same phenomenon occurred with the indices that were found with the measures of bulk and linearity: generally low correlations with skeletal age at the younger and older ages and higher correlations at ages 13 and 14. The highest correlations at ages 13 and 14 were for chest girth $\times$ height (.78 and .81) and weight/height (.68 and .70). Lung capacity/height did not correlate significantly with skeletal age at ages 9 and 11 inclusive, but increased to a high of .68 at age 14. The negative correlations for height/$\sqrt[3]{\text{weight}}$ followed the same negative age correlational pattern as did ectomorphy.

GROSS MUSCULAR STRENGTH. With two exceptions, the gross muscular strength measures did not correlate signicantly with skeletal age at ages 9 and 10; also, nearly one-half of the correlations at age 11 were not significant. Generally, the highest correlations were obtained at age 14; the highest correlations at this age were .81 for right grip, .76 for left grip, and .68 for both the Strength Index and cable-tension average.

OTHER TESTS. While not shown in Table 6, the relative strength test, Physical Fitness Index, and the relative muscular endurance tests, pull-ups and bar push-ups, did not correlate significantly with skeletal age at any age from 9 to 16 inclusive. The same situation prevailed for the motor tests of the 60-yard shuttle run, 10-foot speed, and reaction time. For the standing broad jump, low but significant correlations (.25 to .40) were obtained at ages 13, 14, and 15.

Factor Analyses

As indicated in the preceding section, Phillips (80) conducted a series of factor analyses with the same 62 boys at each age from 9 through 16. The principal axes method of factoring the correlation matrix was employed since it is the method most likely to yield a general factor (51). With this method, each factor extracts the maximum amount of variance, and, consequently, the factor having the highest correlations with the largest number of tests is located. All factors with eigenvalues (sum of squares of factor loadings) above 1.000 were extracted since each contained loadings peculiar to the factor. The varimax criterion for rotation was applied to each of the factor analyses to maximize the loadings on each factor and to avoid the ad hoc quality of subjective rotation (62). A summary of these factor analyses follows.

PRINCIPAL AXES SOLUTIONS. The ages and corresponding number of principal axes factors with eigenvalues of 1.000 or more were as follows: 8 factors at ages 13 and 15, 9 factors at 14 and 16, 10 factors at 9 and 12, and 11 factors at 10 and 11. The first principal axes loadings for each of the eight ages are given in Table 2.7.

The attempt to locate a general maturity factor at the various ages from 9 through 16 was unsuccessful. For each of the analyses, Principal Axes Factor I had the highest loading of skeletal age. These loadings gradually increased for each age from .524 at 9 to .854 at 14, followed by a decline to .626 at 16 years. In all instances, the skeletal age loadings were significant, but were not considered high enough for valid identification of a general maturity factor.

High loadings on the body bulk measures were found for all ages. The highest of these with their ranges were: weight, .885 to .992; arm girth, .852 to .927; buttock girth, .759 to .971; thigh girth, .788 to .967; chest girth, .878 to .951; weight/height squared, .704 to .938; weight/height, .841 to .986; and chest girth × height, .856 to .916. The loadings of the body bulk measures were accompanied by moderately high loadings of the physique and linear measures. The ranges for endomorphy and ectomorphy respectively were .280 to .836 and −.359 to −.696; the mesomorphy loadings ranged from

Table 2.7
FIRST PRINCIPAL AXES FACTORS FOR BOYS FROM 9 THROUGH 16 YEARS OF AGE

Variables	Nine	Ten	Eleven	Twelve	Thirteen	Fourteen	Fifteen	Sixteen
1. Skeletal Age	.524	.571	.602	.657	.776	.854	.811	.626
2. Endomorphy	.630	.816	.836	.773	.504	.280	.312	.700
3. Mesomorphy	.243	.266	.363	.429	.497	.527	.587	.621
4. Ectomorphy	−.437	−.632	−.691	−.667	−.525	−.359	−.362	−.754
5. Height	.659	.663	.641	.638	.727	.801	.699	.361
6. Sitting Height	.496	.556	.598	.590	.717	.802	.709	.448
7. Leg Length	.594	.611	.549	.488	.639	.651	.530	.148
8. Weight	.964	.977	.982	.978	.932	.925	.885	.962
9. Arm Girth	.852	.912	.927	.925	.914	.884	.853	.864
10. Abdominal Girth		.906	.934	.441	.820	.730	.687	.866
11. Buttock Girth		.971	.969	.955	.883	.759	.833	.940
12. Hip Width	.657	.681	.698	.741	.804	.779	.538	.705
13. Thigh Girth		.967	.958	.949	.833	.790	.788	.920
14. Calf Girth	.900	.931	.934	.703	.905	.536	.752	.884
15. Chest Girth	.940	.926	.951	.929	.904	.914	.878	.923
16. Lung Capacity	.323	.223	.330	.377	.594	.741	.672	.306
17. Fat Total				.701	.488	.238	.282	.711
18. Sitting Height/Height	−.281	−.231	.158	−.160	−.054	.080	.205	.205
19. Lung Capacity/Height	.165	.047	.162	.213	.462	.640	.603	.255
20. Height/Cube Root of Weight	−.700	−.797	−.805	−.756	−.572	−.443	−.502	−.842
21. Weight/Height Squared	.876	.938	.929	.916	.789	.738	.704	.936
22. Chest Girth/Height	.647	.623	.737	.658	.525	.557	.559	.761
23. Weight/Height	.960	.986	.980	.979	.912	.884	.841	.979
24. Chest Girth × Height	.916	.931	.903	.932	.908	.938	.893	.856
25. Right Grip Strength	.092	.310	.461	.311	.718	.835	.768	.360
26. Left Grip Strength	.192	.270	.269	.244	.688	.816	.755	.240
27. Leg Lift	.424	.106	.419	.289	.626	.747	.770	.436
28. Back Lift	.242	.228	.306	.243	.716	.357	.690	.191

29. Shoulder Flexion Strength	.362	.101	.263	.211	.525	.494	.699	.457
30. Shoulder Inward Rotation Strength	.157	.186	.133	.238	.430	.460	.664	.181
31. Elbow Flexion Strength	.151	.201	.275	.358	.504	.495	.677	.169
32. Trunk Flexion Strength	-.132	.114	.256	.290	.560	.606	.390	.319
33. Trunk Extension Strength	-.037	.327	.378	.432	.540	.553	.398	.478
34. Hip Flexion Strength	-.018	.029	.300	.481	.402	.651	.651	.255
35. Hip Extension Strength	-.121	.074	.232	.322	.419	.692	.610	.144
36. Knee Flexion Strength	-.005	.111	.103	.476	.642	.710	.762	.390
37. Knee Extension Strength	-.046	.381	.299	.551	.667	.701	.717	.469
38. Ankle Plantar Flexion Strength	.163	.268	.105	.420	.522	.565	.614	.288
39. Cable-Tension Strength Average	.048	.348	.373	.581	.743	.812	.813	.499
40. Strength Index	.307	.079	.320	.244	.681	.777	.748	.220
41. Arm Strength Score	-.516	-.479	-.487	-.296	.275	.405	.492	-.157
42. Push-ups	-.464	-.479	-.573	.385	-.073	-.013	-.175	.278
43. Pull-ups	-.586	-.442	-.486	-.541	-.346	-.300	-.104	-.486
44. Physical Fitness Index	-.301	-.522	-.522	-.411	.079	.129	.134	-.471
45. Standing Broad Jump	-.308	-.319	-.287	-.101	.194	.348	.400	-.147
46. Body Speed (10 Ft.)		.144	.144	.269	-.095	.004	-.042	.209
47. Shuttle Run	.289	.281	.320	.228	.032	-.148	-.169	.304
48. Athletic Rating				.146	.427	.511	.413	.153
49. Total Body Time		.235	.295	.272	-.011	-.013	-.069	.180
50. Total Hand Time		.328	.166	.084	.060	.073	-.069	.222
Eigenvalues	11.093	15.195	16.360	15.926	18.786	19.342	19.012	15.744
Contribution to Variance	26.41%	31.66%	34.08%	31.85%	37.57%	38.69%	38.02%	31.49%

.243 to .621. The linearity measures had loadings on the first principal axes factors which ranged from .361 to .801 for standing height, .448 to .802 for sitting height, and .148 to .651 for leg length.

Generally, the gross strength measures had low loadings on the first principal axes factor at the younger ages and moderately high loadings at the older ages. Consistent negative loadings were obtained for arm and shoulder endurance measures at all ages although the loadings were generally low. Similar connotations exist for the motor tests of 60-yard shuttle run, speed, and reaction time. Low scores on these tests are good, as is true for timed events, so the positive sign has a negative connotation.

ROTATED FACTORS. Space in this monograph does not permit a detailed account of the varimax rotations with accompanying extensive tables, so an attempt at summarization will be made. However, appropriate rotations are shown in subsequent chapters, as related to physique type, body size, strength, and motor ability. These rotations revealed 12 different factors, many of which occurred constantly throughout the eight ages included in the study.

1. *Body Bulk-Physique*. A Body Bulk-Physique factor appeared in the first rotation for six ages and in the second rotation for two ages. The ranges of the loadings for the measures in this factor were: endomorphy, .628 to .916; ectomorphy, −.705 to −.930; weight, .520 to .913; arm girth, .635 to .941; abdominal girth, .304 to .914; buttock girth, .542 to .922; thigh girth, .657 to .948; calf girth, .490 to .918; chest girth, .603 to .941; and fat total, .742 to .891. Body development at age 10 appeared to be more affected by body bulk than during subsequent years, especially age 14. This trend was also evident for endomorphy, but was not found for ectomorphy. Ectomorphic loadings increased steadily from 9 to a high at 14, and then declined to 16 years of age.

2. *Body Linearity*. A Body Linearity factor appeared in the third rotation for six ages and in the first and fifth rotations for two ages. The ranges of loadings for the measures in this factor were: standing height, −.693 to .957; sitting height, .735 to −.930; leg length, −.385 to .839; and chest girth × height, .364 to .886. Negative loadings at 11, 12, 15, and 16 years indicate a failure of the body linearity of boys at these ages to keep pace with general body development. The highest consistent loadings for the linearity mea-

sures occurred at ages 13 and 14. At age 13, the loadings were negative and at age 14 they were positive. The high positive loadings at age 14 corresponded to the lower loadings on the Body Bulk-Physique factor at this age. This result may indicate that growth and development are more affected by linearity than by bulk measures at age 14.

3. *Arm and Shoulder Endurance.* Arm and Shoulder Endurance appeared as a factor in the rotations at all ages. The ranges of the loadings for the measures in this factor were: Rogers' arm strength score, −.780 to .855; push-ups, −.556 to .845; pull-ups, .592 to .859; and Physical Fitness Index, −.210 to −.746. Negative loadings at ages 10, 12, 13, and 15 suggest a failure of the arm and shoulder endurance of boys at these ages to keep pace with general body development. Moderate loadings on many of the motor measures were found with this factor, especially for standing broad jump, 60 yard shuttle run, and athletic rating for ages 13 and 14. These loadings may indicate that motor ability as measured by these variables may be more affected by arm and shoulder endurance at ages 13 and 14 than at other ages in this study.

4. *Body Speed.* Body Speech over a distance of 10 feet appeared as a rotated factor at all ages where the test was used; the range of loadings was from .731 to .911. Positive loadings have negative connotations since a low score on this test is a good score. The positive loadings on this test represent a failure of the body speed of boys at these ages to keep up with general body development.

5. *Relative Sitting Height.* Relative Sitting Height (sitting height/standing height) appeared in rotations at all ages but 9. The loadings ranged from .876 to −.915. At two ages, 11 and 16, these loadings were negative, indicating a lag in this proportion relative to general development at these ages. Leg length was the only other measure to load consistently high with this measure; the loadings ranged from .449 to .824.

6. *Relative Lung Capacity.* Relative Lung Capacity (lung capacity/height) as a factor appeared in rotations at seven ages, all ages but 15; lung capacity had nearly as high loadings at these ages. The ranges of loadings were −.620 to .961 for lung capacity/height and −.426 to .916 for lung capacity. Negative loadings at ages 13 and 14 indicate a lag in relative lung capacity in relation to general development.

7. *Hip-Trunk Strength.* Hip-Trunk Strength was identified as a factor because of high loadings on trunk flexion, trunk extension, hip flexion, and hip extension cable-tension strength tests. This factor appeared at all ages but 15. At ages 12 and 13, the hip strength tests loaded low on this factor. These exceptions to the generally high loadings are probably due to high loadings on these variables on a factor identified later as Lower Body Strength, a factor found to be peculiar to ages 12 and 13.

8. *Arm and Shoulder Strength.* Arm and Shoulder Strength was identified as a factor because of high loadings on shoulder flexion, shoulder inward rotation, and elbow flexion cable-tension strength tests. This factor appeared at five ages, all but 10, 13, and 16 years. Negative loadings obtained at ages 11 and 15 indicate a strength lag at these ages.

9. *Leg-Back Lift Strength.* Leg-Back Lift Strength appeared in five of the rotations, ages 9 to 12 inclusive and age 14. The high loadings on this factor were for the dynamometric strength tests of leg lift and back lift. The factor was not always clear since at some ages one of these tests loaded high and the other loaded low; only at ages 10 and 12 did both tests load high (the range of these loadings was .730 to .866). Negative loadings were found at ages 11 and 12, indicating a strength lag at these ages.

10. *Lower Body Strength.* As mentioned above under Hip-Trunk Strength, a Lower Leg Strength factor was identified at ages 12 and 13. Moderately high loadings were obtained for the following lower body strength tests: hip flexion and extension, knee flexion and extension, and ankle plantar flexion. Certain of these tests also loaded high on this factor at age 9.

11. *Grip Strength.* Grip Strength as a factor appeared in the rotations at ages 9, 10, and 11. Negative loadings occurred at 9 and 11 years and positive loadings were found at 10 years.

12. *Strength.* At ages 15 and 16, a rotated factor identified as Strength was found. Fairly high loadings on all strength tests were obtained. The presence of a total strength factor at these two ages was generally accompanied by an absence of many of the individual strength area factors which were found at the earlier ages. This finding may indicate that as boys grow older, general strength becomes more prominent in their total development.

Summary

Twelve different rotated factors were identified in Phillips' longitudinal factor analysis study of the same boys at each age from 9 through 16. In many instances, the identification of these factors was not consistent with former factor analytic studies. The exceptions to these inconsistencies were found in the rotated factors called Body Bulk-Physique and Body Linearity which were identified at each of the eight ages in this study and were also identified in earlier studies. Much of this inconsistency could be the result of finding many more rotated factors in this study than in former studies. Burt, for example, revealed three rotated factors at age 13 and Willee and Torpey identified five rotated factors each at ages 9 and 16.

Some age differences in dominant factors appear likely, a phenomenon that could be revealed in the Phillips longitudinal study. Only five factors were found at all eight ages where the tests were included: Body-Bulk-Physique, Body Linearity, Relative Sitting Height, Arm and Shoulder Endurance, and Body Speed. Hip-Trunk Strength and Relative Lung Capacity appeared at seven ages and Leg-Back Lift Strength at six ages. At the opposite extreme, Grip Strength and Lower Leg Strength were identified as rotated factors at only three ages.

Ages 9, 10, and 14 were characterized by a large number of positive rotated factors. At age 11, a large number of negative factors was found. The factors of Body Bulk-Physique, Hip-Trunk Strength, and Lower Body Strength did not demonstrate a lag (negative loading) at any age. For the other factors, lag occurred somewhat inconsistently over the eight years of the study. The most consistent negative loadings were for the factors of Body Linearity, Arm and Shoulder Endurance, and Body Speed.

Mean Differences between Maturity Groups

In a Medford Boys' Growth Study, Sekeres (90) investigated the relationships between skeletal maturity and physical, motor, scholastic, and psycho-personal measures by contrasting the means on these measures for advanced, normal, and retarded maturity groups formed at each age 9, 12, 15, and 17. An earlier, similar Medford study by Harrison (29, 52) was limited to physical and motor traits at ages 9, 12, and 15. The study by Sekeres will be reported here with appropriate comparisons to Harrison's results.

Procedures

FORMATION OF MATURITY GROUP. The subjects were 252 Medford boys; the numbers by age were: 9 years, 69; 12 years, 50; 15 years, 70; and 17 years, 63. With skeletal age as the maturity measure, advanced, normal and retarded maturity groups were formed at each of the four chronological ages, as shown in Table 2.8. In order to make distinct groupings, gaps of eight skeletal

Table 2.8

SKELETAL MATURITY GROUPS AT EACH
CHRONOLOGICAL AGE

Chronological Age	Maturity Status	Skeletal Age in Months	Number in Group
9	Retarded	97 and below	18
	Normal	105–111	29
	Advanced	119 and above	22
12	Retarded	133 and below	14
	Normal	141–147	17
	Advanced	155 and above	19
15	Retarded	169 and below	30
	Normal	177–183	18
	Advanced	191 and above	22
17	Retarded	193 and below	14
	Normal	201–207	15
	Advanced	215 and above	34

months were allowed between the advanced and normal and the normal and retarded maturity groups at each age. Illustrations of the X-ray photographs of the hand and wrist of boys who were included in retarded, normal, and advanced maturity groups at age 9 chronologically appear in Fig. 2.2.

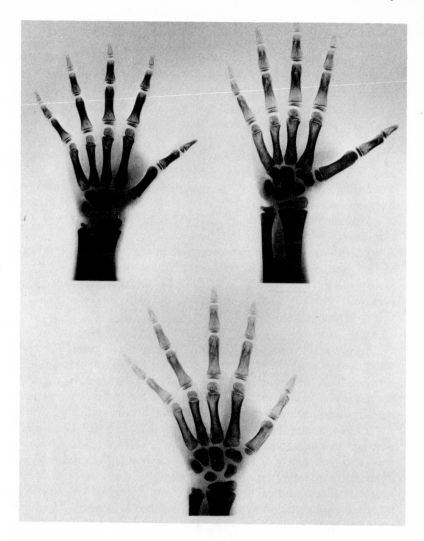

Fig. 2.2   Wrist-hand X-Ray photographs of retarded, normal, and advanced
nine-year-old boys.

EXPERIMENTAL VARIABLES. To secure a broad representation of measures for this study, tests were chosen largely on the basis of their significance in previous Medford boys' growth analyses. The results of the correlational and factor analysis studies by Burt, Willee, Torpey, and Phillips considered above and the study of mean differences between maturity groups by Harrison were given close scrutiny in their selection. The tests included in this study were:

1. *Physique type:* somatotype components of endomorphy, mesomorphy, and ectomorphy.

2. *Body size:* bulk: body weight; linear: standing height; combination: chest girth × height.

3. *Gross muscular strength:* ankle plantar flexion and cable-tension average.

4. *Motor tests:* muscular power: standing broad jump; athletic ability: participation on interschool athletic teams.

Scholastic achievement and personal-social adjustment measures were also included in the study, but will not be reported in this monograph.

ANALYSIS OF THE DATA. The statistical application for this study was one-way analysis of variance whereby the differences between the means of the retarded, normal, and advanced maturity groups on the experimental variables were tested for significance at each age. In those instances where a significant F ratio indicated overall significance among the means for an experimental test, the Scheffé post hoc test of significance for differences between pairs of means was used. The essential feature of this method is the establishment of confidence limits from a confidence interval for a level of significance. If these limits contain .00, the null hypothesis is accepted; if they do not contain .00, the null hypothesis is rejected. In simple application, .00 will not be within the confidence limits if the difference between means exceeds the amount of the confidence interval, since the limits are determined by adding and subtracting the interval from the mean difference. Thus, in this report, mean differences equal to or exceeding their confidence intervals are considered significant. The .05 level of significance was adopted.

Results

PHYSIQUE TYPE. The differences between the endomorphy means of the maturity groups were not significant at all four ages. Non-significant differences were also obtained between the mesomorphy means at ages 9 and 12 and the ectomorphy means at ages 9, 12, and 15.

For mesomorphy, the advanced maturity group had a higher mean than did the normal and retarded groups at age 15: the respective means were 4.61, 3.80, and 3.87. At age 17, the mesomorphy mean of the advanced group was significantly higher than that of the retarded group. The ectomorphy mean of the retarded maturity group at 17 was significantly higher than the mean of the advanced group; the respective means were 3.67 and 2.90.

BODY SIZE. The differences between the means for the three body-size measures with F ratios for boys in the three maturity groups at the four ages appear in Part A of Table 2.9. The Scheffé post hoc tests for those comparisons with significant F ratios are given in Part B of the table.

1. *Weight.* Significant differences between weight means of the three maturity groups were obtained at ages 9, 12, and 15; the respective F ratios were 14.15, 8.77, and 30.30. In the post hoc comparisons, the only differences that were not significant at these ages were between the means of the advanced and normal maturity groups at age 9 and the normal and retarded maturity groups at age 12. In all instances, the more advanced maturity groups had higher means.

2. *Standing height.* Significant differences between standing height means were obtained at ages 9, 12, and 15; the respective F ratios were 9.11, 26.69, and 29.40. In the post hoc comparisons, the only difference that was not significant at these ages was between the means of the advanced and normal maturity groups at age 9. For these comparisons, the more advanced maturity groups had higher means.

3. *Chest girth × height.* Significant differences between chest girth × height means occurred at ages 12 and 15; the F ratios were

Table 2.9
F RATIOS AND SCHEFFÉ POST HOC COMPARISONS FOR BODY SIZE MEASURES: MATURITY GROUPS AT AGES 9, 12, 15 AND 17

Part A: F Ratios

Variable	Age	Means			MS_b	MS_w	F
		Advanced	Normal	Retarded			
Weight	9	71.59	66.33	56.88	1048.56	74.12	14.15*
(pounds)	12	102.16	88.82	79.71	2111.66	240.79	8.77*
	15	150.00	129.37	114.72	7785.50	256.93	30.30*
	17	155.85	149.67	146.14	531.50	375.64	1.41
Standing	9	53.71	52.51	50.85	39.06	4.29	9.11*
Height	12	61.01	58.59	56.02	100.78	3.78	26.29*
(inches)	15	69.19	67.22	64.06	170.87	5.81	29.40*
	17	69.79	70.27	69.60	1.87	5.68	.33
Chest Girth	9	3490	3508	3236	449792	276411	1.63
X	12	4664	4280	3938	2154752	166677	12.93*
Height	15	6178	5662	5093	7427456	193879	38.31*
	17	6415	6306	6286	111616	218188	.51

Part B: Scheffé Tests

Variable	Age	Means			Mean Diff.	Confidence Interval
		Advanced	Normal	Retarded		
Weight	9	71.59	66.33		5.26	6.11
(pounds)		71.59		56.88	14.71*	6.87
			66.33	56.88	9.45*	6.48
	12	102.16	88.82		13.34*	13.09
		102.16		79.71	22.45*	13.81
			88.82	79.71	9.11	14.15
	15	150.00	129.37		20.63*	12.73
		150.00		114.72	35.28*	11.24
			129.37	114.72	14.65*	11.94
Standing	9	53.71	52.51		1.20	1.47
Height		53.71		50.85	2.86*	1.65
(inches)			52.51	50.85	1.66*	1.56
	12	61.01	58.59		2.42*	1.64
		61.01		56.02	4.99*	1.73
			58.59	56.02	2.57*	1.77
	15	69.19	67.22		1.97*	1.91
		69.19		64.06	5.13*	1.69
			67.22	64.06	3.16*	1.80
Chest Girth	12	4664	4280		384*	344
X		4664		3938	726*	363
Height			4280	3938	342	372
	15	6178	5662		516*	350
		6178		5093	1085*	309
			5662	5093	569*	328

* Part A Level of Significance: 3.13 at ages 9 and 15, 3.18 at age 12, and 3.15 at age 17.

* Part B: Significant at .05 level.

12.93 and 38.31 respectively. In the post hoc comparisons, the only difference which was not significant at these ages was between the means of the normal and retarded maturity groups at age 12. At both ages, the more advanced maturity groups had higher means.

GROSS MUSCULAR STRENGTH. The differences between the means for the two muscular strength measures with F ratios for boys in the three maturity groups at the four ages appear in Part A of Table 2.10. The Scheffé post hoc tests for those comparisons with significant F ratios are given in Part B of the table.

1. *Ankle plantar flexion.* Significant differences between ankle plantar flexion strength means of the three maturity groups were obtained at ages 12 and 15; the respective F ratios were 4.53 and 20.99. In the post hoc comparisons, all differences between means were significant at age 15. At age 12, the only significant difference was between the means of advanced and retarded maturity groups. In all instances, the more advanced maturity groups had higher means.

2. *Cable-tension average.* Significant differences between cable-tension strength average means occurred at ages 9, 12, and 15; the respective F ratios were 5.09, 4.84, and 59.84. In the post hoc comparisons, all differences between means were significant at age 15. At ages 9 and 12, the only significant differences were between the advanced and retarded maturity groups. In all instances, the more advanced maturity groups had higher means.

MOTOR ABILITY. Two tests related to motor ability were included in this study. One of these, standing broad jump, had a significant F ratio for the differences between the means of the maturity groups at age 15 only. The Scheffé post hoc tests revealed that the means of the advanced and normal groups were significantly higher than the mean of the retarded group.

For the other motor ability evaluation, the skeletal age means of participants and nonparticipants on interschool athletic teams were tested for significance by application of the t ratio at ages 12, 15, and 17. The only significant difference was at age 15. The mean skeletal ages were 192.69 and 177.18 for the athletes and nonparticipants respectively; the difference between means was 15.51 months and the t ratio was 3.19.

Table 2.10

F RATIOS AND SCHEFFÉ POST HOC COMPARISONS FOR STRENGTH TESTS:
MATURITY GROUPS AT AGES 9, 12, 15, AND 17.

Variable	Age	Part A: F Ratios Means			MS_b	MS_w	F
		Advanced	Normal	Retarded			
Ankle	9	76.90	68.90	63.70	87.80	29.10	3.01
Plantar	12	157.30	137.20	124.10	464.20	102.50	4.53*
Flexion	15	276.30	239.20	192.50	4473.40	213.20	20.99*
(pounds)	17	337.80	331.90	317.60	200.60	461.80	.43
Cable-	9	52.27	48.23	43.47	371.84	73.04	5.09*
Tension	12	88.74	79.47	70.57	1343.56	277.70	4.84*
Average	15	146.41	122.95	97.72	14948.84	249.80	59.84*
(pounds)	17	163.59	152.80	150.57	1119.50	531.23	2.11

Variable	Age	Part B: Scheffé Tests Means			Mean Diff.	Confidence Interval
		Advanced	Normal	Retarded		
Ankle	12	157.30	137.20		20.10	27.00
Plantar		157.30		124.10	33.20*	28.50
Flexion			137.20	124.10	13.10	29.20
(pounds)	15	276.30	239.20		37.10*	36.70
		276.30		192.50	46.70*	34.40
			239.20	192.50	46.70*	34.40
Cable-	9	52.27	48.23		4.04	6.06
Tension		52.27		43.47	8.80*	6.82
Average			48.23	43.47	4.76	6.44
(pounds)	12	88.74	79.47		9.27	14.05
		88.74		70.57	18.17*	14.83
			79.47	70.57	8.90	15.19
	15	146.41	122.95		23.46*	12.55
		146.41		97.72	48.69*	11.08
			122.95	97.72	25.23*	11.77

* Part A Level of Significance: 3.13 at ages 9 and 15, 3.18 at age
12, and 3.15 at age 17.
* Part B: Significant at .05 level.

Summary

1. For all variables, except ectomorphy, when the differences between paired means were significant, the more advanced maturity groups had the higher means.

2. Significant differences between the means of all experimental variables were most often obtained when the 15-year-old maturity groups were compared. The frequency of significant differences between the means of the 12-, 9-, and 17-year-old maturity groups followed in that order.

3. The most frequent significant differences between means were found for standing height. The differences between the standing height means were significant at ages 9, 12, and 15 for all paired mean comparisons, except the advanced-normal comparison at age 9. Other test variables with many significant mean differences were body weight and cable-tension strength average.

4. Differences between the means of the maturity groups were frequently found for body size and gross strength measures. Some relationships between skeletal age and the motor tests were shown.

Harrison's Study (52)

Sekeres' study followed the same general design adopted earlier by Harrison. However, Harrison's investigation differed in the following respects: (1) the ages were 9, 12, and 15 years, thus excluding 17 years; (2) the variables were limited to measures of body size, muscular strength and endurance, and muscular power, although many more tests of these types were included; and (3) the *t* ratio was the statistic used for testing the differences between the means of the maturity groups on the experimental tests. Following are some of the significant results from this study.

1. As in Sekeres' study, the highest and most significant differences between the means on the experimental variables were obtained at age 15; the frequency of significant differences at ages 12 and 9 followed in that order.

2. A greater difference was found between the mean body weights of the three maturity groups at the three ages than for any test variable; without exception, these differences were significant. Other tests for which the differences between the means were relatively high in significance were hip width, grip strength, sitting height, upper arm girth, and calf girth.

3. In the comparisons of the advanced and retarded maturity groups, significant differences between means were obtained at all three ages for the following variables: body weight, chest girth,

sitting height, upper arm girth, grip strength, calf girth, mean cable-tension strength, Rogers' Strength Index, hip width, leg strength, standing height, and elbow flexion strength. Other variables in which the differences reached significance at one or two ages were lung capacity at 12 and 15 years, back lift at 9 and 15 years, Wetzel physique channel and shoulder inward rotation strength at 12 and 15 years, leg length at 12 years, shoulder flexion strength, Rogers' arm strength score, standing broad jump, and Rogers' Physical Fitness Index at 15 years.

4. The only variables in which the differences between the means of the advanced and retarded maturity groups were not significant were push-ups and pull-ups. These variables, in fact, did not produce significant differences between means for any of the maturity groups at any age. This result is logical, since an increase of strength in the muscles performing push-ups and pull-ups is necessary to compensate for the greater size and weight of the body in the advanced maturity groups. Thus, both body weight and muscular strength increase with maturity, one compensating somewhat for the other. The same conclusion may be generally expressed for the Rogers' Physical Fitness Index, since the norms upon which these scores were calculated are based in large part on body weight.

Chapter Summary

In this chapter, primary emphasis was placed on skeletal age, based on an X ray of the hand and wrist, as a test of physical maturation. The origins of skeletal age, dating from 1905, ten years after the discovery of the roentgen ray, was briefly traced to the present use of the Greulich-Pyle atlas. Skeletal age is based on the maturing of the skeleton, which is continuous from birth to adult status, the age of 19 being the terminal age in the atlas.

The equipment and procedures for taking the hand-wrist X rays were explained. Evaluation of the X rays involves the skeletal age assessments of some 30 bones, depending on the age of the boy. In a Medford study, a multiple correlation of .9989 was obtained between assessment of all bones and the following four bones:

capitate, metacarpal III, proximal phalanx III, and middle phalanx III.

Inter-age correlations for skeletal age were determined for boys ages 7 to 12 and ages 12 to 17. The magnitude of these correlations decreased with increases in time lapses between the two years correlated. With one-year lapses, the median correlations were .879 for the 7 to 12 boys and .915 for the 12 to 17 boys. The standard deviations over eleven years of the Medford study ranged from 11.9 to 15.1 months; the ranges varied from 58 to 85 months.

Skeletal age was found to be superior to pubescent assessment as a physical maturity measure at ages 10, 13, and 16. Pubescent assessment was most valuable for this purpose at age 13, of no value at age 10 and of limited value at age 16.

In factor analysis of the same boys at each age 9 through 16, twelve different rotated factors were identified. The following five factors were found at all eight ages: Body Bulk-Physique, Body Linearity, Relative Sitting Height, Arm and Shoulder Endurance, and Body Speed. Ages 9, 10, and 14 were characterized by a large number of positive rotated factors; at age 11, a large number of negative factors was found. The attempt to locate a general maturity factor at the various ages with skeletal age as the criterion was unsuccessful.

At each age 9, 12, 15, and 17, advanced, normal, and retarded maturity groups were formed based upon skeletal age. The differences between means of the maturity groups at each age were tested for significance on physique type, body size, strength, and motor tests. For all variables, except ectomorphy, when the differences between paired means were significant, the more advanced maturity group had the higher mean. Significant mean differences were obtained most frequently at age 15. The differences between the standing height means were significant at all ages but 17 for all paired means comparisons, except the advanced-normal comparison at age 9. Other test variables with many significant mean differences were body weight and cable-tension strength average.

Chapter **3** / **Physique Type**

Sheldon's system of somatotype components was used for describing the physique types of boys in the Medford Boys' Growth Project. This chapter presents the use of the somatotype in understanding growth and development and the relationships of the components to the body size, muscular strength and endurance, and motor ability of boys.

Origins

Man has long held the notion that associations exist between his physical make-up and many other aspects of his constitution. These associations have been related not only to morphological and biological aspects of his being but also to his intelligence, temperament, and proclivity for certain diseases. Early writers expressed the belief that an individual's character is portrayed by his outward appearance. In the ancient sacred literature of the Hindus, for example, reference was made to three physical types, called hare, bull, and horse in man, and deer, mare, and elephant in woman. Each type was associated with specified physical and emotional traits (65). Few periods of recorded history are without mention of some scheme of physique classification.

The most extensive summaries of early developments in the study of constitutional, or physique, types were presented by Tucker and Lessa (105) and by Krogman (65). Tucker and Lessa cite more than three hundred authors from the time of Hippocrates to the present century. Hippocrates designated two physical types, the phthisic habitus and the apoplectic habitus. The phthisic had a long, thin body, which was considered particularly subject to tuberculosis; the apoplectic was a short, thick individual with a predisposition toward diseases of the vascular system leading to apoplexy. The relationship between body and mind has been a popular area of study since Aristotle wrote that a specific body type was associated with a specific mental character. Galen, and later Avicenna, stressed the importance of temperament in the study of man and his physical constitution. Between ancient and modern times, many other physique classifications were proposed and their relationships with other human traits were studied.

Of several typologists who advanced ideas relative to body types during the twentieth century up to the time of Sheldon, Kretschmer (64) made the most lasting impact. Searching for relations between physique and psychic types which could be expressed in the form of some law, this German psychiatrist suggested that the psychopathological types of manic-depressive and schizophrenia were associated with physical characteristics. He proposed a constitutional scheme containing more than seventy observable physique determinants from which he identified three body types, which he named asthenic, athletic, and pyknic. The essential characteristics of these three types are:

1. *Asthenic:* Deficiency in thickness combined with an average unlessoned length...a lean narrowly-built man, who looks taller than he is, with a skin poor in secretion and blood, with narrow shoulders, from which hang lean arms and thin muscles; and delicately boned hands; a long, narrow, flat chest on which the ribs can be counted, with a sharp rib angle.

2. *Athletic:* Middle-sized to tall man, with particularly wide projecting shoulders, a superb chest, a firm stomach, and a trunk

which tapers in its lower region, so that the pelvis and the "magnificent legs" sometimes seem almost graceful compared with the size of the upper limbs and particularly the hypertrophied shoulders.

3. *Pyknic:* Middle height, rounded figure, a soft broad face on a short, massive neck, sitting between the shoulders; the "magnificent fat paunch" protrudes from the deep vaulted chest which broadens out towards the lower part of the body.

These descriptions of body types bear a strong resemblance to Sheldon's. However, Kretchmer defined three specific body types into one or the other of which all individuals were classified, whereas Sheldon's physique types were combinations of his three components, each of which was possessed in some degree by all persons.

Sheldon's Somatotype

The numerous classifications of constitutional types found throughout history, although arising from different methodological approaches, nevertheless exhibit definite similarities with respect to the basic variations of human morphology they attempt to identify. Man has long recognized the fat individual, the thin form, and the aesthetic physique epitomized in Greek sculpture. With the development of the somatotype in 1940 by Sheldon and his associates (94), these three elements of body structure were more clearly defined and described. Thus, the somatotype, as a quantification of these primary components, reflects the basic structural orderliness so long observed in human life.

Primary Components

The names of Sheldon's three components were derived from the layers of the embryo, as follows: (a) First component, *endomorph,* named after the endoderm from which come functional elements of the digestive system; (b) second component, *mesomorph,* named after the mesoderm from which come the muscles and bones; and (c) third component, *ectomorph,* named after the ectoderm from which develop the sensory organs. Brief descriptions of these components follow (12).

In *endomorphy,* the digestive viscera dominate the body economy. A predominance of soft roundness throughout the various body regions is evident, with mass concentration in the center. Other characteristics are: large, round head; short, thick neck; broad, thick chest, with fatty breasts; short arms, with "hammy" appearance; large abdomen, full above the navel and pendulous; heavy buttocks; and short, heavy legs.

In *mesomorphy,* muscle, bone, and connective tissue dominate. The mesomorphic physique is heavy, hard, and rectangular in outline, with rugged, massive muscles and large, prominent bones. Other characteristics are: prominent facial bones; fairly long, strong neck; thoracic trunk dominant over abdominal volume; broad shoulders with heavy prominent clavicles; muscular upperarm and massive forearms, wrists, hands, and fingers; large, heavily muscled abdomen; slender, low waist; heavy buttocks; and massive forelegs.

In *ectomorphy,* linearity and fragility predominate. The dominant ectomorph has a frail, delicate body structure, with thin segments, anteroposteriorly. Other characteristics are: relatively large cranium, with bulbous forehead; small face, pointed chin, and sharp nose; long slender neck; long narrow thorax; winged scapula and forward shoulders; long arms, muscles not marked; flat abdomen, with hollow above navel; inconspicuous buttocks; and long, thin legs.

Each of the three components is rated on a 7-point scale to indicate its relative predominance in the total physique. This scale is read in half units for finer differentiation. In each instance, the first numeral in the sequence refers to endomorphy; the second, to mesomorphy; the third, to ectomorphy. Thus, a somatotype with the greatest endomorphic dominance is 7-1-1; with the greatest mesomorphic dominance, 1-7-1; with the greatest ectomorphic dominance, 1-1-7.

Development

The process of somatotyping originally designed by Sheldon was a laborious task involving photography and numerous measurements, combined with considerable assessment and calculation to arrive at the final rating. His original study on somatotyping was based on a sample of 4,000 college men. Standard somatotype photographs with front, back, and side views were taken in the nude. Seventeen anthropometric measurements were obtained from these photographs; height and weight were determined by subject measurement. From these measurements and an inspection of the photographic print, the subject's somatotype was assessed. The assessment included not only an over-all somatotype, but also a somatotype designation for each of five regions of the body: head, face, and neck; arms, shoulders, and hands; thoracic thrunk; abdominal trunk; legs and feet.

In 1954, Sheldon, Dupertuis, and McDermott (92) published the *Atlas of Men*, which presented a simplified method of somatotyping. This method was based on the study of 46,000 men ranging in age from 18 to 65 years. By this method, the index, height-over-cube-root-of-weight, was used to identify from tables the possible somatotypes for various intervals of the index. The final assessment was made by comparing the subject's somatotype photograph with illustrations found to be possible in the *Atlas*.

Slight modifications of Sheldon's somatotype procedures were made by Heath (54) and employed in the Medford Boys' Growth Project. All somatotype assessments in the study were made by her. The modifications were: (a) The rating scale was opened at both ends; thus component values less than 1 and more than 7 were possible. (b) The tables of possible somatotypes for various intervals of height-over-cube-root-of-weight were revised to provide a more linear relationship between changes in component ratings and this ratio.

In considering various aspects of physique deviation, Sheldon observed three secondary variations: dysplasia, gyandomorphy, and textural aspect. Dysplasia (d-index) refers to any inconsistency or uneven mixture of the three primary components in the five bodily regions. Gyandomorphy (g-index) is the extent to which a physique trait ordinarily associated with the opposite sex is present. The textural aspect (t-index) is a quality variable which deals with differences in the texture of human materials, that is, the graduation from very fine to very coarse physical texture.

Trunk Index

Despite the prominence of Sheldon's method of assessing physique type, a number of objections to his concepts and procedures were raised by various investigators. Sheldon (91) stated that at least four of the objections were made so often that answers to them became mandatory. These were: (a) the somatotype does change from age to age; (b) somatotype determination is basically subjective, with special difficulty found in differentiating between endomorphy and mesomorphy; (c) two not three primary components exist; and (d) the somatotype ignores the factor of body size. These criticisms motivated Sheldon to search for a new method of somatotyping, a method that would reflect the basic physique pattern and remain constant through life.

Sheldon's investigations led to an objective differentiation between *phenotype* and *genotype*. The phenotype refers to the individual's physique type at the time his somatotype picture is taken. As will be shown later, the phenotype does change during growth and thereafter, at least for some individuals. The genotype refers to the individual's hereditary physique. Thus, the genotype is unchanged throughout life, and is not affected by nutritional conditions, developmental activities, the ravages of disease, and the like.

The genotype assessment is based on three parameters: trunk index, minimum height-over-cube-root-of-weight during growth, and adult height. The trunk index is obtained by dividing thoracic dorsal area by abdominal dorsal area; the areas are determined by use of a planimeter applied to a standard photograph. Sheldon has indicated that this method provides a dependable quantitative differentiation between endomorphy and mesomorphy; the somatotype remains constant from three years to old age and is not affected by nutritional changes; the process is completely objective and can be derived on a computer; the factor of size is included by using stature in the determination of the somatotype; and three first-order criteria are identified as shown in the reduction of the high negative correlation among the primary components.

Also, in his studies, Sheldon determined the trunk-index for 2,000 young men and 2,000 young women from his extensive file of somatotypes. He found that this index was a constant for those somatotypes in which endomorphy and mesomorphy were equal. The variations among trunk-indices were completely independent, having a zero correlation with ectomorphy for both males and females. High positive and negative correlations were obtained between the index and mesmorphy and ectomorphy respectively.

Those high in mesomorphy had a large thoracic segment in relation to their abdominal segment, while the reverse was true for endomorphy. Sheldon found that the trunk-index varies from .85 for a person with an endomorphic rating of 7 and a mesomorphic rating of 1 to 2.05 for an individual with an endomorphic rating of 1 and a mesomorphic rating of 7. Where a subject's endomorphic and mesomorphic ratings are equal, the trunk-index is 1.45.

Somatotype Procedures

The somatotype procedures employed in this study followed the techniques developed by Sheldon as described in *Atlas of Men* (92).

Photographic Equipment

An illustration of the photographic equipment in place appears in Fig. 3.1.

SCREEN. A white, silk-mesh photographic screen, 9 feet by 4 feet 2 inches, was used to furnish a constant background for the photographs. It was mounted on a retractable roller to make it easily portable.

PEDESTAL. The pedestal consisted of a circular turntable, ball-bearing mounted on a square stand 5 inches high. The turntable had three stop positions, so that when rotated, front, side, and rear photographic views of the subject could be taken. Cardboard footprints were glued to the surface of the turntable to facilitate placement of the subject on it. The rear edge of the pedestal was placed parallel to the screen with the center of the turntable 1 foot 9 inches from the screen.

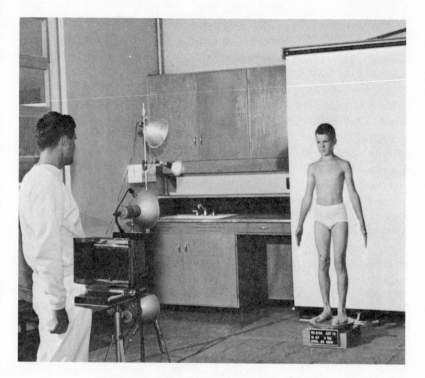

Fig. 3.1 Somatotype photographic equipment

Subject Identification Plate. A subject identification plate was placed on the front of the pedestal below the turntable. The plate was 5 inches by 10 inches, covered with black felt into which were placed 1-inch plastic letters and numerals. The subject's project number, age, height, weight, and date of the photograph appeared on the plate.

Camera. A Rembrandt portrait camera, manufactured by Burke and James, Inc., Chicago, Illinois, was used. It was equipped with a No. 4 Universal lens and shutter unit, f4.5, E.F.8.5, series number 49008, produced by Ilex Optical Company, Rochester, New York. The lens opening was set midway between f5.6 and f8.0 with a time of .01 second. A yellow filter, Wratten series III, K-2, was used to provide contrast for skin texture. The center of the lens was at a height of 4 feet from the floor; the distance from center of the pedestal to a plumb line extending from lens to floor was 15 feet 5 inches. The camera stand was equipped with leveling screws; a bubble-type level was used to insure proper balance of the camera.

FILM. Standard (5″ by 7″) Kodak Royal Pan safety film was used. The films were placed in cardboard holders and kept in a portable lead-lined chest for storage before and after exposures. A sliding panel on the rear of the camera permitted taking the three poses of each subject on a single film.

LIGHTS. Four flood lamps illuminated the subject. One set of two lights was placed at the subject's left at an angle of 45 degrees with the front of the pedestal, at a distance of 7 feet 8 inches from the center of the pedestal; one 500-watt lamp, RFL 2, was placed in a reflector 7 feet from the floor, and a 375-watt lamp, BFA, was adjusted on the same stand at a height of 4 feet 6 inches. In a similar manner, two lights were placed to the subject's right, but at a distance of 5 feet 10 inches; the heights of the two lamps from the floor were 7 feet and 2 feet 8 inches. In addition, a flash unit manufactured by the Lightning-Lite Company, Cleveland, Ohio, was attached to the camera with one light above and one light below the camera lens. These synchonous lights were powered by a transformer-amplifier operated by the camera shutter.

Posing Subjects

Subjects wore only tight-fitting shorts or athletic supporters; all jewelry, neck chains, and glasses were removed. The three poses are described below.

FRONT. Position of attention, standing on pedestal footprints; face toward camera, with head on eye-ear plane; chest relaxed, shoulders down and centered in mid-frontal plane, with arms in forced extension; wrists approximately 5 inches sideward from thighs, with digits hyperextended and pointing perpendicularly to floor.

SIDE. Right arm out of sight; left arm in forced hyperextension, locked at elbow; triceps muscle standing out; left arm in the center of body, but not obscuring back or front lines of body; body and face in profile; legs in alignment with no flexion or hyperextension at knees.

BACK. Same position as frontal view. Head level, shoulders down and not rolled forward or backward; arms may be somewhat wider at sides to clear latissimus dorsi muscle.

Somatotype Assessments

All somatotype assessments were made by Barbara Honeyman Heath, Monterey, California, somatotype consultant for the Medford Boys' Growth Project. The procedures were as follows:

1. The ratio, height-over-cube-root-of-weight (inverse ponderal index) was determined by use of a nomograph appearing in the *Atlas of Men.*

2. The revised table by Heath, mentioned above, was used to identify the possible somatotypes associated with a particular ratio. This process restricts the possible somatotype to some half dozen.

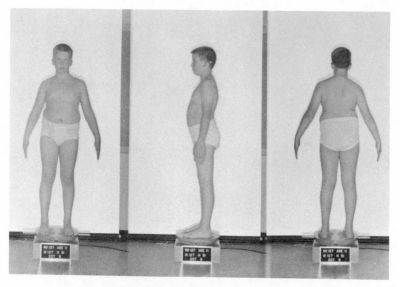

Fig. 3.2 Dominance in somatotype components.
(A) Dominant endomorph somatotype (6–3–2).

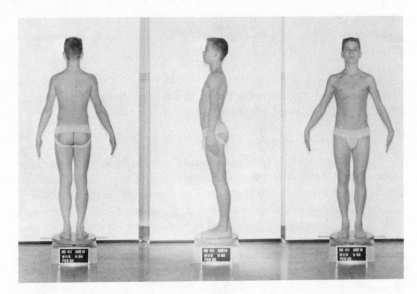

Fig. 3.2 (B)   Dominant mesomorph somatotype (2–6–3).

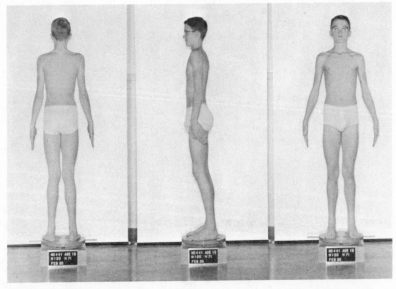

Fig. 3.2 (C)   Dominant ectomorph somatotype (2–2–7).

3. The final assessment was made through anthroposcopy with reference to the standard photographs in the *Atlas,* utilizing the age of 18 years. The component ratings were made in half-unit intervals. Illustrations of boys with dominant endomorphic, mesomorphic, and ectomorphic physiques appear in Fig. 3.2.

The foregoing procedures are commonly followed in present-day somatotyping. High objectivity coefficients have been obtained among trained assessors. Tanner (100) compared the ratings of three experienced somatotype evaluators (Barbara Honeyman Heath, C. Wesley Dupertuis, and himself) and reported correlations between assessors' ratings ranging from .83 to .92 for the three components. These raters agreed within a half-interval on the 7-interval scale 90 percent of the time; there was never a difference between assessors greater than 1 interval.

The Trunk Index

Since somatotype photographs had been taken of the same boys over a period of years in the Medford Boys' Growth Project, it was possible to make comparisons of the anthroposcopic and trunk-index methods of assessing physique types; thus, comparisons of phenotypes and genotypes could be made. As a consequence, Morton (76) contrasted the two methods of assessing somatotype components and their relationships to the maturity, structural, strength, and motor ability characteristics of the same 106 boys 9 through 16 years of age. The anthroposcopic method of somatotype determination was in accordance with the procedures described above in this chapter; the trunk-index method will be described below. Sheldon, Lewis, and Tenney (93) have described this process in detail.

Trunk-Index Determination

As indicated earlier, the trunk-index method of somatotyping is based on the trunk-index, the adult height, and the minimum height-over-cube-root-of-weight ratio (maximum ponderosity) during the growth process. Dr. William H. Sheldon made the actual genotype assessments from the data supplied to him. The procedures follow.

1. Photograph the subject in the same manner as for the anthroposcopic method.

2. Determine the trunk-index. The thoracic and abdominal trunk areas are measured with a planimeter from the somatotype photograph. These measures are made as follows:

a. Divide the trunk into thoracic and abdominal areas at the closest approximation to the plane of the anatomical waist. This plane is midway between the lowermost level of the ribs and uppermost level of the pelvis. The position of this plane is located on the somatotype photographs as follows: (i) Mark the point of intersection of the line of pouparts ligament and the lateral outline of the body in the frontal view. (ii) On the profile view, locate the apex of the lumbar angle and draw a horizontal line through this point and continue it across to the frontal and dorsal view photographs. (iii) If this plane is not coincident with the horizontal plane through the point determined in (i), a line which is midway between these two planes is used to represent the anatomical waist.

b. Determine the upper limit of the thoracic trunk. This is a line connecting the points of intersection of the sternocleidomastoid muscles and the trapezius muscles. The most lateral point of the thoracic trunk is the apex of the angle of the detoideous muscle. This can usually be located on the dorsal view photograph by continuing the line of the posterior axillary crease, formed by the junction of the musculature of the upper extremity and the thoracic trunk, until it intersects the body outline at the tip of the shoulder.

c. Determine the lower limit of the abdominal trunk by locating a horizontal plane through the photographic center of the subgluteal fold.

d. Apply a planimeter to determine the areas of the thoracic and abdominal trunks.

e. Divide the area of the thoracic trunk by the area of the abdominal trunk. The quotient is the trunk index.

3. Determine the adult height. In Morton's study, since the oldest age of the subjects was 16 years, the adult height was predicted from the subject's 16-year height and his skeletal age using tables prepared by Bayley and Pinneau (2).

4. Determine the subject's minimum inverse ponderal index (height-over-cube-root-of-weight). This index was found at the point in the subject's development when he was relatively most massive, i.e., the lowest index recorded for the subject over the period of his participation in the Medford Boys' Growth Project.

5. Determine the somatotype by reference to tables which utilize the measures of trunk index, adult height, and minimum inverse ponderal index. These tables for various ages and the two sexes appear in the publication by Sheldon, Lewis, and Tenney (93).

Comparison of Somatotype Methods

DIFFERENCES BETWEEN MEANS. The differences between the means of the somatotype components as assessed by the trunk-index and anthroposcopic techniques for the 106 Medford boys at each age 9 to 16 years inclusive appear in Table 3.1. The differences between the means were tested for significance by application of the t ratio; t ratios of 1.98 and 2.63 are needed for significance at the .05 and .01 levels respectively. The slight differences in trunk-index means for each component at the different ages are due to occasional instances of missing somatotype photographs at single ages.

The differences between the means for the endomorphic component assessed by the two methods were significant at the .01 level at all ages. These differences ranged from .34 to 1.01; the t ratios ranged from 4.86 to 14.43. The largest mean difference occurred at age 14 and the smallest mean difference was found at the age when each subject attained his minimum inverse ponderal index. This component was rated higher by the trunk-index than by the anthroposcopic method; the respective medians for the various ages were 4.30 and 3.38.

The differences between the mesomorphic means assessed by the two methods were significant at the .01 level at all ages except at age 16 and the age of attaining the minimum inverse ponderal index. The significant differences between the means ranged from .21 to .34; the t ratios ranged from 2.63 to 5.67. At all ages where significant differences occurred, the higher means were obtained again by the trunk-index method; the respective medians for the various ages were 4.39 and 4.15.

Table 3.1

DIFFERENCES BETWEEN MEANS OF SOMATOTYPE COMPONENTS
WHEN ASSESSED BY TRUNK-INDEX AND
ANTHROPOSCOPIC TECHNIQUES

Age	Means Truck Index	Anthroposcopy	Mean Diff.	σD_m	t Ratio
		Endomorphy			
9	4.27	3.38	.89	.08	11.13**
10	4.36	3.55	.81	.13	6.23**
11	4.23	3.41	.82	.09	9.11**
12	4.29	3.49	.80	.07	11.43**
13	4.31	3.51	.80	.08	10.00**
14	4.30	3.29	1.01	.07	14.43**
15	4.28	3.29	.99	.07	14.14**
16	4.31	3.42	.99	.15	6.60**
MP	4.29	3.95	.34	.07	4.80**
		Mesomorphy			
9	4.43	4.22	.21	.08	2.63**
10	4.36	4.15	.21	.07	3.00**
11	4.41	4.17	.24	.07	3.43**
12	4.39	4.05	.34	.06	5.67**
13	4.37	4.03	.34	.08	4.25**
14	4.40	4.08	.32	.08	4.00**
15	4.40	4.12	.28	.07	4.00**
16	4.36	4.20	.16	.12	1.33
MP	4.34	4.37	—.03	.06	.50
		Ectomorphy			
9	3.43	2.90	.53	.08	6.63**
10	3.47	2.85	.62	.08	7.75**
11	3.41	3.18	.23	.09	2.55*
12	3.45	3.20	.25	.08	3.13**
13	3.40	3.17	.23	.11	2.09*
14	3.40	3.35	.05	.11	.45
15	3.39	3.47	—.08	.08	1.00
16	3.51	3.43	.07	.11	.64
MP	3.48	2.51	.97	.09	10.78**

MP : *Age of minimum inverse ponderal index.*
  * *Significant at .05 level (1.98).*
 ** *Significant at .01 level (2.63).*

The differences between the ectomorphic means assessed by
the two methods were significant at the .01 level at ages 9, 10, and
12 and at the age of minimal inverse ponderal index, and at the
.05 level at ages 11 and 13; the mean differences at ages 14, 15, and
16 were not significant. The significant differences between the

means ranged from .23 at age 13 to .97 at the age of minimum inverse ponderal index; the significant *t* ratios ranged from 2.09 to 10.78. At all ages where significant differences occurred, once more the higher means were obtained by the trunk-index method; the respective medians for the various ages were 3.43 and 3.18.

CORRELATIONS BY AGE. The correlations between the trunk-index and anthroposcopic assessments for the three somatotype components at all ages and at the age of minimum inverse ponderal index were significant beyond the .01 level. With the exception of age 9, the endomorphy correlations varied closely between .692 and .758; at age 9, the correlation was .483. For mesomorphy, the correlations between the two assessments ranged from .394 to .580; for ectomorphy, the correlational range was from .554 to .695. The differences between the correlations for the same somatotype component for the various ages were not significant, except when the endomorphy correlation at age 9 was compared with the correlations at the other ages.

SOMATOTYPE DISTRIBUTIONS. At each age and at the age of minimum inverse ponderal index, the subjects were classified into five somatotype categories in accordance with the trunk-index and with the anthroposcopic methods of somatotype assessment. The categories were formed as follows: (1) Primary endomorph: endomorphic component of 5 and over; no other component over 4.5. (2) Primary mesomorph: mesomorphic component of 5 and over; no other component over 4.5. (3) Primary ectomorph: ectomorphic component of 5 and over; no other component above 4.5. (4) Endomesomorphy: endomorphic and mesomorphic components of 5 or greater; ectomorphic component less than 5. (5) Mid-type: none of the three components exceeding 4.5. The differences between the distributions of the subjects into the five categories as assessed by the two somatotype methods were tested for significance at the various ages by application of chi square; these results are presented in Table 3.2. Chi-squares of 9.49 and 13.28 are needed for significance at the .05 and .01 levels respectively.

The distributions of subjects into somatotype categories on the basis of an anthroposcopic assessment were significantly different from the distribution of these subjects when assessed by the trunk-

Table 3.2

DIFFERENCES BETWEEN DISTRIBUTIONS OF SOMATOTYPES WHEN
SUBJECTS WERE ASSESSED BY TRUNK-INDEX AND
ANTHROPOSCOPIC TECHNIQUES

Age	Variable	Endo-morph	Meso-morph	Ecto-morph	Endo-meso-morph	Mid-type	Chi-square
9	Trunk-Index Frequencies	14	21	10	10	38	51.05**
	Anthroposcopic Frequencies	4	17	1	1	70	
10	Trunk-Index Frequencies	17	20	12	10	42	38.91**
	Anthroposcopic Frequencies	7	15	3	4	72	
11	Trunk-Index Frequencies	16	22	10	10	42	32.29**
	Anthroposcopic Frequencies	6	13	9	3	69	
12	Trunk-Index Frequencies	17	23	11	10	43	28.25**
	Anthroposcopic Frequencies	9	17	11	0	67	
13	Trunk-Index Frequencies	16	23	10	9	44	35.24**
	Anthroposcopic Frequencies	5	12	12	2	71	
14	Trunk-Index Frequencies	15	23	12	10	41	38.17**
	Anthroposcopic Frequencies	3	13	16	2	67	
15	Trunk-Index Frequencies	16	22	10	9	41	24.85**
	Anthroposcopic Frequencies	7	14	19	3	55	

16	Trunk-Index Frequencies	17	22	10	9	41	9.64*
	Anthroposcopic Frequencies	8	21	14	4	52	
M. P.†	Trunk-Index Frequencies	17	23	12	10	44	24.49**
	Anthroposcopic Frequencies	8	20	2	10	66	

† M. P.: Age of minimum inverse ponderal index.
* Significant at the .05 level (9.49).
** Significant at the .01 level (13.28).

index technique at all ages. The chi-squares ranged from 9.64 at 16 to 51.05 at 9 years of age. The chi-square at age 16 was significant at the .05 level; all other chi-squares were significant well beyond the .01 level (24.29 and above).

At all ages except 15 and 16 years, larger discrepancies in the distributions occurred for the mid-type category by the anthroposcopic than by the trunk-index method. At all ages, the reverse was true for the endomorphic and the endomesomorphic categories (except for endomesomorphy at the age of minimum inverse ponderal index) with the trunk-index method having predominate frequencies. The frequencies were more evenly divided in the mesomorphic category, although the trunk-index assessments showed considerable dominance from ages 11 to 15 inclusive. For ectomorphy, the distributions varied: a fairly even division of frequencies at ages 11, 12, and 13; larger frequencies by the trunk-index method at ages 9 and 10; and greater frequencies by the anthroposcopic method at ages 14, 15, and 16.

Correlations with Selected Variables

At the ages of 10, 13, and 16, zero-order correlations were computed for each of the somatotype components as assessed by the two somatotype methods with the following selected variables: maturity, by skeletal age; body size, by skinfold total (three sites), hip width, chest girth, sitting height, abdominal girth, chest girth/sitting height, chest girth/standing height, chest girth/hip width, hip width/sitting height, chest girth/abdominal girth, and inverse ponderal index; motor ability, by standing broad jump, 60-yard shuttle run, 10-foot speed, and total-body reaction time; muscular endurance, by bar push-ups; and gross and relative muscular strength, by cable-tension strength average (11 tests) and Rogers' Physical Fitness Index respectively. The differences between the correlations by the two somatotype assessment methods were tested for significance by Hotelling's *t*-ratio formula for correlated correlations (55).

ENDOMORPHY. The correlations between endomorphy and skeletal age were significant by both somatotype assessment methods at age 10 only; the correlations of .266 and .331 were not significantly different.

For the body size measures, the correlations with endomorphy were significant at the .01 level and beyond, except for sitting height and chest girth/hip width. In general, the correlations were higher by the anthroposcopic than by the trunk index method. For three of these variables, the anthroposcopic method produced significantly higher correlations at the .05 level and above for all three ages. These correlations plus those for abdominal girth, where the correlational differences were significant at two ages only, are tabulated below; correlations of .195 and .254 are needed for significance at the .05 and .01 levels respectively.

Variable	Trunk-Index			Anthroposcopy		
	10 Yrs.	13 Yrs.	16 Yrs.	10 Yrs.	13 Yrs.	16 Yrs.
Skinfold Total	.714	.693	.693	.887	.816	.815
Abdominal Girth	.660	.706	.700	.792	.754	.748
Chest Girth/Sitting Ht.	.286	.582	.525	.537	.697	.683
Chest Girth/Standing Ht.	.554	.620	.482	.722	.714	.655

The only other significant correlational differences among these variables were for chest girth and chest girth/hip width at age 10 and inverse ponderal index at age 16. The correlations with the inverse ponderal index were negative, between −.640 and −.712 by trunk-index and −.795 and −.807 by anthroposcopic assessments.

The correlations between endomorphy and the various motor and muscular endurance and strength tests were substantially lower than for the body size measures by both somatotype assessment methods. The significant correlations obtained were either negative or had negative connotations, as for positive correlations with timed events where the lower scores are best. Although the differences were mostly insignificant, generally higher correlations were obtained by anthroposcopic assessment. The highest such correlations are tabulated below.

Variable	Trunk-Index			Anthroposcopy		
	10 Yrs.	13 Yrs.	16 Yrs.	10 Yrs.	13 Yrs.	16 Yrs.
Standing Broad Jump	—.304	—.431	—.448	—.418	—.495	—.495
60-Yd. Shuttle Run	.307	.318	.384	.329	.453	.405
10-Ft. Speed	.169	.233	.379	.136	.333	.486
Bar Push-ups	—.252	—.359	—.362	—.316	—.377	—.391
Physical Fitness Index	—.401	—.371	—.431	—.467	—.510	—.546

The only significant differences between correlations at the .05 level by the two assessment methods were for the 60-yard shuttle run and Physical Fitness Index at age 13. Total-body reaction time and cable-tension strength average did not reach significance at the .05 level at any age by either assessment method.

Mesomorphy. The correlations between mesomorphy and skeletal age were significant above the .01 level at age 13 by both somatotype assessment methods (.317 and .278) and at the .05 level at age 16 by the trunk-index method (.227). The differences between these correlations by the two assessment methods were not significant.

For the body size measures, the correlations with mesomorphy were much lower than with endomorphy by both assessment methods; in fact, of the 33 such correlations by each method, only 7 were significant at the .01 level by trunk-index and 15 by anthroposcopic assessments. Generally, the correlations of this component with these measures were higher by anthroposcopic than by trunk-index assessments. The only differences between the correlations by the two assessments that were significant at the .05 level and above at all three ages were chest girth/standing height and inverse ponderal index; the correlations were positive with the former and negative with the latter index. For skinfold total and abdominal girth, the correlational differences were significant at ages 13 and 16. A tabulation of these correlations follows.

Variable	Trunk-Index			Anthroposcopy		
	10 Yrs.	13 Yrs.	16 Yrs.	10 Yrs.	13 Yrs.	16 Yrs.
Chest Girth/Standing. Ht.	.197	.103	.391	.568	.516	.659
Inverse Ponderal Index	—.187	—.105	—.292	—.621	—.625	—.685
Skinfold Total	.125	—.120	—.141	.316	.339	.179
Abdominal Girth	—.005	.050	.084	.174	.397	.364

The only other significant correlational differences among these variables were for chest girth at age 13 and chest girth/abdominal girth at age 16.

The correlations between mesmorphy and the various motor and muscular strength and endurance measures were mostly non-significant at the .05 level; of the 33 correlations by each somototype assessment method, only 11 by the trunk-index and 6 by the anthroposcopic method were significant. The highest of these correlations appear below.

Variable	Trunk-Index			Anthroposcopy		
	10 Yrs.	13 Yrs.	16 Yrs.	10 Yrs.	13 Yrs.	16 Yrs.
Standing Broad Jump	.190	.292	.271	.008	.064	.097
Bar Push-ups	.186	.271	.382	.208	.151	.320
Cable-Tension Strength Av.	.129	.242	.464	.253	.442	.393

The only significant correlational differences between the two assessment methods at the .05 level were for standing broad jump and cable-tension strength average at age 13.

ECTOMORPHY. The correlations between ectomorphy and skeletal age were significant at the .05 level and above by both somatotype assessment methods at all ages but 10 by the trunk-index method. The correlations were negative, ranging from $-.137$ to $-.295$. The correlational differences by the two assessment methods were not significant.

The correlations between ectomorphy and the body size measures were mostly negative (excepting inverse ponderal index) and significant by both assessment methods, but were higher by the anthroposcopic method. The differences between the correlations by the two methods were significant at the .01 level and above at all three years for skinfold total, chest girth, abdominal girth, chest girth/sitting height (.05 level at age 10), chest girth/standing height, and inverse ponderal index; at the .05 level, the correlational differences were significant for hip width at the three ages. These correlations appear in the following tabulation for the three ages.

Variable	Trunk-Index			Anthroposcopy		
	10 Yrs.	13 Yrs.	16 Yrs.	10 Yrs.	13 Yrs.	16 Yrs.
Skinfold Total	—.392	—.176	—.194	—.751	—.686	—.547
Hip Width	—.002	—.116	.018	—.195	—.348	—.161
Chest Girth	—.288	—.311	—.247	—.610	—.570	—.454
Abdominal Girth	—.184	—.211	—.210	—.545	—.703	—.547
Chest Girth/Sitting Ht.	—.358	—.321	—.446	—.744	—.481	—.693
Chest Girth/Standing Ht.	—.575	—.476	—.597	—.799	—.815	—.802
Inverse Ponderal Index	.614	.506	.649	.902	.958	.924

The highest correlations between ectomorphy and the motor and muscular strength and endurance measures by the two somatotype assessment methods were obtained for the standing broad jump, bar push-ups, and cable-tension strength average. These correlations are given in the following tabulation.

Variable	Trunk-Index			Anthroposcopy		
	10 Yrs.	13 Yrs.	16 Yrs.	10 Yrs.	13 Yrs.	16 Yrs.
Standing Broad Jump	.079	—.034	.035	.242	.246	.309
Bar Push-ups	—.245	—.248	—.348	.002	.095	—.022
Cable-Tension Strength Av.	—.131	—.250	—.257	—.242	—.319	—.174

All correlations were positive for standing broad jump and all correlations were negative for cable-tension strength average; for bar push-ups, the correlations were negative by the trunk-index and non-significant by the anthroposcopic method. The differences between the correlations were significant at the .05 level and above at all three ages for standing broad jump and bar push-ups; for cable-tension strength average, the correlational differences were not significant.

Summary

1. Generally, the trunk-index method produced higher somatotype designations for the three components at all ages than did the anthroposcopic method. The differences between the component means for all endomorphy and all but two mesomorphy and three ectomorphy comparisons were significant.

2. The correlations between trunk-index and anthroposcopic assessments for the various ages ranged from .394 to .758. The endomorphy and ectomorphy correlations were higher than those for mesomorphy.

3. The distributions of somatotypes into the five categories of primary endomorphs, primary mesomorphs, primary ectomorphs, endomesomorphs, and mid-types by the two assessment methods were significantly different. The trunk-index assessments produced a more proportionate distribution over the five categories at all ages. Generally, more subjects were located in the endomorph, endomesomorph, and ectomorph categories by the trunk-index method and in the mid-type category by the anthroposcopic method; the subjects were more evenly divided in the mesomorph category.

4. The following results were obtained from correlating maturity, structural, motor, and muscular strength and endurance measures with the three somatotype components as assessed by the two methods at the ages of 10, 13, and 16:

   a. For skeletal age, significant positive correlations were found with endomorphy at age 10 and with mesomorphy at ages 13 and 16 by both assessment methods; with ectomorphy, the correlations were significant but negative at the three ages. The differences between correlations by the two methods were not significant.

   b. For body size measures, the correlations were much higher by the anthroposcopic than by the trunk-index assessments with endomorphy in a positive and ectomorphy in a negative direction; with mesomorphy, the correlations by the anthroposcopic method were also higher but not so high, and they were in a positive direction. The tests showing significant correlational differences at the .05 level and above at all three ages were: chest girth/standing height for all three components; skinfold total and chest girth/sitting height for endomorphy and ectomorphy; inverse ponderal index for mesomorphy and ectomorphy; and hip width, chest girth, and abdominal girth for ectomorphy only.

   c. For the motor and muscular strength and endurance measures, the correlations with the somatotype components as assessed by the two methods were low and mostly insignificant. The correlations with endomorphy were negative or had negative connotations (as for timed events); the reverse was true for mesomorphy and ectomorphy. The highest correlations with somatotype components were for standing broad jump, bar push-ups, and cable-tension strength average. With few exceptions, the correlational differences by the two assessment methods were insignificant.

Somatotype Stability

As indicated above in the discussion of the phenotype versus genotype in somatotype determination, the issue of phenotype changes during growth has been resolved. Initial studies refuting Sheldon's early contention that the somatotype is stable were reported by Hunt and Barton (58) and Lasker (67). Hunt and Barton longitudinally studied 71 boys in order to compare the 10-year-old physique with its subsequent status at the time it reached Tanner's terminal maturation stage. Inasmuch as some boys fatten, others stabilize, and still others thin down during adolescence, the investigators commented that this period of growth is often a "calorie revolution whose intensity cannot be efficiently forecast from a nude photograph. . . ." Consequently, similar adult physiques may be realized by quite different developmental paths in different individuals. Lasker studied the effects of nutritional deprivation on the somatotype; the mean rating for endomorphy decreased 49 percent, mesomorphy decreased 43 percent, and ectomorphy increased 77 percent. Investigators in the Medford Boys' Growth Project have studied the stability of the somatotypes (phenotypes) of boys; these studies are reported below.

Inter-Age Correlations

Kurimoto (66) studied the somatotype designations of the same boys from ages 15 through 18. The inter-age correlations of the somatotype components ranged from .69 to .87 for endomorphy, .81 to .91 for mesomorphy, and .83 to .93 for ectomorphy.

In two Medford studies, Sinclair followed the somatotype assessments of 100 boys from ages 9 through 12 (96) and 106 boys from ages 12 through 17 (97). The inter-age correlations of the

Table 3.3

INTER-AGE CORRELATIONS FOR THE SOMATOTYPE COMPONENTS
OF BOYS FROM 9 THROUGH 17 YEARS OF AGE*

Part A

Component	Age		*Age* 10	11	12
Endomorphy	9		.79	.78	.77
	10			.85	.76
	11				.82
Mesomorphy	9		.90	.88	.83
	10			.93	.80
	11				.83
Ectomorphy	9		.85	.80	.79
	10			.89	.84
	11				.86

Part B

Component	Age	13	14	*Age* 15	16	17
Endomorphy	12	.80	.70	.60	.59	.50
	13		.82	.73	.63	.54
	14			.85	.73	.66
	15				.83	.73
	16					.80
Mesomorphy	12	.94	.88	.80	.75	.60
	13		.91	.81	.77	.62
	14			.89	.84	.68
	15				.89	.73
	16					.84
Ectomorphy	12	.90	.80	.74	.74	.67
	13		.86	.85	.80	.71
	14			.90	.83	.73
	15				.86	.76
	16					.89

* *Significant at .01 level : .25.*

somatotype components appear in Table 3.3: Part A for ages 9
through 12 and Part B for ages 12 through 17. The highest inter-age
correlations were found for adjacent ages; the greater the gaps
between ages, the lower were these correlations. For the various
inter-age gaps, the ranges of correlations for the three somatotype
components are shown in the following tabulation.

Gaps	*Endomorphy*	*Mesomorphy*	*Ectomorphy*
One Year	.79 to .85	.83 to .93	.85 to .90
Two Years	.70 to .78	.73 to .88	.76 to .85
Three Years	.63 to .77	.68 to .83	.73 to .80
Four Years	.54 to .59	.62 to .75	.71 to .74
Five Years	.50	.60	.67

Mean Differences

In Kurimoto's study of boys from ages 15 through 18, the mean amount of mesomorphy increased from 4.05 to 4.65 and the mean amount of ectomorphy decreased from 3.71 to 3.18 as the subjects became older; the amounts of increases and decreases for these components were significant each succeeding year. The mean amount of endomorphy increased from ages 15 to 16, but returned to the 15-year-old level at ages 17 and 18.

Sinclair also tested the differences between the means of the somatotype components for successive ages in his two studies. For the 100 boys tested from ages 9 through 12, none of the differences between the means of the components during the four-year period was significant; the t ratios ranged from .05 to .76. The mean ranges for the components were as follows: endomorphy, 3.42 to 3.59; mesomorphy, 4.07 to 4.18; and ectomorphy, 2.80 to 3.18.

For the 106 boys from ages 12 through 17 tested by Sinclair, the following results were obtained:

ENDOMORPHY. The endomorphy means of these boys remained essentially the same, 3.32 and 3.35, at ages 12 and 13; a decrease to a mean of 3.14 occurred at 14, followed by an increase to 3.22 at 15 and a decline to 3.15 and 3.07 at 16 and 17 years. Six of the 15 differences between the means, or 40 percent, were significant at the .05 level; the significant t ratios ranged from 2.03 to 3.88. Only one of the significant differences occurred between adjacent ages, which was between 13 and 14 years. The remaining significant differences were between age 12 and ages 14, 16, and 17 and between age 13 and ages 14 and 16.

MESOMORPHY. The mesomorphy means of these boys remained approximately the same, 3.93 to 3.97, at ages 12, 13, and 14; then, a steady rise to means of 4.02, 4.20, and 4.48 occurred during the last three years. Eight of the 15 differences between means, or 54 percent, were significant well beyond the .05 level; the significant *t* ratios ranged from 4.61 to 9.88. Only one of these differences involved adjacent ages, which was between 16 and 17 years. The other significant differences primarily involved the ages of 16 and 17: 12, 13, and 14 years with both of these ages and age 15 with 17 years only.

ECTOMORPHY. The ectomorphy means of these boys displayed a steady rise from 3.37 at age 12 to 3.47 and 3.70 at ages 13 and 14, followed by a gradual decline as the means decreased to 3.62, 3.52, and 3.27 during the last three years. Eight of the 15 mean differences, or 53 percent, were significant at the .05 level: the significant *t* ratios ranged from 1.99 to 5.12. Three of these differences involved the adjacent ages of 12 and 13, 13 and 14, and 16 and 17. The remaining significant differences occurred between age 14 and ages 12, 13, 16, and 17 and between age 17 and ages 13 and 15.

Changes and Fluctuations

In Sinclair's studies, inspection of the annual somatotype assessments of the subjects revealed greater instability than was portrayed by the mean differences. As a consequence, he studied the magnitude of changes and maximum fluctuations for his two longitudinal series.

Magnitude of change was determined as the difference between a boy's initial and final ratings on a component during the period of study. For example, if a subject's annual endomorphic ratings were 4^2, 4, 4, 3^2, 3^2, 2^2, this pattern constitutes a change of 2, the difference between 4^2 and 2^2. Changes of .5 in component assessments were disregarded, since a change of this magnitude is an acceptable assessment error in accordance with the reliability of somatotyping.

Maximum fluctuation was determined as the greatest difference between any two ratings of a component during the period of study. For example, if a subject's annual endomorphic ratings were 5^2, 7^2, 6^2, 5^2 5, 5^2, this pattern shows no change at the first and last ages, since both assessments were 5^2; however, the maximum fluctuation was 2.5, as represented by the amount between the minimum and maximum ratings of 5 and 7^2.

AGES 9 THROUGH 12. The numbers of changes of one full unit or more for the 100 boys from ages 9 through 12 were 46 for endomorphy, 7 for mesomorphy, and 52 for ectomorphy. Further analysis revealed that for the endomorphic component, 35 boys changed 1.0, 8 changed 1.5, 1 changed 2.0, and 2 changed 2.5 units. The mesomorphic component had 6 changes of 1.0 and 1 change of 1.5 units. Ectomorphy showed 41 changes of 1.0, 9 changes of 1.5, and 2 changes of 2.0 units.

AGES 12 THROUGH 17. For the 106 boys from ages 12 through 17, the magnitude of change in endomorphy was 1.0 or more for 48 boys; 26 changes were by 1.0, 12 by 1.5, 6 by 2.0, 3 by 2.5, and 1 by 3.0 units. For 60 subjects, various fluctuations in this component occurred during this period. For 11 subjects who displayed no change at ages 12 and 17, 8 showed fluctuations of 1.0 and fluctuations of 1.5, 2.0, and 2.5 occurred for the other subjects. Twenty-one subjects had a 12-17-age difference of .5, but had the following fluctuations: 1.0 for 16, 1.5 for 4, and 2.5 for 1. For 18 subjects with a 12-17-age difference of 1.0, the fluctuations were 1.0 for 5, 1.5 for 12, and 2.0 for 1. The other fluctuations were scattered and mostly related to their magnitude of changes.

The mesomorphic assessments change by 1.0 or more for 34 of the subjects over the six-year period; 21 changes were by 1.0, 11 by 1.5, and 1 each by 2.0 and 2.5 For 16 boys, various fluctuations in this component occurred during the six-year period. A single subject showed no change at ages 12 and 17, but showed a fluctuation of .5. Thirteen subjects had a 12-17-age difference of .5 with 11 fluctuations of 1.0 and 2 of 1.5; 2 subjects had a 12-17-age difference of 1.0, which was the amount of their fluctuations.

The ectomorphic assessments varied by 1.0 or more for 39 of the boys over the six-year period; 22 changes were by 1.0, 11 by 1.5, 4 by 2.0, and 2 by 2.5. For 61 subjects various fluctuations in this component occurred during this period. For 13 subjects who had no change at ages 12 and 17, 9 showed a fluctuation of 1.0, 3 of

1.5, and 1 of 2.5. Twenty-eight subjects had a .5 12-17-age difference, but had the following fluctuations: 1.0 for 21, 1.5 for 5, and 2.0 and 2.5 for 1 each. For 10 subjects with a 1.0 12-17-age difference, the fluctuations were 1.0 for 1, 1.5 for 5, and 2.0 for 4. For 6 subjects with a 1.5 12-17-age difference, the fluctuations were 1.5 for 1, 2.0 for 2, 2.5 for 2, and 3.5 for 1. The remaining fluctuations were scattered and mostly related to their magnitude of changes.

Summary

1. The highest inter-age correlations of somatotype components were obtained for adjacent years; the ranges of these correlations were .79 to .85 for endomorphy, .83 to .93 for mesomorphy, and .85 to .90 for ectomorphy. The lowest such correlations were for the five-year gap, .50, .60, and .67 respectively for the three components.

2. For the 15 differences between each of the component means for the various ages, 6 were significant for endomorphy and 8 each for mesomorphy and for ectomorphy. Most of these significant differences occurred when more than one year intervened. The differences between component means for ages 9 to 12 were not significant; the ages most involved with significant differences were 17 with 5 and 12, 13, and 14 with 4 each.

3. Inspection of somatotype assessments of the subjects revealed even greater instability of somatotype components. The numbers of changes for the 100 boys ages 9 through 12 and the 106 boys ages 12 through 17 were 94 for endomorphy, 42 for mesomorphy, and 91 for ectomorphy. Additional fluctuations occurred during the respective age spans.

Correlations between Somatotype Components

In Sinclair's studies (96,97), the correlations between somatotype components at each age 9 through 17 were determined. The correlations between endomorphy and mesomorphy were not significant at the .05 level for ages 9 and 17; for the intervening years, the correlations ranged between .212 and .366. Ectomorphy correlated negatively with both endomorphy and mesomorphy; the ranges of the correlations were comparable, −.644 to −.748 for endomorphy and −.643 to −.758 for mesomorphy.

Somatotype Categories

Irving (31,59) studied the differences in the maturity, body size, and muscular strength of Medford boys grouped into various somatotype categories.

Procedures

The subjects consisted of 37 boys chosen at random at each age 9 through 15, a total of 259 boys, covering the upper elementary and junior high school grades. Five somatotype categories were formed, according to the following specifications:

Endomorphs (18 subjects): endomorphic component of 5 and over; no other component above 4.
Mesomorphs (54 subjects): mesomorphic component of 5 and over; no other component above 4.
Ectomorphs (63 subjects): ectomorphic component of 5 and over; no other component above 4.
Endomesomorphs (26 subjects): mesomorphic component of 5 and over; endomorphy of 4 and above; ectomorphy below 4.
Mid-types (98 subjects): no component exceeding 4.

Twenty-two experimental variables were included in this study, as follows:

Maturity measure: skeletal age.
Body size measures: body weight, standing height, sitting height, leg length, chest girth, flexed-tensed upper arm girth, calf girth, hip width, and lung capacity. Two derived measures were included based on the above body size measures, Wetzel physique channels and McCloy's Classification Index I (20 Age + 6 Height + Weight).
Relative muscular strength and endurance measures: pull-ups or chins, push-ups from the parallel bars, and Rogers' Physical Fitness Index.

In grouping the subjects into the five somatotype categories, it was assumed that the distributions of somatotypes by age would be comparable for these classifications. A check on this assumption revealed that it was reasonably well met for endomorphs, endomesomorphs, and mid-types. However, there were more mesmorphs in the younger ages and more ectomorphs in the older ages. Inasmuch as most of the experimental variables increase with age, the mesomorphs were at a disadvantage and the ectomorphs had an advantage in comparison with the other somatotype categories.

The data were analyzed for the five categories with all ages included; this procedure is known herein as the *original* analysis. In addition, a second analysis was made, known as the *supplementary* analysis. Since there were sufficient numbers of boys at ages 10 and 14 in the mesomorph, ectomorph, and mid-type categories to permit comparisons, the differences between these groups for certain of the variables were determined. Thus, for the supplementary analysis, the effect of age upon the results was eliminated. It may still be contended, however, that the mesomorphs were at a disadvantage and the ectomorphs had an advantage for some tests when compared with the endomorphs and endomesomorphs.

The basic statistical procedure used in the analysis of data consisted of testing the significance of the differences between the means of the experimental variables for the various somatotype categories by application of the t ratio. For some variables, the means of the highest and lowest 25 percents of the boys were also compared in the same manner. A problem was encountered in reaching conclusions where findings in the original analysis differed from the supplementary analysis of the 10- and 14-year-old boys. In these instances, findings based on the data from the 10- and 14-year-old boys took precedence, as the variances introduced by age were not present. For this study, significance for the difference between means was accepted at the .05 level.

Results

MATURITY. None of the t ratios reached significance at the .05 level when the means in skeletal age for boys in the five somatotytpe categories were compared. When the highest and lowest 25 percents of the boys in skeletal age were compared, however, the following results were obtained: A significantly greater percentage of boys were advanced than were retarded for the endomesomorph category; the reverse was true for the mid-type boys, as a significantly greater percentage of these boys were retarded than were advanced in skeletal age.

BODY SIZE. A summary of the results obtained in testing the differences between the means of the body size measures for the various somatotype categories follows.

1. The means of the endomorphs and the endomesomorphs significantly exceeded the means of the other somatotype categories in body weight, chest girth, upper arm girth, and calf girth. The endomorphs had a greater mean hip width than did all other somatotype categories except the endomesomorphs. In all probability, the heavier flesh folds distributed generally over the bodies of the endomorphs and endomesomorphs account for their greater girth measures. No significant mean difference was found between these two categories and the others in standing height, sitting height, Classification Index, and lung capacity. For all body size measures, the differences between the means of the endomorphs and the endomesomorphs were not significant.

2. In the original analysis, the means of the ectomorphs were significantly higher than those of the mesomorphs in standing height and leg length. However, these differences were not significant in the supplementary analysis of the 10- and 14-year-old boys; thus it is concluded that differences between these categories are due to sampling. The mesomorphs had a significantly higher mean upper arm girth and calf girth than did the ectomorphs.

3. For all body size measures in the original analysis, the differences between the means of the mesomorphs and mid-types were not significant. However, in the supplementary analysis, the mesomorphs had significantly higher means in calf girth at both 10 and 14 years and in upper arm girth at 10 years.

4. In the original analysis, the means of the ectomorphs were significantly higher than the means of the mid-types in standing height, sitting height, and leg lift. In the supplementary analysis, the ectomorphs were superior to the mid-types in standing height,

at age 10 only. Also, in the supplementary analysis, the ectomorphs had a significantly higher mean hip width at age 10 than did the mid-types.

5. High t ratios were obtained for the differences between the five somatotype categories when compared by Wetzel physique channels. The endomorphs and the endomesomorphs were predominantly in channels A-4, A-3, and A-2; the mesomorphs and mid-types, in channels A-1, M, and B-1; and the ectomorphs, in channels B-2, B-3, and B-4.

GROSS MUSCULAR STRENGTH AND ENDURANCE. A summary of the differences between the means of the gross muscular strength and endurance measures for the five somatotype categories follows.

1. In the original analysis, no significant difference was found between the sum of grips and leg lift means for the various somatotype categories. In the supplementary analysis, the means of the mesomorphs were significantly higher than the means of the mid-types and ectomorphs in sum of grips at 10 years of age, the means of the mid-types in leg lift at 10 and 14 years, and the mean of the ectomorphs in leg lift at 14 years. In the original analysis, the mean of the mesomorphs in back lift was significantly lower than the means of the ectomorphs, endomesomorphs, and mid-types. When adjusted for age by comparing the 10- and 14-year-old boys, however, the differences in back lift were reversed in favor of the mesomorphs with significant differences between the means.

2. The Rogers' arm strength mean of the endomorphs was significantly lower than the means of the other somatotype categories. The mean of the mesomorphs significantly exceeded the means of endomesomorphs and the mid-types in the original analysis and the means of the mid-types at 10 and 14 years and of the ectomorphs at 14 years of age. The ectomorphs had a significantly higher mean than did the endomesomorphs. For McCloy's arm strength score, the mean of the endomesomorphs was significantly higher than the means of the ectomorphs and mid-types in the original analysis; the means of the mesomorphs significantly exceeded the means of the ectomorphs and mid-types. When the

highest and lowest 25 percents of the boys were compared, a significantly greater percentage of mesomorphs was found in the higher scoring group.

3. In the original analysis, the mean of the endomorphs was significantly lower than the means of the endomesomorphs and mid-types for the cable-tension strength average; and the mean of mid-types was higher than the mean of the ectomorphs. No significant difference between means for this measure was obtained on the supplementary analysis. When the highest and lowest 25 percents of the boys on the cable-tension tests were compared, significantly greater percentages of mesomorphs and endomesomorphs were found in the upper 25 percent and a significantly greater percentage of ectomorphs was found in the lower 25 percent.

RELATIVE MUSCULAR STRENGTH AND ENDURANCE. The results of the differences between the means of the relative muscular strength and endurance measures for the five somatotype categories follow.

1. Sixteen of the 18 boys in the mesomorph category were unable to perform a single pull-up; the mean number of pull-ups for this group was .06. For the other comparisons, the mesomorphs had significantly higher means than did the endomesomorphs, ectomorphs, and mid-types; and both the ectomorphs and mid-types had significantly higher means than the mean of the endomesomorphs. Much the same results were obtained with the push-up test, performed supporting full body weight on parallel bars.

2. The Physical Fitness Index means of the endomorphs and the endomesomorphs were significantly lower than the means for the boys in the other somatotype categories; the mean of the endomorphs was significantly lower than the mean of the endomesomorphs. The mean of the mesomorphs was significantly higher than the mean of the mid-types; the difference between the means of the mesomorphs and ectomorphs was not significant. When the highest and lowest 25 percents of the boys on this test were compared, the following results were obtained: Significantly greater percentages of endomorphs and endomesomorphs were found in the lower 25 percent; significantly greater percentages of mesomorphs and

ectomorphs were found in the upper 25 percent; the mid-types were fairly evenly distributed between these high and low Physical Fitness Index groups.

Summary

ENDOMORPHS: The endomorphs had greater body weight, chest girth, upper arm girth, calf girth, and hip width than did the mesomorphs, ectomorphs, and mid-types. They were generally found in Wetzel's physique channels A-4, A-3, and A-2. This group was able to perform only a few, if any, pull-ups and push-ups and had lower Rogers' arm strength scores and Physical Fitness Indexes than all other categories. They also had lower cable-tension strength test means than the endomesomorphs and mid-types and lower Strength Indexes than the ectomorphs. (Quite possibly, the Strength Index superiority of the ectomorphs is due to their being generally older; also, the mesomorphs' lack of superiority on this test could logically be due to their relatively younger ages.)

ENDOMESOMORPHS: No significant difference was found between the endomorphs and the endomesomorphs in the various body size measures; however, the endomesomorphs did show superiority to the endomorphs in number of pull-ups and push-ups, Rogers' arm strength scores, cable-tension strength tests, and Physical Fitness Indexes. This group had greater body weight, chest girth, upper arm girth, and calf girth than did the mesomorphs, ectomorphs, and mid-types. They were generally found in Wetzel's physique channels A-4, A-3, and A-2. The endomesomorphs also had lower Strength Indexes and Rogers' arm strength scores than the ectomorphs; their McCloy's arm strength scores were superior to those of the ectomorphs and mid-types.

MESOMORPHS: The mesomorphs were smaller than the endomorphs in body weight, chest girth, upper arm girth, calf girth, and hip width; they were also smaller than the endomesomorphs, except for hip width. The situation for these body size measures is not conclusive, however, as the mesomorphs generally were younger, a fact which would naturally result in lower means on these tests than for the generally older endomorphs and endomesomorphs. Compared with the ectomorphs and mid-types, the mesomorphs had larger upper arm and calf girths. Generally their Wetzel physique channels were A-1, M, and B-1. The mesomorphs had higher means than the ectomorphs and mid-types on the following muscular strength and endurance measures: back lift, leg lift, Strength Index, pull-ups, push-ups, and both Rogers' and McCloy's arm strength scores. For the Physical Fitness Index, they exceeded the mid-types but not the ectomorphs. As for the structural measures, the comparisons of mesomorphs with endomorphs and endomesomorphs on strength tests were obscured by the differences in age; however, it was clear that the mesomorphs were superior in pull-ups, push-ups, Rogers' arm strength, and Physical Fitness Indexes.

ECTOMORPHS: The ectomorphs were smaller than the endomorphs and endomesomorphs in body weight, chest girth, upper arm girth, calf girth, and hip width; with the exception of hip width, the ectomorphs were also smaller than the endomesomorphs on these tests. Further, the ectomorphs were smaller than the mesomorphs in chest and calf girths and were larger than the mid-types in hip width. The boys in this category were found largely in Wetzel physique channels B-2, B-3, and B-4. For the muscular strength and endurance measures, the ectomorphs were superior to the endomorphs and endomesomorphs in pull-ups, push-ups, and Physical Fitness Indexes, and to the endomorphs in Strength Index, although this latter superiority was probably due to the fact that the ectomorphic boys were generally older. The ectomorphs were inferior to the mesomorphs in sum of grips, back and leg lifts, Strength Index, pull-ups and push-ups, and Rogers' and McCloy's arm strength scores. The only strength difference between the ectomorphs and mid-types was that the ectomorphs were stronger on the cable-tension tests.

MID-TYPES: Although there were a number of exceptions, the mid-types followed somewhat the pattern of the ectomorphs in their comparison with the other somatotype categories. The exceptions were: no difference in chest girth in comparison with mesomorphs, no superiority to endomesomorphs in Rogers' arm strength, and inferiority to mesomorphs in Physical Fitness Index. The only significant differences noted between the mid-types and the ectomorphs were that the ectomorphs had greater standing height and hip width at age 10 and the mid-types were stronger on cable-tension strength tests. The mid-types were generally found in Wetzel physique channels A-1, M, and B-1.

The only tests in this study where no significant mean difference was found between the five somatotype categories were sitting height, leg length, Classification Index, and lung capacity. For standing height, only one difference was obtained, between the ectomorphs and mid-types. A significantly greater percentage of endomesomorphs were advanced than were retarded in skeletal age; the reverse was true for the mid-type boys.

Somatotype Correlations

In his longitudinal studies mentioned earlier, Sinclair determined the relationships between somatotype components and experimental variables consisting of maturity, body size, muscular strength and endurance, and motor tests for the same Medford boys at each age from 9 through 12 (96) and from 12 through 17 (97). Multiple correlations and multiple regression equations were also computed with each of the somatotype components serving as the dependent variable in turn. Earlier, Munroe (77) conducted a similar study with 12-year-old Medford boys, but included partial correlations as well. The results of these studies will be presented here.

Product-Moment Correlations

In each of Sinclair's longitudinal series, the differences between Fisher z-coefficient equivalents of the product-moment correlations were tested for significance by application of the *t* ratio. The correlations needed for significance at the .05 level were .195 and .192 for the ages 9 through 12 and 12 through 17 respectively.

AGES 9 THROUGH 12. The product-moment correlations between the somatotype components and the experimental variables for the

100 boys from ages 9 through 12 appear in Table 3.4. A summary of these results follows.

1. *Endomorphy.* The highest correlations with endomorphy for all four ages were found with measures of body bulk (positive) and with inverse ponderal index (negative); these correlations ranged between .707 and .814 for weight and arm girth and between −.714 and −.854 for the index. Skeletal age and the linear measures had low but significant correlations with this component, ranging between .224 and .372. Physical Fitness Index and bar dips had negative correlations with endomorphy, ranging between −.248 and −.422. The cable-tension strength average showed a steady progression from .214 at 9 years to .524 at 12 years. For the motor ability elements, all correlations with the shuttle run were insignificant. An insignificant correlation with the standing broad jump was found at age 12; for the other three ages, significant correlations between −.198 and .254 were obtained.

Only three significant differences between the correlations of endomorphy with the experimental variables at the four ages were obtained. These differences were between 9 and 10 years for negative correlations with the two indices and between 9 and 12 years for the positive correlations with cable-tension strength average. The age 9 boys had the higher correlation for the indices but the lower correlation for the strength average.

2. *Mesomorphy.* The inverse ponderal index had the highest correlations with mesomorphy; these correlations were negative, ranging from −.592 to −.685. Arm girth had the next highest correlations, between .406 and .503. Skeletal age, weight, and cable-tension strength average had low positive but significant correlations with this component; the highest such correlation was .359 for cable-tension strength average at age 12. Sitting height/standing height had comparable significant correlations at three of the ages. Leg length correlated significantly but negatively with mesomorphy; for the four ages, the coefficients ranged between −.207 and −.267. Four variables did not correlate significantly with mesomorphy at any age; these variables were height, Physical Fitness Index, standing broad jump, and shuttle run.

None of the differences between the correlations of mesomorphy with the experimental variables at the four ages was significant.

Table 3.4

PRODUCT MOMENT CORRELATIONS BETWEEN SOMATOTYPE COMPONENTS AND EXPERIMENTAL VARIABLES FOR THE SAME BOYS FROM 9 THROUGH 12 YEARS OF AGE

Variables	Endomorphy				Mesomorphy				Ectomorphy			
	9	10	11	12	9	10	11	12	9	10	11	12
Skeletal Age	.224*	.339*	.350*	.340*	.207*	.257*	.197*	.238*	−.287*	−.329*	−.265*	−.277*
Height	.308*	.305*	.342*	.372*	−.170	−.157	−.169	−.058	.035	.037	.037	.017
Leg Length	.352*	.237*	.304*	.279*	−.217*	−.207*	−.267*	−.250*	.031	.084	.094	.147
Weight	.714*	.771*	.799*	.765*	.233*	.318*	.282*	.320*	−.548*	−.562*	−.583*	−.536*
Arm Girth	.707*	.814*	.767*	.792*	.406*	.503*	.494*	.442*	−.686*	−.717*	−.731*	−.695*
Inverse Ponderal Index	−.714*	−.854*	−.829*	−.791*	−.592*	−.685*	−.658*	−.650*	.896*	.926*	.950*	.943*
Sitting Ht./Standing Ht.	−.302*	−.019	−.108	−.276*	.193	.201*	.341*	.333*	.029	−.120	−.160	−.050
C-T Strength Average	.214*	.328*	.418*	.524*	.248*	.255*	.314*	.359*	−.219*	−.276*	−.347*	−.472*
Physical Fitness Index	−.248*	−.422*	−.358*	−.330*	.028	.002	.142	.102	.158	.239*	.191	.110
Bar Dips	−.352*	−.307*	−.362*	−.366*	.249*	.230*	.195*	.154	.079	.042	.103	.078
Standing Broad Jump	−.249*	−.198*	−.254*	−.145	.065	.029	−.013	.060	.225*	.119	.289*	.105
60-Yd. Shuttle Run	.184	.090	.102	.045	−.155	−.191	−.097	−.109	−.014	.062	−.060	.021

* Exceeds .05 level of significance (.195).

3. *Ectomorphy.* The highest correlations with ectomorphy were obtained for the inverse ponderal index; the range of coefficients was from .896 to .950. The body bulk measures of arm girth and weight showed moderately high negative relationships with this component; the ranges were −.686 to −.731 and −.536 to −.583, respectively. The correlations with skeletal age were negative and significant at all ages, ranging from −.265 to −.329. Cable-tension strength average displayed a steady increase in negative correlations over the four-year period; these correlations rose from −.219 at age 9 to −.472 at age 12. Non-significant correlations were obtained at all ages for height, leg length, sitting height/standing height, bar dips, and 60-yard shuttle run.

Only three differences between the correlations of ectomorphy with the experimental variables at the four ages were significant. These differences were: between ages 9 and 11 for inverse ponderal index and between ages 9 and 12 for inverse ponderal index and cable-tension strength average.

AGES 12 THROUGH 17. The product-moment correlations between the somatotype components and the experimental variables for the 106 boys from ages 12 through 17 are shown in Table 3.5. These results are summarized below.

1. *Endomorphy.* The highest correlations with endomorphy ranged from −.762 to −.835 for inverse ponderal index over the six-year span and from .804 to .845 for skinfold total during the last three years when this measurement was made. Moderately high correlations, between .499 and .729, were obtained for the body bulk measures of weight, arm girth, and calf girth; for sitting height × chest girth, the range was between .271 and .502. The correlations between this component and Physical Fitness Index, Rogers' arm strength score, and bar dips were all significant but negative; the respective ranges were −.336 to −.657, −.338 to −.502, and −.364 to −.449. The motor ability elements had correlations of comparable magnitude and were negative or were positive with negative connotations (timed events). The correlations with skeletal age were significant (.198 to .293) during the first three years only. All correlations between endomorphy and height,

Table 3.5

PRODUCT-MOMENT CORRELATIONS BETWEEN SOMATOTYPE COMPONENTS AND EXPERIMENTAL VARIABLES
FOR THE SAME BOYS FROM 12 THROUGH 17 YEARS OF AGE

Variables	Endomorphy						Mesomorphy						Ectomorphy					
	12	13	14	15	16'	17	12	13	14	15	16	17	12	13	14	15	16	17
Skeletal Age	.255*	.293*	.198*	.127	.111	.160	.243*	.305*	.401*	.453*	.447*	.396*	−.198*	−.277*	−.202*	−.201*	−.291*	−.373*
Height	.066	.039	.041	−.035	−.101	.014	−.072	−.025	.037	.052	−.116	−.178	.183	.135	.208*	.257*	.293*	.338*
Lung Capacity	.077	.191	.078	.078	.090	.018	.168	.246*	.253*	.298*	.293*	.186	−.019	−.128	−.041	−.035	−.161	−.042
Weight	.644*	.577*	.508*	.499*	.567*	.656*	.418*	.452*	.481*	.534*	.472*	.386*	−.520*	−.512*	−.402*	−.421*	−.538*	−.557*
Arm Girth	.729*	.637*	.547*	.499*	.520*	.553*	.531*	.571*	.610*	.672*	.643*	.498*	−.679*	−.629*	−.558*	−.539*	−.676*	−.650*
Calf Girth	.646*	.593*	.540*	.550*	.599*	.607*	.552*	.600*	.548*	.625*	.562*	.512*	−.699*	−.600*	−.489*	−.577*	−.618*	−.631*
Skinfold Total				.804*	.810*	.845*				.318*	.295*	.160				−.606*	−.640*	−.612*
Inverse Ponderal Index	−.835*	−.834*	−.777*	−.763*	−.779*	−.726*	−.702*	−.753*	−.676*	−.727*	−.712*	−.630*	.957*	.970*	.965*	.931*	.949*	.942*
Sitting Height X Chest Girth	.502*	.387*	.307*	.271*	.311*	.380*	.350*	.371*	.438*	.480*	.427*	.356*	−.376*	−.334*	−.240*	−.225*	−.362*	−.356*
C-T Strength Average	.171	.181	.205*	.120	.072	.073	.256*	.277*	.358*	.299*	.359*	.402*	−.266*	−.244*	−.233*	−.191	−.257*	−.271*
Left Grip Strength	.146	.190	.172	.185	.093	.153	.068	.267*	.359*	.326*	.279*	.077	−.121	−.227*	−.179	−.172	−.228*	−.115
Physical Fitness Index	−.418*	−.336*	−.440*	−.496*	−.576*	−.657*	−.201*	−.058	−.011	−.021	−.039	.017	.327*	.256*	.244*	.257*	.340*	.342*
Rogers' Arm Strength	−.459*	−.338*	−.384*	−.333*	−.416*	−.502*	−.076	.029	.180	.281*	.206*	.289*	.329*	.194*	.157	.112	.127	.143
Bar Dips	−.393*	−.384*	−.432*	−.364*	−.375*	−.449*	−.011	.008	.144	.194*	.163	.288*	.251*	.185	.111	.101	.086	.065
Standing Broad Jump X Weight	.335*	.307*	.188	.241*	.214*	.266*	.298*	.233*	.391*	.436*	.469*	.495*	−.273*	−.294*	−.170	−.216*	−.345*	−.381*
Standing Broad Jump Distance	−.379*	−.340*	−.458*	−.264*	−.420*	−.490*	−.129	−.123	.020	.068	.153	.266*	.304*	.265*	.306*	.185	.138	.146
60-Yard Shuttle Run	.270*	.164	.370*	.243*	.232*	.262*	.136	.112	−.021	−.096	−.094	−.227*	−.268*	−.169	−.235*	−.047	−.056	−.030
Total Body Completion Time		.209*	.374*	.237*	.251*	.287*		.170	−.006	−.143	−.045	−.178		−.244*	−.235*	−.089	−.090	−.134

* Exceeds .05 level of significance (.192).

lung capacity, cable-tension strength average, and left grip strength were insignificant.

The only significant differences between correlations at the six ages were: for arm girth, when the highest correlation at 12 years (.729) was compared with those at 14, 15, 16, and 17 years (.499 to .547); for inverse ponderal index, when the lowest correlation at 17 years (−.726) was compared with the coefficients at 12 and 13 years (−.835 and −.834); and for Physical Fitness Index, when 17 years (−.657) was compared with 12, 13, and 14 years (−.336 to −.440) and when 16 years (−.576) was compared with 13 years (−.336).

2. *Mesomorphy*. The highest correlations with mesomorphy were with inverse ponderal index, between −.676 and −.727. The correlations with body bulk measures ranged from .512 to .672 for arm and calf girths and from .386 to .534 for weight. Skeletal age, sitting height × chest girth, cable-tension strength average, and standing broad jump × weight correlated significantly with this component at the six ages; the correlations were comparable, ranging from .233 to .495. The correlations were low but significant at four ages for lung capacity and left grip strength (13 to 16 years) and at three ages for Rogers' arm strength score (15 to 17 years). The variables without significant correlations at any age were height and total-body completion time.

Some significant differences between correlations with mesomorphy at the different ages were obtained. However, they were of minor importance, since low correlations were compared with insignificant correlations or low positive and low negative correlations were compared; these significant differences could well be within the limits imposed by the .05 level.

3. *Ectomorphy*. Especially high correlations were obtained between ectomorphy and inverse ponderal index; the correlational range was .931 to .970. The correlations with body bulk measures were negative, ranging from −.402 to −.699. Skeletal age and sitting height × chest girth had low negative but significant correlations with this component at all ages (−.198 to −.376); the same was found for Physical Fitness Index but the correlations were positive (.256 to .342). The correlations were low and significant

at five ages for cable-tension strength average (negative) and standing broad jump × weight (negative), at four ages for height (positive), at three ages for standing broad jump distance (positive), at two ages for left grip strength (negative) and 60-yard shuttle run (positive, but negative connotation), and at one age for Rogers' arm strength score (positive) and bar dips (positive). Insignificant correlations were obtained at all ages for lung capacity and total-body completion time.

The only significant differences between correlations with ectomorphy at the different ages were for inverse ponderal index. The correlation of .970 at 13 years was significantly higher than the .931 and .942 at 15 and 17 years, and the correlations of .965 at 14 years was significantly higher than the .931 at 15 years.

Partial Correlations

Partial correlations were computed by Munroe (77, 78) with 12-year-old boys in order to analyze the relationships between each of his experimental variables and the somatotype components without the possible interference of the other experimental variables. Somatotype ratings indicate the shape of the body rather than size, and therefore, the true relationship of physique to structure and performance may be masked by differences in body size.

Of the 2,268 partial correlations computed, the majority was not significantly different from the corresponding zero-order correlations. However, the relationships between somatotype components and measures of body structure increased significantly when contrasting structural measures were held constant. The greatest differences were obtained with ectomorphy and linearity when body bulk measures were held constant; only 3 of the 28 differences were not significant. The zero-order correlation between ectomorphy and standing height was .164, but with weight constant, the partial correlation was .926.

For endomorphy, the zero-order correlations with measures of body bulk were moderately high, yet when linear measures were partialed, a significant increase was obtained. Partialing standing height increased the correlation between endomorphy and body weight from .708 to .862. Reversing these variables had a greater effect. The zero-order correlation between endomorphy and standing height was .187, but with weight held constant, the partial correlation was −.709.

The correlation coefficients for mesomorphy were generally lower than for the other two somatotype components, yet the partial correlations increased significantly in several instances. The pattern of increase indicated that mesomorphy was associated with a large upper body and relatively short, thick limbs. The zero-order correlation between mesomorphy and leg length was −.300; with weight held constant, the partial correlation was −.697. Calf girth correlated .420 with mesomorphy, but when leg length was partialed, the coefficient was .723.

Multiple Correlations and Regression Equations

In Sinclair's studies (96, 97) multiple correlations and their regression equations were computed for all ages from 9 through 17 by stepwise regression procedures. For each multiple correlation, a somatotype component was the dependent variable and the experimental tests were the independent variables. From ages 12 through 17, two such correlations and equations were computed. For one of these, the somatotype components other than the one serving as the dependent variable were included; for the other, the somatotype components were excluded. The multiple correlations and regression equations thus obtained follow: for ages 12 through 17, the A designations include the somatotype components and the B designations do not.

Endomorphy:

Age	Part	R	Regression Equation	SE est
9		.911	−.86(meso) −.39(ecto) −.25 (height) +.09(weight) +15.58	.38
10		.935	−.81(meso) +.12(arm girth) − 2.17(inv. ponderal index) +32.58	.35
11		.947	−.80(meso) −.46(height) +.13 (weight) +22.29	.36
12	A	.933	−2.54(inv. ponderal index) −.78 (meso) +.06(height) +36.23	.36
	B	.891	−.65(inv. ponderal index) +.16 (chest girth) −.02(arm strength) −.01(sitting height × chest girth) +.39(weight) +6.94	.46

13	A	.939	−3.37(inv. ponderal index) −.83 (meso) +.52(ecto) +53.40	.33
	B	.880	−.77(inv. ponderal index) −.02 (bar dips) +.03(arm girth) −.27(height) +.30(weight) +18.53	.45
14	A	.934	−4.28(inv. ponderal index) −.94 (meso) +.66(ecto) +61.41	.33
	B	.876	−.68(inv. ponderal index) −.03 (bar dips) −.27(standing broad jump) +.31(weight) −.22(height) +18.06	.45
15	A	.922	.17(skinfold total) −2.04 (inv. ponderal index) −.75 (meso) +.05(height) +29.73	.36
	B	.861	.29(skinfold total) −.85(inv. ponderal index) −.01(arm strength) +13.80	.47
16	A	.932	.13(skinfold total) −2.04(inv. ponderal index) −.71(meso) +32.63	.33
	B	.891	.21(skinfold total) −.48(inv. ponderal index) −.01(arm strength) −.21(height) +.18(weight) +13.97	.42
17	A	.921	.22(skinfold total) −.19(st. broad jump) −1.55(inv. ponderal index) −.56(meso) +26.73	.42
	B	.888	.33(skinfold total) −.33(standing broad jump) −.67(inv. ponderal index) +13.47	.49

Mesomorphy: *

12	A	.878	−.04(ecto) −.65(endo) −1.77 (inv. ponderal index) +.07 (calf girth) +27.56	.33
	B	.798	−1.52(inv. ponderal index)+.01 (arm strength) +.31(height) −.53(weight) +.17(calf girth) +13.92	.42
13	A	.913	.14(ecto) −.64(endo) −2.14 (inv. ponderal index) +.06 (calf girth) +32.13	.26
	B	.842	−1.28(inv. ponderal index) +.01(arm strength) −.15(calf girth) −.36(weight) +.18(height) +13.81	.35
14	A	.926	−2.01(inv. ponderal index) −.56 (endo) +.08(height) +29.90	.26
	B	.826	−1.72(inv. ponderal index) +.01 (arm strength) −.09(completion time) +.23(height) −.22(weight) +22.83	.35

15	A	.906	−1.66(inv. ponderal index) −.58 (endo) +.10(arm girth) +25.07	.31
	B	.847	−1.23(inv. ponderal index) +.01 (arm strength) −.15(height) +.10 (calf girth) −.05(C-T strength av.) +17.59	.39
16	A	.913	−.05(ecto) −.73(endo) −1.93 (inv. ponderal index) +.07(calf girth) +29.68	.31
	B	.856	−1.73(inv. ponderal index) +.01 (arm strength) −.13(skinfold total) +.18(height) −.23(weight) +.12(calf girth) +19.60	.40
17	A	.901	−.24(ecto) −.48(endo) +.12 (calf girth) +.02(bar dips) −.83 (inv. ponderal index) +12.76	.33
	B	.854	−1.25(inv. ponderal index) +.01 (arm strength) −.20(height) +.12(calf girth) −.06(left grip) +17.50	.40

Ectomorphy:

9		.918	−.30(endo) −.54(meso) +1.06 (inv. ponderal index) −7.6	.38
10		.926	2.10(inv. ponderal index) −24.54	.38
11		.949	2.27(inv. ponderal index) −26.67	.34
12	A, B	.957	2.26(inv. ponderal index) −26.48	.33
13	A, B	.970	2.42(inv. ponderal index) −28.55	.30
14	A, B	.965	2.50(inv. ponderal index) −29.63	.31
15	A, B	.931	2.37(inv. ponderal index) −27.77	.43
16	A	.960	2.92(inv. ponderal index) +.30(endo) −35.98	.33
	B	.949	2.45(inv. ponderal index) −28.89	.37
17	A, B	.942	2.24(inv. ponderal index) −26.14	.38

* *The multiple correlations with mesomorphy are not given at ages 9 through 11, as they were too low to warrant prediction.*

Summary

1. Considerable consistency existed between the product-moment correlations of somatotype components and the experimental variables from age to age. Few differences between such

inter-age correlations were significant; in Sinclair's studies, the numbers were 6 out of 252 differences, or 2.4 percent, from ages 9 through 12, and 30 out of 858 differences, or 3.5 percent, from ages 12 through 17. The main significant differences for the three components were:

ENDOMORPHY. At age 9, the negative correlations with the two indices were higher than at age 10 and the positive correlation with cable-tension strength average was lower than at age 12. The positive arm girth correlation at age 12 was higher than at ages 14, 15, 16, and 17; at age 17, the correlation was higher with Physical Fitness Index than at ages 12, 13, and 14, and was lower with the inverse ponderal index than at ages 12 and 13.

MESOMORPHY. The correlational differences between mesomorphy and the experimental variables were of little significance.

ECTOMORPHY. The significant correlational differences between ectomorphy and the experimental variables mostly involved the inverse ponderal index (all positive correlations). These differences were higher at age 11 than at 9 years, higher at age 13 than at 15 and 17 years, and higher at age 14 than at 15 years.

2. The inverse ponderal index had the highest product-moment correlations with somatotype components from ages 9 through 17. The ranges of these correlations for the nine years were from $-.714$ to $-.854$ for endomorphy, $-.592$ to $-.753$ for mesomorphy, and .896 to .970 for ectomorphy.

3. The body bulk measures of weight, arm girth, and calf girth had moderately high correlations with the somatotype components. The directions of these correlations were opposite those for the inverse ponderal index, positive for endomorphy and mesomorphy and negative for ectomorphy. The highest correlations with endomorphy were for skinfold total for the three years this measure was available; the coefficients ranged from .804 to .845.

4. Other correlations between somatotype components and experimental variables that were significant for the nine years of the studies were: skeletal age, positive for mesomorphy and negative for ectomorphy; cable-tension strength average, positive for mesomorphy; Physical Fitness Index, bar dips, and standing broad jump distance, negative for endomorphy. For the age span 12 through

17 years, the following correlations were significant at all ages: sitting height × chest girth, positive for endomorphy and mesomorphy and negative for ectomorphy; Rogers' arm strength score, negative for endomorphy; standing broad jump × weight, positive for mesomorphy; total-body completion time, positive (negative connotation) for endomorphy.

5. The variables with the fewest significant correlations with somatotype components were height, leg length, lung capacity (except for mesomorphy), and total-body completion time (except for endomorphy).

6. The relationships between somatotype components increased considerably when contrasting structural measures were held constant. The greatest differences were obtained with ectomorphy and linearity when body bulk measures were partialed out.

7. Multiple correlations between somatotype components as dependent variables and the experimental tests as independent variables were high enough to warrant prediction of individual components. For endomorphy and mesomorphy, the multiple correlations were highest when the other somatotype components were included in the computations. The inverse ponderal index appeared most frequently by far in the multiple correlations; in fact, regression equations based on this variable alone were justifiable for predicting ectomorphy at all ages. Other variables found frequently in the multiple correlations were height, weight, Rogers' arm strength score, skinfold total, and calf girth.

Chapter Summary

This chapter was devoted to the somatotype as a means of designating physique type. Sheldon's original phenotype assessment through anthroposcopy was compared with his later genotype assessment through the trunk index. Generally, the trunk-index method produced higher somatotype designations than did the anthroposcopic method. However, the correlations between somatotype components and body size measures were much higher from age to age by anthroposcopic than by trunk-index assessments. The

inter-age correlations between adjacent years ranged from .79 to
.93; when four years intervened, the correlational range was from
.50 to .67, and various fluctuations in component designations
occurred.

From age to age, considerable consistency was found between
the correlations of somatotype components with measures of maturity, body size, muscular strength and endurance, and motor elements. The inverse ponderal index had the highest correlations with
somatotype components; the correlations were negative with endomorphy and positive with ectomorphy. The reverse was true for
body bulk measures, although the correlations were not so high.
The relationships with somatotype components increased considerably when contrasting structural measures were held constant.
Other significant correlations with somatotype components were:
skeletal age, positive for endomorphy and mesomorphy and negative for ectomorphy; cable-tension strength average, positive for
mesomorphy; Physical Fitness Index, bar dips, and standing broad
jump distance, negative for endomorphy. For the age span 12
through 17 years, the following correlations were significant at all
ages: height × chest girth, positive for endomorphy and mesomorphy and negative for ectomorphy; Rogers' arm strength score,
negative for endomorphy; standing broad jump × weight, positive
for mesomorphy; total-body completion time, positive (negative
connotations) for endomorphy.

Chapter **4** / **Physical Structure**

It is not startling to contend that the individual's physical structure is an essential factor in his motor performances. Evidence of this relationship is everywhere. Observe the well-proportioned physique of boxers, wrestlers, and gymnasts, the superstructure of great basketball competitors, the solidarity of top-flight football players, the wiriness of champion distance runners, and the massive builds of great shot-putters and discus throwers.

Anthropometry is the oldest type of body measurement known, dating back to the beginning of recorded history. The concepts of the ideal proportions varied over periods of time. For example, Polycletus fashioned Doryphorus, the Spear-Bearer, as a fighter and an athlete, broad shouldered, thick set, and square chested, the perfect man. This ideal lasted for nearly a century. As the arts of civilization became more refined, however, grace rather than ruggedness appealed to the Greeks; the ideal man then became slender, graceful, and skillful, albeit also well proportioned.

In the United States, anthropometric measurement was the first type of testing used in physical education.

On the theory that exercise should be prescribed to affect muscle size, emphasis was placed upon body symmetry and proportion. In 1861, Hitchcock, and later Sargent, prepared profile charts to reveal how individuals compared with standards. Stargent's chart, which was widely used at the time, required 44 separate anthropometric measurements, as well as certain strength tests, before the instructor could analyze a student's body proportions. Fifty such measurements were recommended by the American Association for the Advancement of Physical Education. While physical education has been concerned with many types of measurement during the century since Hitchcock's early studies, the physical structure of the body as it relates to motor performance has been a consistent, although not always an intense, interest of researchers in the field.

This chapter is devoted to significant findings pertaining to the physical structure of the subjects in the Medford Boys' Growth Project. The anthropometric measures included for all twelve years were standing height, sitting height, leg length, hip width, weight, arm girth, chest girth, calf girth, and lung capacity. Abdominal, buttocks, and thigh girths were added after the first year and skinfold measures were included beginning in the fourth year. Indices based on the anthropometric tests were also used. These measures will be discussed in this chapter.

Anthropometric Test Descriptions

Following are descriptions of the anthropometric tests employed in the Medford Boys' Growth Study.

Linear Measures

STANDING HEIGHT. Subject stood in stocking feet on stadiometer with heels, buttocks, and shoulders touching a vertical plane; top of head was extended forcefully upward. The square in the stadiometer groove was brought down with enough force to crush the hair. Reading made to nearest tenth of an inch.

SITTING HEIGHT. Subject sat on 12-inch bench placed on stadiometer with buttocks and shoulders against the vertical plane, head extended forcefully upward, and feet flat on base of instrument. The square in the stadiometer groove was brought down with enough force to crush the hair. Reading made to nearest tenth of an inch.

LEG LENGTH. Leg length was obtained as the difference between standing and sitting heights.

Body Bulk Measures

WEIGHT. Subject stood in shorts and stocking feet in the center of beam-type platform scales. Reading made to nearest pound.

ARM GIRTH. Subject stood in normal standing position with left upper arm abducted slightly with forearm flexed. A Gulick tape* was placed around largest part of upper arm at right angles to its axis; subject flexed muscles to greatest size. Reading made to nearest tenth of a centimeter. The Gulick tape, i.e., anthropometric tape with Gulick handle, is shown in Fig. 4.1, as applied to the arm girth measures.

CHEST GIRTH. Subject stood in a relaxed position with elbows flexed to 90 degrees and upper arms held away from body. Gulick tape was located around thorax at nipple level and held horizontally. Readings to nearest tenth of a centimeter were taken after maximum inspiration and after maximum expiration. Chest girth was the average of these readings.

ABDOMINAL GIRTH. Subject stood in relaxed position. Gulick tape was located around trunk at level of umbilicus. Subject was instructed to hold abdomen in normal position, neither sucked in nor extended. Reading made to nearest tenth of a centimeter.

---

* The Gulick tape has a handle with a spring in it which permits constant pressure when making measurements over soft tissue. This tape may be obtained from J. A. Preston, Corporation, 71 Fifth Avenue, New York, N. Y. 10003.

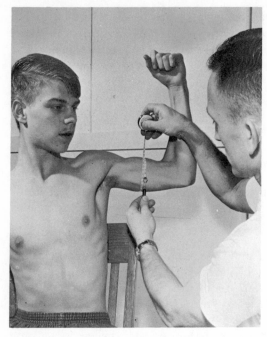

Fig. 4.1 Arm girth test with Gulick tape

BUTTOCKS GIRTH. Subject stood in relaxed position, including gluteal musculature, with feet together. Gulick tape was located horizontally around buttocks at point of greatest girth. Reading made to nearest tenth of a centimeter.

THIGH GIRTH. Subject stood in relaxed position, including thigh muscles, with feet slightly apart and weight evenly distributed. Gulick tape was located horizontally around left thigh at point of greatest girth. Reading made to nearest tenth of a centimeter.

CALF GIRTH. Subject stood in relaxed position, including muscles of lower leg, with feet slightly apart and weight evenly distributed. Gulick tape was located horizontally around calf at point of greatest girth. Reading made to nearest tenth of a centimeter.

SKINFOLD TOTAL. Skinfold tests are described in a later section of this chapter under "Skinfold Measures."

Hɪᴘ Wɪᴅᴛʜ. Subject stood with feet together, weight evenly distributed and arms hanging loosely at sides. Wooden sliding caliper was applied to lateral surfaces of iliac crests with enough force to feel bone resistance. Reading made to nearest tenth of a centimeter.

Lung Capacity

Lung capacity was measured with a wet spirometer, graduated in cubic inches. Subject took one or two deep breaths. Then, after fullest possible inhalation, subject placed mouthpiece attached to hose in mouth and exhaled slowly and steadily while bending forward until all air within his control was expelled through the hose. Subject was instructed to prevent air from escaping through nose or around mouthpiece. Reading made to nearest cubic inch. This test is illustrated in Fig. 4.2.

Factor Analyses

As presented in Chapter 2, several factor analyses were conducted in the Medford Boys' Growth Study in attempts to identify a general maturity factor. These factor analyses will not be described again here. However, additional details will be given about the rotated factors related to physical structure obtained by Phillips (80) in his longitudinal analyses of 62 boys from 9 through 16 years of age.

Body Bulk-Physique

The rotated loadings for Body Bulk-Physique for the eight ages, 9 through 16, are shown in Table 4.1. This factor appeared in the first rotation at six ages and the second rotation at two ages. Its identification was based on high loadings of the body bulk and physique type measures. The linearity measures loaded low on this rotated factor at all ages.

For this factor, endomorphy loaded positively and ectomorphy loaded negatively. Height/$\sqrt[3]{\text{weight}}$, also, loaded negatively, which

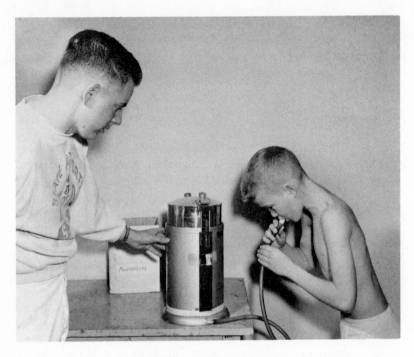

Fig. 4.2 Lung capacity test

is logical due to the high correlation between this index and ecto-morphy (around .96, as reported in Chapter 3). The mesomorphy loadings were moderate but positive. The loadings for weight/height^2 were consistently high, between .852 and .984 for the various ages.

The bulk measures increased from age 9 to high loadings at 10, decreased yearly to low loadings at 14, and finally increased to high loadings at 16 years. The body development at age 10 appeared to be more affected by body bulk than for other ages, especially 14 years. This trend was also evident for endomorphy, but was not found for ectomorphy, height/$\sqrt[3]{\text{weight}}$, and chest girth/height. For these indices, the trend was a decrease in loadings from 9 to 10 followed by a steady increase to a high at 13, and a

Table 4.1

BODY BULK-PHYSIQUE ROTATED FACTOR LOADINGS FOR BOYS
FROM AGES 9 THROUGH 16

	Ages							
Variables	9	10	11	12	13	14	15	16
Endomorphy	.628	.869	.916	.908	.871	.728	.835	.861
Mesomorphy	.585	.339	.421	.514	.591	.713	.633	.511
Ectomorphy	−.705	−.731	−.840	−.869	−.922	−.930	−.838	−.785
Weight	.720	.913	.899	.789	.606	.520	.786	.875
Arm Girth	.849	.941	.913	.894	.767	.635	.799	.874
Buttock Girth		.922	.887	.802	.612	.542	.809	.887
Thigh Girth		.948	.908	.843	.746	.657	.840	.903
Calf Girth	.739	.918	.862	.650	.648	.490	.860	.806
Chest Girth	.704	.941	.929	.875	.692	.603	.779	.900
Skinfold Total				.891	.868	.742	.820	.847
Height/$\sqrt[3]{\text{Weight}}$	−.962	−.875	−.942	−.943	−.963	−.956	−.948	−.903
Weight/Height^2	.923	.953	.984	.959	.909	.852	.967	.955
Chest Girth/Height	.823	.764	.897	.901	.922	.900	.900	.875

gradual decline to 16 years of age. The loadings for ectomorphy increased steadily from 9 to a high at 14 and then declined to 16 years of age. These increases in index loadings at age 14 corresponded to the decreases in the bulk measures.

Body Linearity

The rotated loadings for Body Linearity for the eight ages appear in Table 4.2. This factor appeared in the third rotation for six ages and one each in the first (14 years) and fifth (16 years) rotations. Its identification was based on high loadings of the linearity measures. The body bulk and physique measures generally loaded·low on this rotated factor.

For the Body Linearity factor, the loadings were positive at ages 9, 10, and 14 and were negative at the other ages. The negative loadings are interpreted as possible failures of body linearity of boys at these ages to keep pace with general development. The highest consistent loadings for the linearity measures were obtained at ages 13 and 14. At age 13, they were negative; at age 14, they were positive. The high positive loadings of the linearity meas-

Table 4.2

BODY LINEARITY ROTATED FACTOR LOADINGS FOR BOYS
FROM AGES 9 THROUGH 16

Ages	Standing Height	Sitting Height	Leg Length
Nine Years	.950	.875	.761
Ten Years	.762	.735	.637
Eleven Years	−.693	−.778	−.494
Twelve Years	−.821	−.862	−.563
Thirteen Years	−.951	−.930	−.834
Fourteen Years	.957	.900	.839
Fifteen Years	−.909	−.821	−.800
Sixteen Years	−.715	−.794	−.385

ures at age 14 corresponded to the lower loadings of the bulk measures on the Body Bulk-Physique Factor at this age. This result may indicate that at age 14, growth and development are more affected by linearity than by bulk.

Relative Sitting Height

Relative Sitting Height was identified as a rotated factor at all ages but 9 years, due to high loadings of the single index of sitting height/standing height. The loadings were:

Age	Loading	Age	Loading
Ten Years	.894	Fourteen Years	.896
Eleven Years	−.915	Fifteen Years	.876
Twelve Years	.888	Sixteen Years	−.892
Thirteen Years	.881		

Leg length was the only other measure to load moderately high with this factor; these loadings ranged from .449 at 14 to .824 at 16 years of age. The negative loadings at ages 11 and 16 are interpreted as some lag in the relative sitting height of boys at those ages as related to general body development.

Relative Lung Capacity

Relative Lung Capacity was identified as a rotated factor at five ages, although it had higher loadings than other tests at two additional ages. This factor was so named because of high loadings on lung capacity/standing height and on lung capacity. The loadings for the seven ages follow.

Age	Lung Capacity/Height	Lung Capacity
Nine Years	.917	.875
Ten Years	.925	.904
Eleven Years	.961	.916
Twelve Years	.916	.860
Thirteen Years	−.620	−.467
Fourteen Years	−.573	−.426
Sixteen Years	.880	.854

The identification of this factor was somewhat obscured due to the accompanying high loadings of lung capacity. However, the consistently higher loadings for the index accounted for the name given. High positive loadings were obtained at ages 9, 10, 11, 12, and 16. The negative loadings at ages 13 and 14 were only moderate and may indicate some developmental lag in this trait at these ages. This factor was not found at age 15.

Comparisons with Other Studies

The rotated factor identified as Body Bulk-Physique in Phillips' factor analyses was found at all ages from 9 through 16. A similar factor was obtained in other studies by Willee (113), But (10), Torpey (104), and McCloy (71, 72). Direct comparisons were not possible, since most other studies did not include the somatotype components in the correlational matrix. Different names for this factor were used, such as Growth in Cross Section by McCloy, Ectomorphy-Endomorphy by Willee, and Body Bulk by Burt.

In Phillips' factor analyses, Body Linearity was also found as a rotated factor at all eight ages. The same factor was obtained by other investigators, except Torpey with 16-year-old boys. The factor names given by others were Height by Willee, Linearity of Bone Structure by Burt, and General Growth by McCloy. A minor difference existed between the results of Phillips' and McCloy's studies: both studies had negative loadings at ages 11, 12, 13, 15, and 16, but McCloy's loadings were also negative at age 14 while Phillips' were positive at this age.

Phillips identified Relative Sitting Height as a rotated factor at all ages except 9 years. The same factor was obtained by Torpey for 16-year-old boys, but not by Willee and Burt for boys 9 and 13 years of age. McCloy did not use this measure in his factor analysis.

Relative Lung Capacity was found as a factor at all ages in Phillips' study. For the other analyses reviewed, only Willee with 9-year-old boys identified this factor.

Intercorrelations of Structural Measures

Because of the large number of structural measures and indices included in the Medford Boys' Growth Study and the extensive amount of information developed about each of these, some selection of the measures to be presented in this section seemed necessary. Criteria applied in their selection were: (1) Representative of their respective categories as revealed in the factor analysis studies presented above. (2) High correlations with other measures in their respective categories. (3) Highly related to such nonstructural measures as muscular strength and endurance, motor elements, and athletic ability. (4) Revealing distinctive mean growth curves in cross-sectional and longitudinal studies. (5) Distinctive characteristics in other respects, such as low relationships with other structural measures. The tests thus selected are: weight, arm girth, skinfold total, hip width, standing height, lung capacity, and chest girth × height. All correlations, of course, may be found in the studies cited. Most correlations presented here are from the longitudinal factor analysis study by Phillips (80).

Weight

Weight was selected as one of the body bulk measures against which to present the correlations of other anthropometric measures and indices. The correlations for ages 9 through 16 appear in Table 4.3. A summarization of these correlations follows.

Table 4.3

CORRELATIONS BETWEEN WEIGHT AND
OTHER ANTHROPOMETRIC MEASURES AND INDICES
FOR THE SAME BOYS AGED 9 THROUGH 16

Variables	Ages							
	9	10	11	12	13	14	15	16
Body Bulk								
Arm Girth	.828	.864	.904	.893	.913	.918	.870	.801
Chest Girth	.880	.891	.938	.919	.944	.941	.943	.897
Abdominal Girth		.873	.913	.819*	.888	.858	.876	.891
Buttocks Girth		.970	.963	.968	.956	.871	.967	.956
Thigh Girth		.947	.944	.948	.917	.918	.929	.911
Calf Girth	.863	.918	.927	.821*	.924	.837*	.898	.881
Skinfold Total				.697	.591	.454	.575	.677
Hip Width	.608	.675	.669	.751	.828	.776	.655	.726
Linearity								
Standing Height	.725	.761	.700	.726	.775	.805	.686	.533
Sitting Height	.570	.663	.653	.669	.714	.789	.642	.534
Leg Length	.639	.693	.594	.561	.720	.673	.579	.332
Indices								
Wt./Ht.^{2}	.879	.899	.919	.878	.849	.852	.868	.881
Wt./Ht.	.980	.984	.985	.976	.976	.977	.977	.974
Ht./$\sqrt[3]{\text{Wt.}}$	−.671	−.721	−.768	−.676	−.589	−.551	−.654	−.735
Chest Girth × Ht.	.907	.948	.913	.963	.957	.957	.931	.912

Corrections made from original.

The correlations of weight with the various girth measures were generally high, ranging in the high .80's and .90's. The correlations with buttocks and thigh girths were the highest, between .871 and .970 for buttocks girth and .911 and .948 for thigh girth. The correlations of weight with skinfold total and hip width were lower than for the other body bulk measures, between .454 and .697 for skinfold total and .608 and .828 for hip width.

The correlations between weight and the three linear measures were mostly in the .60's and .70's. The lowest of these correlations were at age 16: .533 for standing height, .534 for sitting height, and .332 for leg length. The highest correlations were .805 for standing height and .789 for sitting height at 14 and .720 for leg length at age 16.

Weight had high positive correlations with three of the indices, as follows: weight/height, .976 to .985; chest girth × height, .907 to .963; and weight/height², .849 to .919. The correlations with height/$\sqrt[3]{\text{weight}}$ were negative and lower, between −.551 and −.768.

Arm Girth

Arm girth was selected as a second body bulk measure against which to show the correlations of the other anthropometric measures. The annual correlations for the Medford boys from 9 through 16 years of age are given in Table 4.4. A summarization of these correlations follows.

The correlations of arm girth with weight and the other girth measures were mostly in the .80's. The highest of these correlations were at the middle ages, 10 to 14. A drop in correlations was found

Table 4.4

CORRELATIONS BETWEEN ARM GIRTH AND
OTHER ANTHROPOMETRIC MEASURES AND INDICES
FOR BOYS AGED 9 THROUGH 16

	Ages							
Variables	*9*	*10*	*11*	*12*	*13*	*14*	*15*	*16*
Body Bulk								
Weight	.828	.864	.904	.893	.913	.918	.870	.801
Chest Girth	.788	.889	.899	.878	.906	.890	.846	.798
Abdominal Girth		.830	.863	.768*	.880	.835	.790	.738
Buttocks Girth		.870	.882	.865	.871	.791	.816	.752
Thigh Girth		.910	.875	.904	.880	.854	.837	.807
Calf Girth	.835	.868	.875	.678*	.890	.693*	.811	.702
Skinfold Total				.797	.654	.438	.491	.652
Hip Width	.451	.632	.546	.624	.744	.711	.582	.552
Linearity								
Standing Height	.412	.474	.466	.443	.555	.648	.446	.125
Sitting Height	.293	.400	.460	.451	.531	.634	.461	.249
Leg Length	.380	.423	.377	.366	.503	.545	.332	−.030
Indices								
Wt./Ht.²	.851	.900	.919	.920	.896	.856	.854	.881
Wt./Ht.	.868	.901	.930	.932	.942	.931	.896	.856
Ht./$\sqrt[3]{\text{Weight}}$	−.760	−.819	−.845	−.821	−.741	−.650	−.740	−.751
Chest Girth × Ht.	.706	.829	.802	.817	.834	.857	.765	.665

Corrections made from original.

at 16 with some decline at 15 years of age; at age 16, the correlations were .807 and below. The correlations with skinfold total ranged from .438 to .797 for the four years this measure was included. Some declines in the correlations occurred with calf girth at the ages of 12, 14, and 16. The lowest arm girth correlations among the bulk measures were for hip width; these ranged from .451 at 9 years to .744 at 13 years.

The correlations of arm girth and the three linear measures were highest at ages 13 and 14, between .503 and .648. The lowest such correlations were at ages 9 and 16; those at age 16 were insignificant at the .05 level for standing height and leg length.

Arm girth had high positive correlations with two of the indices, weight/height^2 and weight/height; these correlations ranged from .851 to .942. The correlations with chest girth $\times$ height were lower, .665 to .857; the lowest of these correlations were at ages 9 and 16. Arm girth correlated negatively with height/$\sqrt[3]{\text{weight}}$; the correlational range was $-.650$ to $-.845$.

Skinfold Total

Skinfold tests were given to these subjects from ages 12 through 16. The total of three such measures were included in the correlations, as shown in Table 4.5. The sites of the three measures were over the triceps, the inferior angle of the scapula, and the lateral abdomen opposite the umbilicus. A summarization of these correlations follows.

The correlations between skinfold total and weight and the girth measures were scattered between .438 and .835; 43 percent of these, however, were in the .60's. The highest of these correlations were for abdominal and thigh girths; the respective correlational ranges were .697 to .835 and .648 to .800. Although lower, the most consistent correlations were for calf girth, .580 to .675. The lowest correlations were found at age 14. The correlations with hip width were much lower, between .172 and .522.

None of the correlations between skinfold total and the three linear measures was significant.

For the indices, skinfold total correlated highest with weight/height^2 and height/$\sqrt[3]{\text{weight}}$; the respective correlations ranged

Table 4.5

CORRELATIONS BETWEEN SKINFOLD TOTAL AND
OTHER ANTHROPOMETRIC MEASURES AND INDICES
FOR BOYS AGED 12 THROUGH 16

	Ages				
Variables	12	13	14	15	16
Body Bulk					
Weight	.697	.591	.454	.575	.677
Arm Girth	.797	.694	.438	.491	.652
Chest Girth	.776	.626	.453	.535	.692
Abdominal Girth	.787*	.795	.697	.811	.835
Buttocks Girth	.715	.619	.553	.663	.771
Thigh Girth	.763	.749	.648	.664	.800
Calf Girth	.580	.613	.633*	.634	.675
Hip Width	.338	.370	.172	.332	.522
Linearity					
Standing Height	.163	.086	.015	.004	−.030
Sitting Height	.102	.008	−.024	−.046	.003
Leg Length	.136	.143	.054	.058	−.049
Indices					
Wt./Ht.^{2}	.841	.813	.707	.763	.809
Wt./Ht.	.782	.708	.575	.873	.766
Ht./$\sqrt[3]{\text{Weight}}$	−.800	−.813	−.750	−.754	−.795
Chest Girth × Ht.	.623	.435	.298	.360	.511

Corrections made from original.

from .707 to .841 and −.750 to −.813. The lowest of these correlations was for chest girth × height, between .298 at age 14 and .623 at age 12.

Hip Width

In the correlations presented thus far, those with hip width generally fell between the body bulk and linearity measures. Table 4.6 presents the correlations of hip width with the other structural measures. A summarization of this table follows.

The correlations between hip width and weight and the girth measures were mostly in the .50's, .60's, and .70's. The highest correlations for all of these tests were found at age 13; generally, the lowest correlations were obtained at 9 and 15 years of age. The correlations with skinfold total were between .338 and .384, except for age 16 when the correlation was .522.

Table 4.6

CORRELATIONS BETWEEN HIP WIDTH AND
OTHER ANTHROPOMETRIC MEASURES AND INDICES
FOR BOYS AGED 9 THROUGH 16

Variables	Ages							
	9	10	11	12	13	14	15	16
Body Bulk								
Weight	.608	.675	.669	.751	.828	.776	.655	.726
Arm Girth	.451	.632	.546	.624	.744	.711	.582	.552
Chest Girth	.596	.591	.656	.672	.808	.750	.623	.722
Abdominal Girth		.580	.639	.621*	.750	.588	.567	.742
Buttocks Girth		.698	.664	.714	.806	.667	.677	.725
Thigh Girth		.642	.598	.653	.735	.644	.555	.608
Calf Girth	.538	.647	.618	.525	.728	.488	.569	.578
Skinfold Total				.338	.370	.384*	.362	.522
Linearity								
Standing Height	.545	.586	.574	.638	.677	.725	.459	.359
Sitting Height	.526	.537	.540	.628	.670	.721	.487	.388
Leg Length	.388	.500	.487	.489	.584	.597	.329	.204
Indices								
Wt./Ht.²	.461	.547*	.635	.608	.652	.561	.555	.647
Wt./Ht.	.565	.667*	.550	.712	.793	.720	.642	.715
Ht./∛Weight	−.303	−.441*	−.437	−.430	−.443	−.407*	−.406	−.521
Chest Girth × Ht.	.639	.750*	.684	.752	.830	.801	.618	.706

Corrections made from original.

The correlations between hip width and the linear measures were scattered between .204 and .725 with the largest numbers, 38 percent, in the .50's. The highest of these correlations were at ages 13 and 14; all lowest correlations were at age 16.

For the indices, the highest correlations with hip width were for chest girth × height; the correlational range was from .618 to .830. The correlational ranges for weight/height² and weight/height were .461 to .652 and .550 to .793 respectively. The correlations with height/∛weight were lower and negative, −.303 to −.521. Generally, the highest of these correlations were at age 13; the lowest, at age 9.

Standing Height

The linear measure selected for inclusion in this inter-correlational analysis of structural measures was standing height;

the correlations appear in Table 4.7. A summarization of these correlations follows.

Table 4.7

CORRELATIONS BETWEEN STANDING HEIGHT AND
OTHER ANTHROPOMETRIC MEASURES AND INDICES
FOR BOYS AGED 9 THROUGH 16

Variables	Ages							
	9	10	11	12	13	14	15	16
Body Bulk								
Weight	.725	.761	.700	.726	.775	.805	.686	.533
Arm Girth	.412	.474	.466	.443	.555	.648	.446	.398*
Chest Girth	.629	.553	.555	.523	.658	.712	.626	.361
Abdominal Girth		.557	.505	.494*	.497	.504	.379	.292
Buttocks Girth		.716	.647	.650	.715	.650	.612	.410
Thigh Girth		.635	.574	.571	.560	.599	.520	.302
Calf Girth	.581	.616	.608	.526*	.640	.576*	.469	.368
Skinfold Total				.163	.086	.015	.004	.030
Hip Width	.545	.586	.574	.638	.677	.725	.459	.359
Linearity								
Sitting Height	.818	.858	.850	.908	.918	.902	.899	.780
Leg Length	.875	.909	.913	.826	.930	.908	.879	.823
Indices								
Wt./Ht.^{2}	.327	.410	.372	.330	.335	.387	.246	.079
Wt./Ht.	.580	.638	.570	.579	.624	.665	.522	.333
Ht./$\sqrt[3]{\text{Weight}}$	.012	−.113	−.096	−.012	.042	.036	.089	.169
Chest Girth × Ht.	.859	.811	.762	.792	.877	.890	.852	.706

Corrections made from original.

All lowest correlations between standing height and the body bulk measures were obtained at age 16; the range of these correlations, excepting skinfold total, was from .292 to .533. The highest correlations were with weight and buttocks girth; the respective ranges, excepting age 16, were from .686 to .805 and .612 to .716. The other correlations with the girth measures and hip width ranged between .379 and .805. The highest correlations were at age 14 for weight, arm girth, chest girth, and hip width, and at age 10 for abdominal, buttocks, thigh, and calf girths. None of the correlations with skinfold total was significant.

Generally, leg length correlated slightly higher with standing height than did sitting height, although the differences between the correlations are not significant. The correlational ranges were .780 to .918 for sitting height and .823 to .930 for leg length.

The correlations between standing height and chest girth × height fell between .706 and .890. The respective ranges for weight/height and weight/height², excepting age 16 when they were lowest, were from .522 to .665 and .246 to .410. None of the correlations with height/∛weight was significant.

Lung Capacity

Lung capacity has been a controversial item in physical education testing, especially since Rogers included it in his Strength Index battery. Cureton (38) studied this test and concluded that it was largely a measure of body size. Early in the Medford series, Tomaras (103), also reported by Clarke (19), found that lung capacity had high correlations with anthropometric tests for junior high school boys (three ages combined). Some of his correlations were: .86 with McCloy's Classification Index, .85 with standing and sitting heights, .76 with body weight, .75 with hip width and with leg length, .69 with chest girth, and .65 with arm girth. In general, a higher correlation was found between lung capacity and linear measures of the body than between lung capacity and body bulk measures. Additional information on this test is provided from Phillips' longitudinal investigation of boys 9 through 16 years of age; the correlations with other anthropometric measures and indices are contained in Table 4.8. A summarization of these correlations follows.

The correlations between lung capacity and the body bulk measures were highest for weight, arm girth, chest girth, buttocks girth, and hip width at ages 13, 14, and 15; these correlations ranged between .388 and .641 with nearly one-half of them in the .50's. A number of insignificant correlations were obtained (below .25 at the .05 level) among the other body bulk tests; none of the correlations with skinfold total was significant. The correlations in this study were much lower than in the Tomaras study. However, the correlations in this study were from data obtained in a single year and within two months of the boys' birthdays, while Tomaras combined three years thus allowing chronological age to affect the correlations.

Table 4.8

CORRELATIONS BETWEEN LUNG CAPACITY AND
OTHER ANTHROPOMETRIC MEASURES AND INDICES
FOR BOYS AGED 9 THROUGH 16

Variables	Ages							
	9	10	11	12	13	14	15	16
Body Bulk								
Weight	.256	.271	.293	.382	.545	.641	.528	.329
Arm Girth	.084	.186	.226	.244	.437	.549	.388	.356*
Chest Girth	.241	.261	.293	.345	.525	.624	.547	.311
Abdominal Girth		.084	.203	.270	.351	.371	.250	.180
Buttocks Girth		.269	.288	.331	.503	.493	.462	.231
Thigh Girth		.209	.283	.275	.384	.443	.407	.381*
Calf Girth	.184	.250	.289	.370*	.469	.392	.321	.236
Skinfold Total				−.054	−.085	−.167	−.122	−.134
Hip width	.422	.259	.353	.386	.560	.613	.636*	.602*
Linearity								
Standing Height	.323	.418	.462	.539	.736	.802	.744	.567
Sitting Height	.291	.461	.483	.543	.768	.763	.779	.489
Leg Length	.236	.310	.353	.405	.608	.687	.536	.427
Indices								
Wt./Ht.²	.168	.106	.160	.190	.199	.308	.220	.094
Wt./Ht.	.217	.213	.235	.298	.427	.528	.414	.220
Ht./∛Wt.	−.065	−.004	−.025	−.017	.056	.032	.030	.052
Chest Girth × Ht.	.503*	.648*	.638*	.509*	.671	.748	.688	.482

Corrections made from original.

The correlations between lung capacity and the linear tests were higher than for the body bulk measures, as in the Tomaras study. Again, the highest correlations were at the there ages of 13, 14, and 15; over one-half of the correlations were in the .70's. All but one correlation with the linear tests were significant at the .05 level and above.

With the exception of chest girth × height, the correlations between lung capacity and the indices were mostly insignificant at the .05 level, excepting weight/height at ages 13, 14, and 15. For chest girth × height, the correlations ranged between .482 and .748; the lowest of these correlations were at ages 9 and 16.

Chest Girth × Height

Chest girth × height has frequently been used as a body proportion index in other Medford studies, and thus was chosen as an index against which to present the correlations of the anthropometric measures and other indices. Moreover, the other indices correlated very highly with each other or with body bulk measures. For example, at age 9, weight/height² correlated .953 with weight/height and −.931 with height/$\sqrt[3]{\text{weight}}$; and weight/height correlated .980 with weight. The correlations for ages 9 through 16 appear in Table 4.9. A summarization of these correlations follows.

Table 4.9

CORRELATIONS BETWEEN CHEST GIRTH × HEIGHT AND
ANTHROPOMETRIC MEASURES AND OTHER INDICES
FOR BOYS AGED 9 THROUGH 16

				Ages				
Variables	9	10	11	12	13	14	15	16
Body Bulk								
Weight	.907	.948	.913	.963	.957	.957	.931	.912
Arm Girth	.706	.829	.802	.817	.834	.857	.765	.665
Chest Girth	.940	.936	.896	.934	.937	.952	.940	.913
Abdominal Girth		.820	.848	.780*	.800	.755	.735	.758
Buttocks Girth		.929	.883	.916	.897	.809	.864	.827
Thigh Girth		.916	.838	.882	.808	.822	.807	.771
Calf Girth	.807	.858	.822	.888*	.846	.805*	.763	.728
Skinfold Total				.411*	.435	.298	.360	.511
Hip Width	.639	.829	.684	.752	.830	.801	.618	.706
Linearity								
Standing Height	.859	.811	.762	.792	.877	.890	.852	.706
Sitting Height	.683	.731	.654	.706	.819	.853	.785	.682
Leg Length	.764	.700	.691	.648	.723*	.746	.734	.667
Indices								
Wt./Ht.²	.666	.796	.771	.740	.704	.716	.674	.683
Wt./Ht.	.835	.910	.871	.917	.890	.895	.853	.834
Ht./$\sqrt[3]{\text{Weight}}$	−.398	−.591	−.585	−.553	−.390	−.364	−.394	−.497

Corrections made from original.

Correlations in the .90's were obtained at all ages between chest girth × height and the body bulk measures of weight and chest girth. High but slightly lower correlations were found for buttocks, thigh, and calf girths. The lowest of the body bulk correlations were with skinfold total, ranging from .298 to .511. Excepting skinfold total, only 2 of the 62 correlations with these tests were below .70.

The ranges of correlations between chest girth × height and

the linearity tests were comparable, as follows: .706 to .890 for standing height, .682 to .853 for sitting height, and .648 to .764 for leg length.

The highest correlations between chest girth $\times$ height and the other indices were for weight/height; the correlations ranged from .835 to .917. The correlational range for weight/height^2 was from .666 to .796. The lowest correlations were with height/$\sqrt[3]{\text{weight}}$, from −.364 to −.591.

Correlations with Strength and Motor Tests

The correlations of the physical measures with strength and motor tests will follow a pattern similar to that used above for the intercorrelations of the structural measures. The same anthropometric measures are used in this chapter, although skinfold total will be considered later. The strength and motor tests are Strength Index, cable-tension strength average, Physical Fitness Index, pull-ups, bar dips, standing broad jump, 60-yard shuttle run, and total-body reaction time. Instead of using the correlations from the longitudinal data on 62 subjects in Phillips' study, however, correlations were especially computed for the maximum number of Medford boys at each of the twelve ages, 7 through 18 years. The number of subjects and the correlation needed for significance at the .05 level at each of the ages were:

Age	Number	r needed .05 level	Age	Number	r needed .05 level
7	107	.188	13	231–239	.131
8	72–76	.225	14	215	.135
9	160–176	.148	15	241–338	.108–.128
10	208–216	.135	16	304–316	.113
11	180–181	.148	17	259–261	.125
12	203–287	.116–.138	18	149–151	.159

Weight

The correlations between weight and the muscular strength and endurance and motor tests for ages 7 through 18

Table 4.10

CORRELATIONS BETWEEN BODY WEIGHT AND
MUSCULAR STRENGTH AND ENDURANCE AND MOTOR TESTS
FOR BOYS AGED 7 THROUGH 18

Ages	Strength Index	C-T Strength Average	Physical Fitness Index	Pull-Ups	Bar Dips	Standing Broad Jump	60-Yard Shuttle	Total Body RT
7		.581				.084*	−.119*	.211*
8	.496	.604	−.059*	−.408	−.220*	.105*	−.192*	.097*
9	.375	.348	−.174	−.408	−.341	−.057*	.027*	.050*
10	.385	.556	−.346	−.408	−.336	−.178	.154	.237
11	.430	.497	−.425	−.509	−.390	−.275	.216	.180
12	.460	.539	−.298	−.435	−.347	−.109*	.160	.157
13	.555	.621	−.165	−.424	−.259	−.023*	.121*	.121*
14	.586	.663	−.121*	−.323	−.247	.054*	.108*	.079*
15	.527	.586	−.242	−.251	−.166	.089*	.047*	.050*
16	.411	.570	−.437	−.424	−.266	−.044*	.080*	.030*
17	.326	.482	−.518	−.476	−.304	.013*	.130	.060*
18	.483	.641	−.487	−.455	−.244	−.081*	.034*	

*Non-significant correlations at .05 level.

117

appear in Table 4.10. The highest correlations were with gross strength batteries; the correlational ranges were from .348 to .641 for cable-tension strength average and .326 to .586 for Strength Index. The correlations with Physical Fitness Index, pull-ups, and bar dips were negative and lower than for the strength batteries, but were mostly significant at the .05 level and above. The correlations with standing broad jump, 60-yard shuttle run, and total-body reaction time were also negative or had negative connotations, but were largely insignificant. The only age where all of these correlations were significant was 11 years; all correlations but one were significant at ages 10 and 12.

Arm Girth

The correlations between arm girth and the muscular strength and endurance and motor tests were comparable to those obtained with weight. However, more insignificant correlations were found for Physical Fitness Index, pull-ups, and bar dips. All correlations were significant at ages 11 and 12.

Hip Width

The correlations between hip width and the muscular strength and endurance and motor tests were also comparable to those obtained with weight. However, no age was found to have significant correlations on all tests.

Standing Height

Table 4.11 contains the correlations between standing height and the muscular strength and endurance and motor tests. The highest correlations were with the gross strength batteries; the correlational ranges were .262 to .600 for the Strength Index and .254 to .449 for cable-tension strength average with highest correlations at ages 13, 14, and 15. Six of the correlations with Physical Fitness Index were insignificant; the other correlations were low and negative. Negative and low correlations, mostly significant, were obtained with pull-ups and bar dips. One-half of the height versus standing broad jump correlations were not significant; the other correlations were low and positive. The correlations with 60-yard shuttle run and total-body reaction time were mostly insignificant.

Table 4.11

CORRELATIONS BETWEEN STANDING HEIGHT AND
MUSCULAR STRENGTH AND ENDURANCE AND MOTOR TESTS
FOR BOYS AGED 7 THROUGH 18

Ages	Strength Index	C-T Strength Average	Physical Fitness Index	Pull-Ups	Bar Dips	Standing Broad Jump	60-Yard Shuttle	Total Body RT
7		.449				.183*	-.215	
8	.474	.451	.024*	-.338	-.223*	.245	-.248	.168*
9	.361	.327	-.043*	-.292	-.390	.145*	-.066*	-.082*
10	.386	.449	-.150	-.349	-.242	.051*	.035*	.068*
11	.399	.408	-.241	-.491	-.373	.044*	.057*	.096*
12	.465	.415	-.093*	-.320	-.224	.181*	-.041*	.195
13	.567	.448	.078*	-.297	-.125*	.290	-.035*	.102*
14	.600	.563	.095*	-.178	-.158	.413	-.156	.043*
15	.533	.480	-.017*	-.126	-.051*	.382	-.126*	-.027*
16	.344	.349	-.185	-.297	-.223	.223	-.047	-.033*
17	.262	.254	-.277	-.351	-.308	.165	.043*	.104*
18	.369	.300	-.211	-.326	-.238	-.026*	.033*	.093*

*Non-significant correlations at .05 level.

Table 4.12

CORRELATIONS BETWEEN LUNG CAPACITY AND
MUSCULAR STRENGTH AND ENDURANCE AND MOTOR TESTS
FOR BOYS AGED 7 THROUGH 18

Ages	Strength Index	C-T Strength Average	Physical Fitness Index	Pull-Ups	Bar Dips	Standing Broad Jump	60-Yard Shuttle	Total Body RT
7	.451	.316				.505	-.436	.290
8	.522	.422	.135*	-.209	-.176*	.108*	-.254	-.147*
9	.454	.374	.286	-.078*	-.066*	.156	-.236	.047*
10	.506	.441	.048*	-.093*	-.015*	.101*	-.047*	.017*
11	.534	.495	.016*	-.216	-.148	.052*	-.062*	.125*
12		.444	.086*	-.180	-.081*	.178	-.102*	.001*
13	.670	.554	.238	-.103*	.010*	.311	-.133	.022*
14	.673	.603	.231	-.033*	-.010*	.417	-.186	-.059*
15	.604	.555	.107*	.004	.064*	.389	-.190	.032*
16	.310	.386	-.321	-.355	-.206	.105*	.037*	.020*
17	.416	.378	-.107*	-.223	-.089*	.181	-.104*	.043*
18	.464	.456	-.201	-.248	-.068*	-.116*	-.108*	

*Non-significant correlations at .05 level.

Lung Capacity

The correlations between lung capacity and the muscular strength and endurance and motor tests are shown in Table 4.12. The highest correlations were with the gross strength batteries; the correlational ranges were .416 to .673 for Strength Index and .316 to .603 for cable-tension strength average, with highest correlations at ages 13, 14, and 15. Six of the correlations with Physical Fitness Index were insignificant; the balance of the correlations were low and positive. The correlations between lung capacity and the other measures were low and mostly insignificant.

Chest Girth × Height

The correlations between chest girth × height and the muscular strength and endurance and motor tests were comparable to those obtained with weight, although no age was found to have significant correlations on all tests.

Growth Studies

Seven dissertations involving growth analyses have been completed within the Medford Boys' Growth Project; five of these studies have included measures of body size. The statistics employed were the mean, standard error of the mean, high and low scores, range, standard deviation, and coefficient of variation. The mean growth curves for the structural measures in these studies are described in this section.

Cross-Sectional Study

An early cross-sectional growth study of boys from 9 through 15 years of age was conducted by Wickens (37,111). The subjects were 40 different boys at each of the seven ages. A summary of these growth data follows.

1. The mean growth curves for body weight and chest girth had characteristics in common, namely: a relatively slight increase from 9 to 10, a pronounced nearly straight-line rise to 12, a slight

acceleration at 14, and a deceleration at 15 years of age. The mean growth curve for calf girth resembled these curves, except that a slight acceleration occurred at age 13. The mean body weight of the 15-year-old boys was nearly twice as great as that at 9 years; the percentage increases for chest girth and calf girth between these ages were 27 and 25 percent respectively.

2. The mean growth curves were comparable for standing height, sitting height, and leg length. The curve for standing height approached a straight-line rise from 9 to 15 years, except for some acceleration at 14 years. The curves for sitting height and leg length showed more irregularities than did the curve for standing height; this was especially true for sitting height. At all ages, the sitting height means of the subjects exceeded the means of their leg lengths. The percentages of mean increases between 9 and 15 years of age were 29 for standing height, 24 for sitting height, and 32 for leg length.

3. The mean growth curve for arm girth showed a slight decrease from 9 to 10, followed by a steep rise to 15 years of age. The increase in mean growth from 9 to 15 years for this measure was 33 percent.

4. The mean growth curves for lung capacity and hip width were similar. The curves were convex, especially from 9 to 13 years of age, after which they became essentially linear in form. The mean lung capacity of the boys at 15 years was over twice (115 percent) as great as that for the 9-year-old boys; for hip width, the corresponding gain was 28 percent.

Convergence Study

Watt (107) conducted a convergence growth analysis of boys 7 through 17 years of age; four structural measures were included: weight, arm girth, standing height, and lung capacity. As explained in Chapter 1, the convergence method of growth analysis consists of short longitudinal studies connected at overlapping ages. In Watt's study, the ages and numbers of subjects were: 7 to 9 years, 62; 9 to 12 years, 48; 12 to 15 years, 41; 15 to 17 years, 52. Thus, the overlapping years were 9, 12, and 15; the first and last longitudinal series were for three years and the two middle series were for four years.

Although not specified in the proposal for convergence analysis, the difference between the means of the independent samples was tested for significance by application of the *t* ratio at the overlapping years for each of the growth tests. None of these mean differences was significant at any age for weight, standing height, and lung capacity; consequently, complete convergence analyses from ages 7 to 17 were made for these tests. The difference between the arm girth means was significant at age 9; as a consequence, the convergence analysis for this test was from ages 9 to 17.

The means growth curves were straight line in form for standing height and arm girth and concave for weight and lung capacity.

Longitudinal Studies

The first longitudinal growth study in the Medford series was conducted by Kurimoto (66) after the graduation from high school of the original 15-year-old boys. Actually, he did two longitudinal analyses due to the graduation of some boys at age 17 and others at age 18; the analyses were from ages 15 through 17 with 70 boys and from 15 through 18 with 45 boys. Five body size measures were included: weight, standing height, arm girth, calf girth, and lung capacity. Inasmuch as much more extensive longitudinal growth studies were subsequently conducted with the Medford boys, the results of this study will not be presented here.

However, Kurimoto established the pattern for longitudinal growth studies in the Medford series. Three types of analysis were made, as follows: (a) Description of the physical growth process for the same subjects tested annually over a time period. (b) Examination of individual differences in the growth process for the time period. (c) The testing of hypotheses regarding factors involving growth. Answers to the following questions, which reflect the hypotheses, were sought:

1. What degrees of consistency exist for the various measures from age to age?
2. What are the mean growth patterns and the extent of individual differences in the growth variables studied?
3. Based on skeletal age assessments made at the first year of

the longitudinal sequence, what differences in growth patterns exist between those who are advanced and those who are retarded in maturity?

4. What differences in growth patterns exist for boys who demonstrate high gross strength scores at the first year of the longitudinal sequence as compared with those low on such strength measures?

5. What differences in growth patterns exist for boys who demonstrate high relative strength scores at the first year of the longitudinal sequence as compared with those low on this strength measure?

6. What differences in growth patterns occur for boys who are heaviest at the first year of the longitudinal series as compared with those who are lightest?

7. What differences in growth patterns are found for boys who are tallest at the first year of the longitudinal series as compared with those who are shortest?

Two doctoral dissertations in the Medford series concentrated on longitudinal growth analyses of structural measures from 7 through 17 years of age: Day (39) followed boys from 7 through 12 years and Santa Maria (86) did likewise for boys from 12 through 17 years. Day's subjects were 49 boys at ages 7 and 8, continuing to age 12, and 50 additional boys (99 in all) from ages 9 through 12. The combining of the subjects at age 9 was justified by demonstrating that the means of the two groups at this age, the original 7's and the original 9's, were not significantly different on tests under scrutiny. In Santa Maria's study, 123 boys were tested annually from ages 12 through 17. For both analyses, the means of the boys who dropped from the Medford study during the longitudinal periods (with rare exceptions, because of moving away) were compared with those who remained; the differences between means were not significant on the growth tests at the respective initial ages of 9 and 12.

Both Day and Santa Maria included the same 17 tests for their longitudinal growth analyses. These tests were: weight; arm, chest, abdominal, buttocks, thigh, and calf girths; hip width; lung capacity; standing and sitting heights and leg length; and the indices of chest girth $\times$ height, sitting height/standing height, chest girth/standing height, height/$\sqrt[3]{\text{weight}}$, and chest girth/buttocks girth. Both mean growth and mean velocity curves were constructed.

Longitudinal Mean Growth Curves

Descriptions of the longitudinal mean growth curves obtained by Day (39) and Santa Maria (86) for boys ages 7 through 17 are presented in this section. When growth curves are illustrated, the mean curves from the two studies are joined at age 12.

Body Bulk Measures

BODY WEIGHT. The mean growth curve for weight is presented in Fig. 4.3; the means for the ages appear at the bottom of the figure. This curve has a nearly straightline rise from age 7 to age 11; the slope of the curve is steeper, increasing in a concave manner to age 16; at age 17, the mean weight is still higher but the curve decelerates. The mean weights increased from 52 lbs. at 7 to 152 lbs. at 17 years of age, a gain of 100 lbs., or 192 percent.

ARM GIRTH. The mean growth curve for arm girth is similar to the weight curve, except for a greater relative increment at age 9. The mean arm girths increased from 18.6 cm. at 7 to 30.0 cm. at 17 years of age, a gain of 11.4 cm., or 61 percent.

CHEST GIRTH. The mean chest girth curve is linear until age 10; a deceleration and subsequent acceleration occurs at ages 11 and 12; the curve is similar to the weight curve from ages 12 through 17. The mean chest girths increased from 61.6 cm. at 7 to 91.0 cm. at 17 years of age, a gain of 29.4 cm., or 48 percent.

ABDOMINAL GIRTH. The mean growth curve for abdominal girth is shown in Fig. 4.4; the means for the ages appear at the bottom of the figure. This growth curve is irregular from ages 7 to 12, with pronounced acceleration at age 10; the slope is concave from ages 12 to 16, with a deceleration at age 17. The mean abdominal girths increased from 55.9 cm. at 8 to 77.1 cm. at 17 years of age, a gain of 21.2 cm., or 38 percent.

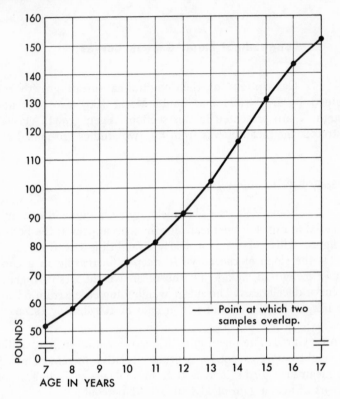

Fig. 4.3 Body weight mean growth curve

MEAN WEIGHTS IN POUNDS

Ages	Means	Ages	Means
7	52	12	91
8	58	13	102
9	67	14	116
10	74	15	131
11	81	16	143
12	91	17	152

BUTTOCKS GIRTH. The mean growth curve for buttocks girth is similar to the curve for abdominal girth, although the acceleration is not so much at age 10. The mean buttocks girth increased from 63.6 cm. at 8 to 91.2 cm. at 17 years of age, a gain of 27.6 cm., or 43 percent.

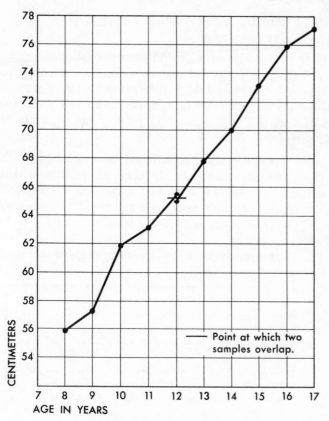

Fig. 4.4 Abdominal girth mean growth curve

MEAN ABDOMINAL GIRTHS IN CENTIMETERS

Ages	Means	Ages	Means
		12	65.0
8	55.9	13	67.8
9	57.2	14	70.0
10	61.9	15	73.1
11	63.1	16	75.9
12	65.4	17	77.1

THIGH GIRTH. The mean growth curve for thigh girth is comparable to the curves for abdominal and buttocks girths, although this curve is steeper from ages 15 to 16. The mean thigh girths increased from 37.3 cm. at 8 to 53.2 cm. at 17 years of age, a gain of 15.9 cm., or 43 percent.

CALF GIRTH. The mean growth curve for calf girth has a steeper rise at 9 than at 10 years of age, as contrasted with the curves for abdominal, buttocks, and thigh girths; also, final deceleration begins at 16 rather than 17 years of age. The mean calf girths increased from 24.6 cm. at 7 to 36.3 cm. at 17 years of age, a gain of 11.7 cm., or 48 percent.

HIP WIDTH. Hip width is included here as a body bulk measure, inasmuch as it correlates higher with such tests than with linear tests. In Table 4.6, hip width correlated mostly in the .60's and .70's with body bulk tests, although the .80's were reached at age 13. The correlations with linear tests were largely in the .50's and .60's.

The mean growth curve for hip width is given in Fig. 4.5; the

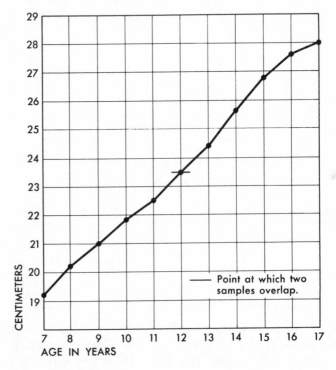

Fig. 4.5 Hip width mean growth curve

MEAN HIP WIDTHS IN CENTIMETERS

Ages	Means	Ages	Means
7	19.2	12	23.5
8	20.2	13	24.4
9	21.0	14	25.6
10	21.8	15	26.8
11	22.5	16	27.6
12	23.5	17	28.0

means for the ages appear at the bottom of the table. This curve is slightly convex from ages 7 to 11; a slightly steeper concave rise follows to age 15; finally, a deceleration extends over the last two years. The mean hip widths increased from 19.2 cm. at 7 to 28.0 cm. at 17 years of age, a gain of 8.8 cm., or 46 percent.

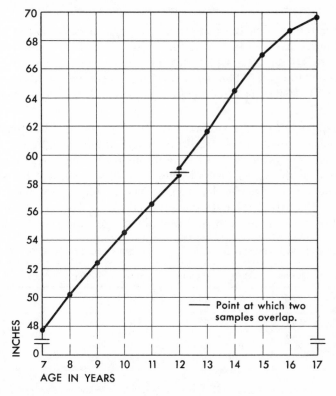

Fig. 4.6   Standing height mean growth curve

Linear Measures

Descriptions of the mean growth curves for the linear measures are presented here.

STANDING HEIGHT. The mean growth curve for standing height is shown in Fig. 4.6; the means for the ages appear at the bottom

MEAN HEIGHTS IN INCHES

Ages	Means	Ages	Means
7	47.7	12	59.0
8	50.1	13	61.6
9	52.4	14	64.5
10	54.5	15	67.0
11	56.5	16	68.7
12	58.6	17	69.6

of the table. With the exception of a slight acceleration at age 8, this curve has a nearly straightline rise to age 12; acceleration follows to age 14, after which the curve is convex in shape as it decelerates to age 17. The mean standing heights increased from 47.7 in, at 7 to 69.6 in. at 17 years of age, a gain of 21.9 in., or 46 percent.

SITTING HEIGHT AND LEG LENGTH. For comparative purposes, the mean growth curves for sitting height and leg length are shown on the same graph, Fig. 4.7. The means for the ages appear at the bottom of the table. Overall, these curves are concave for sitting height and convex for leg length. The sitting height means are higher than the leg length means at all ages.* The two curves are farthest apart at the youngest and oldest ages; they converge until

MEAN SITTING HEIGHTS IN INCHES				MEAN LEG LENGTHS IN INCHES			
Ages	Means	Ages	Means	Ages	Means	Ages	Means
7	26.3	12	30.6	7	21.4	12	28.3
8	27.3	13	31.8	8	22.8	13	29.7
9	28.1	14	33.2	9	24.3	14	31.3
10	28.9	15	34.6	10	25.5	15	32.4
11	29.7	16	35.8	11	26.8	16	32.9
12	30.4	17	36.4	12	28.2	17	33.2

* It should be observed that sitting height is measured from the top of the head and is not confined to the trunk.

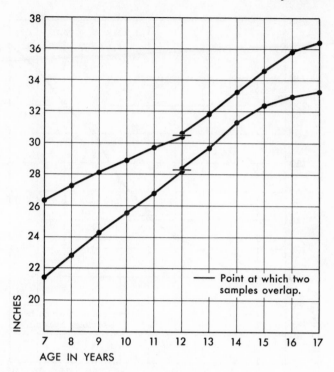

Fig. 4.7 Sitting height and leg length mean growth curve

the age of 14, after which they separate. The mean sitting heights increased from 26.3 in. at 7 to 36.4 in. at 17 years of age, a gain of 10.1 in., or 38 percent. For leg length means, the increase was from 21.4 in. to 33.2 in., a gain of 11.8 in., or 55 percent.

Lung Capacity

Lung capacity is presented here as a separate category, since it does not generally correlate well with either body bulk

MEAN LUNG CAPACITIES IN CUBIC INCHES

Ages	Means	Ages	Means
7	78	12	145
8	93	13	167
9	104	14	201
10	118	15	220
11	128	16	246
12	141	17	262

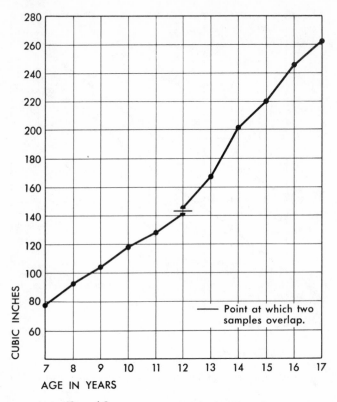

Fig. 4.8 Lung capacity mean growth curve

or linear measures. As shown in Table 4.8, the correlations are low, except with linear measures, at ages 13, 14, and 15, where they reach the .70's and .80's.

The mean growth curve for lung capacity is shown in Fig. 4.8; the means for the ages appear at the bottom of the table. This

MEAN GROWTH CURVE FOR CHEST GIRTH × HEIGHT

Ages	Means	Ages	Means
7	2942	12	4356
8	3206	13	4737
9	3483	14	5192
10	3759	15	5671
11	3975	16	6060
12	4292	17	6334

growth curve is somewhat irregular. It starts with a straightline rise from ages 7 to 10, takes a slight dip to age 12, then becomes a wandering convexity during the older ages. The lung capacity means increased from 78 cu. in. at 8 to 262 cu. in. at 17 years of age, a gain of 184 cm., or 236 percent.

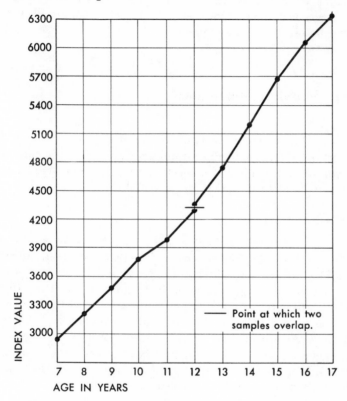

Fig. 4.9   Chest girth × height mean growth curve

Indices

Descriptions of the mean growth curves for the indices are given below.

CHEST GIRTH × HEIGHT. The mean growth curve for this index is shown in Fig. 4.9; the means for the ages appear at the bottom of the table. This curve resembles the curve for body weight: nearly a straightline rise to age 12, with a slight dip at 11 years; a steeper straightline rise to age 15; some deceleration at ages 16 and 17. The means for chest girth × height increased from 2,942 at 7 to 6,334 at 17 years of age, a gain of 3,392, or 115 percent.

OTHER INDICES. The mean growth curves for the other indices were largely horizontal from ages 7 to 17. The changes in means were negligible over this age span.

Individual Differences

This section presents the extent of individual differences for structural measures for boys from ages 7 through 18. For each table shown, the number of subjects, mean, low and high scores, range, and standard deviation, are given at each age.

Body Bulk Measures

WEIGHT. The individual differences for body weight are shown in Table 4.13. The standard deviations increased steadily from 6.3 lbs. at age 7 to 22.6 lbs. at age 14; thereafter, they were fairly consistent, ranging between 19.2 and 22.6 lbs. The ranges varied with the presence of extreme scores at some of the ages; the lowest range was 33 lbs. at 7 years and the highest was 141 lbs. at 17 years. At all but one age (7 years), the heaviest boy was at least twice as heavy as the lightest boy; at some ages, this differential was nearly three times as great. At ages 12 to 15, the ranges nearly reached or exceeded their respective means.

ARM GIRTH. The individual differences for arm girth are given in Table 4.14. The standard deviations increased slightly from 1.4 to 2.2 cm. from ages 7 to 10; little change occurred until age 13, when it reached 2.6 cm. The ranges were erratic, due to the pressure of extreme scores at some of the ages; the lowest range was 6.2 cm. at 7 and the highest was 16.9 cm. at 15. Generally, boys with the highest arm girths were 50 to 100 percent greater than boys with the smallest girths.

Table 4.13

WEIGHT INDIVIDUAL DIFFERENCES
(Pounds)

Age	N	Mean	Low	High	Range	S.D.
7	113	52.5	38	71	33	6.3
8	93	58.8	41	82	41	7.9
9	176	65.6	44	100	56	10.1
10	221	74.3	48	127	79	13.1
11	189	81.0	51	129	78	14.8
12	297	91.2	56	144	88	16.6
13	246	102.8	59	180	121	19.9
14	224	116.6	64	179	115	21.3
15	345	132.2	76	207	131	21.1
16	322	143.7	91	213	122	19.2
17	295	150.7	72	213	141	21.1
18	165	158.1	111	228	117	22.6

Table 4.14

ARM GIRTH INDIVIDUAL DIFFERENCES
(Centimeters)

Age	N	Mean	Low	High	Range	S.D.
7	113	18.8	16.0	22.2	6.2	1.4
8	93	19.3	16.0	23.9	7.9	1.6
9	176	20.5	17.2	26.0	8.8	1.9
10	221	21.2	16.1	28.7	12.6	2.2
11	186	22.0	17.0	30.6	13.6	2.3
12	296	23.1	17.3	31.9	14.6	2.3
13	244	24.3	18.8	35.2	16.4	2.6
14	223	26.0	19.7	34.0	14.3	2.6
15	345	27.7	18.2	35.1	16.9	2.6
16	322	29.2	23.8	38.1	14.3	2.4
17	295	30.0	22.5	38.4	15.9	2.5
18	165	31.0	25.5	37.7	12.2	2.5

HIP WIDTH. The individual differences for hip width are presented in Table 4.15. The standard deviations gradually increased from 1.1 cm. at 7 to 2.1 cm. at 14 years of age; thereafter, some decline occurred. The ranges varied erratically from 5.3 cm. at 7 and 8 to 18.6 cm. at 14 years of age.

Table 4.15

HIP WIDTH INDIVIDUAL DIFFERENCES
(Centimeters)

Age	N	Mean	Low	High	Range	S.D.
7	111	19.3	16.5	21.8	5.3	1.1
8	93	20.2	16.6	21.9	5.3	1.0
9	174	20.9	18.0	24.0	6.0	1.2
10	221	21.8	18.3	26.0	7.7	1.4
11	185	22.6	17.7	29.7	12.0	1.6
12	294	23.4	19.5	28.4	8.9	1.6
13	242	24.4	20.2	29.6	9.4	1.7
14	224	25.6	21.3	39.9	18.6	2.1
15	343	26.9	22.1	37.6	15.5	1.9
16	319	27.7	22.7	35.0	12.3	1.6
17	294	28.2	22.7	34.5	11.8	1.6
18	166	28.4	24.0	32.6	8.6	1.7

Linear Measures

STANDING HEIGHT. The individual differences for standing height appear in Table 4.16. The standard deviations increased gradually from 2.0 in. at 7 to 3.4 in. at 14 years of age; thereafter, some decline occurred. The ranges were erratic, varying between 11 in. at 7 and 22.2 in. at 17 years of age.

Table 4.16

STANDING HEIGHT INDIVIDUAL DIFFERENCES
(Inches)

Age	N	Mean	Low	High	Range	S.D.
7	113	48.1	42.0	53.0	11.0	2.0
8	93	50.5	43.3	54.8	11.5	2.1
9	176	52.3	44.9	57.3	12.4	2.2
10	221	54.6	46.7	61.0	14.3	2.3
11	189	56.6	48.4	63.4	15.0	2.4
12	297	58.9	49.8	69.0	19.2	2.8
13	246	61.5	51.2	69.4	18.2	3.2
14	223	64.4	55.8	72.6	16.8	3.4
15	344	67.1	58.8	76.0	17.2	3.1
16	321	69.0	61.2	76.8	15.6	2.6
17	298	69.7	54.0	76.2	22.2	2.7
18	165	70.1	64.2	77.2	13.0	2.5

Lung Capacity

The individual differences for lung capacity are given in Table 4.17. The standard deviations increased steadily from 11.9 cu. in. at 7 to 39.6 cu. in. at 15 years of age; thereafter, they remained constant, except for a decrease at age 17. A similar pattern was found for the ranges, which varied from 50 to 263 cu. in. For most ages, the ranges nearly reached or exceeded their respective means.

Table 4.17

LUNG CAPACITY INDIVIDUAL DIFFERENCES
(Cubic Inches)

Age	N	Mean	Low	High	Range	S.D.
7	34	81.5	54	104	50	11.9
8	92	95.1	52	142	90	14.4
9	176	105.6	59	170	111	16.4
10	223	119.2	74	178	104	19.0
11	184	130.4	85	250	165	21.1
12	300	144.8	80	230	150	23.0
13	239	165.9	90	290	200	29.0
14	224	199.4	120	320	200	36.4
15	354	224.6	130	392	262	39.6
16	322	249.5	117	380	263	39.8
17	288	261.4	160	374	214	36.4
18	156	268.4	176	410	234	40.6

High and Low Structural Groups

In the longitudinal growth analyses by Day (39) and Santa Maria (86), heavy and light groups and tall and short groups were formed at the ages of 9 and 12 years. Between 20 and 24 boys composed each group. The growth patterns of these groups were followed for four years, ages 9 through 12 in Day's study and for six years, ages 12 through 17, in Santa Maria's investigation. The differences between the means of these groups for all structural measures and indices included in their studies were tested annually for significance by application of the *t* ratio.

Heavy-Light Groups

For the heavy and light groups formed at age 9, the body weight means were 83.7 lbs. and 53.7 lbs. respectively; the difference between the means was 30.0 lbs, and the *t* ratio was 19.04. The difference between mean weights continued significant at each age through 12 years; the lowest *t* ratio was 14.98 at 11 years. A similar situation prevailed for the heavy-light groups formed at age 12: the respective means were 113.4 lbs. and 73.0 lbs., a difference of 40.4 lbs. with a *t* ratio of 16.81; significant mean differences were obtained at the subsequent ages with the lowest *t* ratio of 10.26 at age 17.

The boys in the heavy as contrasted with the light weight groups in both studies had significantly higher means on maturity, girth, and linear measures at all ages. The *t* ratios were greatest for the girth tests, ranging from 7.50 to 17.26. The *t* ratios ranged between 2.61 and 10.91 for the linear measures and between 4.55 and 9.67 for skeletal age.

The means for the indices, chest girth × height and chest girth/height, also favored the heavy weight groups; the respective *t*-ratio ranges were 8.50 to 16.07 and 3.91 to 5.61. The mean indices for height/$\sqrt[3]{\text{weight}}$ and chest girth/buttocks girth were higher for the light weight groups; the *t* ratios clustered between 2.55 and 7.36 over the age spans. The sitting height/standing height means were also higher for the light weight groups; the differences between the means were significant for the 9-year group at all ages and for the 12-year group at the age of 12 only.

Tall-Short Groups

For the tall-short groups formed at age 9, the standing height means were 55.3 in. and 49.4 in. respectively; the difference between the means was 4.9 in. and the *t* ratio was 15.22. The differences between mean standing heights continued significant at each age through 12 years; the lowest *t* ratio was 13.28 at 12 years. The situation was similar for the tall-short groups formed at age 12:

Table 4.18

INTER-AGE CORRELATIONS FOR ANTHROPOMETRIC TESTS AND INDICES

Tests	Adjacent Ages Medians		5-Year Span Correlation	
	7–12 Group	12–17 Group	7–12 Group	12–17 Group
Weight	.944	.954	.873	.816
Arm Girth	.909	.918	.834	.777
Chest Girth	.923	.917	.782	.774
Abdominal Girth	.880	.906	.746*	.765
Buttocks Girth	.936	.916	.809*	.829
Thigh Girth	.880	.919	.889*	.750
Calf Girth	.919	.938	.653	.766
Hip Width	.877	.823	.794	.772
Standing Height	.982	.956	.922	.755
Sitting Height	.914	.920	.901	.746
Leg Length	.899	.914	.868	.644
Lung Capacity	.676	.830	.747	.577
Chest Girth × Height	.964	.940	.856	.776
Chest Girth/Height	.884	.890	.708	.756
Height/$\sqrt[3]{}$ Weight	.918	.928	.792	.797
Sitting Ht./Standing Ht.	.783	.814	.689	.644
Chest Girth/Abdominal Girth	.755	.762	.452*	.620

*Only four ages intervened for these tests.

the respective means were 62.9 in. and 55.4 in., a difference of 7.48 in. with a *t* ratio of 24.43; significant mean differences were obtained at all ages with the lowest *t* ratio of 11.09 at 17 years.

The boys in the tall as contrasted with the short height groups in both studies had significantly higher means on maturity, linear, and body bulk measures at all ages. The *t* ratios were greatest for sitting height and leg length, ranging from 7.33 to 20.49. The *t* ratios ranged between 2.57 and 10.54 for all other anthropometric measures and skeletal age.

The means for the index, chest girth × height, also favored the tall height groups; the respective *t* ratios were 8.29 to 10.38 and 10.45 to 13.14. The mean indices of sitting height/standing height and chest girth/buttocks girth were higher for the low height groups. The mean differences were significant for both indices at all ages, 9 through 12, with *t* ratios ranging between 2.91 and 4.91; the mean differences were significant at the .05 level and above for sitting height/standing height for ages 12 through 14 and for chest girth/buttocks girth at age 12 only. No significant difference between means was obtained for chest girth/height; for height/$\sqrt[3]{\text{weight}}$, a mean difference significant at the .05 level was obtained at age 13.

Inter-Age Correlations

Inter-age correlations were obtained for the various anthropometric tests and indices for boys aged 7 through 12 and 12 through 17 in the longitudinal growth studies by Day (39) and Santa Maria (86). The median correlations obtained for adjacent ages and the correlations found when a span of five years intervened between the tests* are presented in Table 4.18.

The adjacent inter-age correlations, as might be expected, were the highest obtained for both groups. The median correlations were in the .90's or nearly so for weight, all girth measures, the three linear tests, and the indices of chest girth × height, chest girth/height, and height/$\sqrt[3]{\text{weight}}$. The median correlations for the 7–12

---

* Only four ages intervened for abdominal, buttocks, and thigh girths in the 7-to-12-year-old group.

and 12–17 age groups respectively were .877 and .823 for hip width. The lowest median correlations were obtained for lung capacity, sitting height/standing height, and chest girth/abdominal girth; these correlations ranged bewteen .676 and .830.

As the number of intervening years increased, the magnitude of the inter-age correlations declined. The highest of these correlations were between .889 and .922 for thigh girth (four-year span) and the three linear measures for the 7–12 age group; however, the comparable correlations for the 12–17 age group were lower, between .746 and .755. The five-year inter-age correlations were .873 and .816 for weight and .856 and .776 for chest girth × height. With the exception of chest girth/abdominal girth, the remainder of the correlations ranged between .577 and .794. The correlation for lung capacity was substantially lower (.577) for the 12–17 age group than for the 7–12 age group (.747); the reverse was true for chest girth/abdominal girth where the correlations were .452 and .620.

Skinfold Measurements

Skinfold measurement has been developed to evaluate the status of adipose tissue on the human body. Franzen (43) presented evidence that the amount of subcutaneous tissue for a given skeletal conformity yields dependable distinctions in children and that various amounts of such tissue exist which are entirely independent of skeletal measures and girths. Brozek recommended skinfold measurements as a better indication of fatness than is deviation from a standard weight table (8) and as a better means of interpreting deviation from reference weight in terms of approximate body composition (6). Mayer (74) indicated that the use of calipers to measure skinfolds is apparently the most precise method of measuring the fat content of the body and the degree of obesity when tested against other methods, the densimetric method in particular.

Caliper Measurements

Most of the early use of calipers in making skinfold measurement was by investigators in Europe. In the United States,

Franzen (43) introduced a spring equipped type of skinfold caliper which was widely used. McCloy (71, 72) provided an extensive survey of the problems associated with measurements of subcutaneous thickness and offered criticisms of earlier studies.

Caliper measurements of skinfolds by competent testers give good results. Tanner and Weiner (101) took a series of caliper measurements of subcutaneous tissue over five body areas on 65 to 70 adults; their reliability coefficients were of the same magnitude as for other anthropometric tests. Clarke, Geser, and Hunsdon (27) reported an objectivity coefficient of .98 for the pinch-caliper method of measuring the amount of adipose tissue over the biceps muscle with college men as subjects.

Garn and Gorman (44) obtained a correlation of .88 between fat-shadow measurements from X-ray and pinch-caliper measurements made at the same sites. Clarke, Geser, and Hunsdon (27) reported a .79 correlation between these methods of measurement at the same site, over the biceps muscle.

Many sites have been proposed for taking skinfold measurements, including chest front, chest back, abdomen, suprailiac, back of arm, thigh above knee cap, front and rear thigh, inferior angle of scapula, mid-axillary line at level of umbilicus, cheek, and calf. Brozek (7) completed many studies with skinfold measures as related to the leanness and fatness of individuals. After considering various criteria for determining the most appropriate sites for such measurements, the following were found most significant, in the order given: (a) back of upper arm, mid-posterior over the triceps muscle at a point halfway between the tip of the shoulder and the tip of the elbow; (b) inferior angle (tip) of the scapula; and (c) mid-axillary line at the level of the umbilicus.

Skinfold Tests

The Lange Skinfold Caliper was the instrument used in the Medford Boys' Growth Project.* This instrument conforms to the recommended specifications for such instruments (7), as follows: constant pressure of 10 grams per square millimeter; size

---

* The Lange Skinfold Caliper may be obtained from Cambridge Scientific Instruments, Inc., 18 Poplar Street, Cambridge, Md. The instrument may be seen in Fig. 4.10.

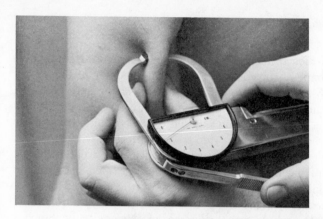

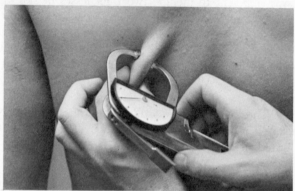

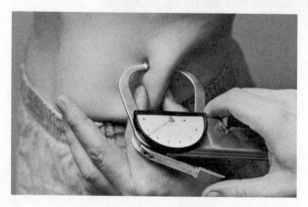

Fig. 4.10 Skinfold measures with
Lange Caliper A: Back of
upper arm B: Scapular C:
Lateral abdomen

143

of contact surface from 20 to 40 square millimeters, depending in part on the shape of the contact surface. Any opening of the caliper arms up to 65 millimeters applies the amount of pressure specified. The contact surface of one caliper arm is on a swivel, so that it may conform to the slope of varying skinfold contacts. Calibration of the caliper can be checked with a "step tester" furnished with it.

In the Medford project, all skinfold measures were made on the left side of the body. The skinfolds were grasped between the thumb and index finger with the span of the grasp dependent upon the thickness of the skinfold. The amount of skinfold held was sufficient to include two thicknesses of skin and subcutaneous fat but not muscle and fascia. To insure against including such structures when the tester was in doubt, the subject was instructed to tense the muscles underlying the skinfold held in the grasp. The caliper was applied about 1 cm. above the fingers holding the skinfold. All measurements were recorded to the nearest millimeter.

The skinfold sites utilized in the Medford project were the same three recommended above by Brozek. These tests are illustrated in Fig. 4.10 and are described below:

BACK OF UPPER ARM. This skinfold was taken at the back of the upper arm, mid-posterior over the triceps muscle, at a point halfway between the tip of the shoulder (acromial process) and the tip of the elbow (olecranon process). The point was located with the forearm flexed to 90 degrees; in making the measurement, however, the arm hung free. The fold was lifted parallel to the long axis of the arm.

SCAPULAR. This skinfold was taken at the inferior angle (tip) of the scapula with the subject in a relaxed standing position. The fold was lifted in the diagonal plane at about 45 degrees from the vertical and horizontal planes medially upward and laterally downward.

LATERAL ABDOMEN. This skinfold was taken at the side of the abdomen on the mid-axillary line at the level of the umbilicus. The fold was lifted parallel to the long axis of the body.

12-Year-Old Boys

In the Medford growth series, Geser (46) studied skin-fold measures of 212 boys 12 years of age as related to 19 maturity, physique, body size, muscular strength and endurance and motor ability tests. Seven skinfold criteria were utilized consisting of the three skinfold measures described above, the total of these measures, and three indices. The indices were derived as follows:

$$\text{Arm Skinfold Index} = \frac{\text{Arm Skinfold}}{\text{Arm Girth}} \times 100$$

$$\text{Scapular Skinfold Index} = \frac{\text{Scapular Skinfold}}{\text{Chest Girth}} \times 100$$

$$\text{Abdominal Skinfold Index} = \frac{\text{Abdominal Skinfold}}{\text{Abdomen Girth}} \times 100$$

Some results of this study are presented below.

CORRELATIONS AMONG SKINFOLD CRITERIA. The intercorrelations of the skinfold measures were .810 between scapula and abdomen, .804 between arm and abdomen, and .797 between arm and scapula. The correlations of these skinfolds with total skinfold were .912 for arm, .908 for scapula, and .963 for abdomen. Each of the skinfold measures correlated highly with their respective index, as follows: .977, arm skinfold and index; .989, scalpular skinfold and index; and .983 abdominal skinfold and index. The intercorrelation of the skinfold indices were .763 between scapular and abdominal indices, .733 between arm and abdominal indices, and .731 between arm and scapular indices.

MATURITY. All zero-order correlations between skeletal age and the skinfold measures were low but significant, ranging between .265 and .379. When partial correlations were computed, only the body bulk measures showed significant changes in the relationship between skeletal age and the skinfold measures. When measures of body bulk were partialed, the relationship generally reversed direction, although the magnitudes of the correlations did not change appreciably.

PHYSIQUE TYPE. All zero-order correlations between skinfold measures and somatotype components were significant. The correlational ranges for the three components were: .719 to .824 for endomorphy, .303 to .351 for mesomorphy, and −.578 and −.657 for ectomorphy. In the partial correlation analysis, only the body bulk measures produced significant changes from the corresponding zero-order correlations; generally, the partial correlations maintained the same direction but were lower. Partialing arm girth resulted in significantly lower correlations with all skinfold measures. Also, partialing chest girth and buttock girth significantly lowered all skinfold correlations with ectomorphy.

MUSCULAR STRENGTH. Rogers' Strength Index and the average of 11 cable-tension strength tests were utilized as measures of gross strength; Rogers' Physical Fitness Index was used as a measure of relative strength. The zero-order correlations between skinfold measures and gross strength batteries were significant but low, ranging from .173 for scapular skinfold and Strength Index to .441 for abdominal skinfold and cable-tension strength average; the correlations with cable-tension strength average were consistently higher than with Strength Index. As for skeletal age, partialing body bulk measures changed the directions of the correlations from positive to negative without appreciable change is their magnitude. The Physical Fitness Index correlated negatively with the skinfold measures, clustering between −.246 and −.278.

MUSCULAR ENDURANCE. The muscular endurance test used was bar push-ups. The correlations of skinfold measures with this test were similar to those with the Physical Fitness Index; the range of correlations was from −.255 to −.346.

MOTOR ABILITY ELEMENTS. The motor ability elements included a muscular power test, standing broad jump, and a speed-agility test, 60-yard shuttle run (10-yard distance). All correlations between the skinfold measures and these tests were significant. The correlational ranges were −.306 to −.345 for standing broad jump and .182 to .268 (negative connotation) for 60-yard shuttle run. None of the partial correlations were significantly different from the corresponding zero-order correlations.

SKINFOLD INDICES. The use of the skinfold indices did not significantly change the magnitude or direction of the correlations with the various experimental variables included in the study, so they are not reported here.

Wetzel Grid

The Wetzel Grid (109) was devised as a direct reading control chart on the quality of growth and development in individual boys and girls. In his original work with 2,093 school children, kindergarten through twelfth grade, Wetzel obtained 94 percent agreement between grid ratings and physicians' estimates of growth quality. Bruch (9) confirmed the usefulness of the Grid technique in the early recognition of abnormal changes in the height-weight relationship.

The Grid

Three components of the Wetzel Grid have been used in the Medford Boys' Growth Project, as follows: physique channels, developmental levels, and developmental ratios. Descriptions of these components follow.

PHYSIQUE CHANNELS. The grid contains nine channels, A4 to M to B4. In terms of physique types, or "clinical ratings," the channels are designated as follows: A4, obesity; A3 and A2, stocky; A1, M, and B1, good; B2, fair; B3, borderline; and B4, poor. The child's position on the physique channels is plotted from his height and weight; weights are scaled horizontally and heights are scaled vertically. For purposes of statistical computation in the Medford project, the nine channels were numbered from 1 to 9, with B4 as 1 and A4 as 9.

DEVELOPMENTAL LEVELS. The physique channels are crossed by iso-developmental lines; these lines have values from 0 to 180. A boy's developmental level is determined by the point at which his height-weight lines intersect (which also determines his physique channel, as noted). This point of intersection will lie on or near one of the iso-developmental lines crossing the physique channels.

DEVELOPMENT RATIOS. The right side of the grid contains age schedules of development (auxodromes). These schedules have percentage values of 2, 15, 67, 82, and 98. The 67 percent auxodrome is taken as the standard of reference for determining whether a child is advanced, normal, or retarded. A developmental age can be determined for each child by reading the age at which the 67 percent norm crosses his developmental level. The developmental ratio is obtained by dividing the child's developmental age by his chronological age.

Ages 9 through 15

In the Medford growth series, Weinberg (108) studied the relationships between the three forementioned components of the Wetzel Grid and various structural, strength, and motor measures. The subjects constituted cross-sectional samples of 40 boys at each age 9 through 15, excepting 39 and 37 respectively at ages 10 and 13, or 276 boys in all. Zero-order, multiple, and partial correlations were computed between each of the three grid criteria as dependent variables in turn and the exprimental variables. The differences between means on the experimental variables were tested for significance by application of the t ratio for the boys grouped into physique types. The physique types and the number of boys in each were as follows: 9, poor; 9 borderline; 53, fair; 161, good; 31, stocky; and 13, obese. Correlation and mean difference significance was accepted at the .05 level.

PHYSIQUE CHANNELS. Of the three Wetzel Grid criteria, the physique channels had the lowest zero-order correlations with the experimental variables. The highest correlations were with the three body bulk measures of arm girth, chest girth, and calf girth; the respective correlations were .519, .453, and .449. Low but significant correlations were obtained with weight (.380), Physical Fitness Index ($-.328$), McCloy's arm strength score (.208), hip width (.179), and cable-tension strength average (.152). Non-significant correlations were obtained with standing height, sitting height, leg length, lung capacity, Rogers' arm strength score, Strength Index, skeletal age, chronological age, and Wetzel's developmental level and ratio. A multiple correlation of .901 was obtained between the physique channels and arm girth, standing height, and weight; this correlation was increased to .962 with the addition of sitting height and leg length.

The means of the body bulk measures of weight, calf girth, arm girth, and chest girth increased in the same order as the physique categories; all mean differences were significant except for the differences betwen the stocky and obese groups in calf and arm girths. For each of the three linear measures of standing and sitting heights and leg length, the borderline group had the lowest mean and the fair group had the highest mean; the differences between these adjacent means were significant for all linear measures. Other significant mean differences are listed as follows:

> *Hip width:* obese group higher than all but the stocky group; borderline group lower than all other groups.
> *Lung capacity:* good group higher than borderline group.
> *Physical Fitness Index:* borderline, fair, and good groups higher than stocky and obese groups.
> *McCloy's arm strength score and cable-tension strength average:* borderline group lower than all other groups.
> *Rogers' arm strength score and Strength Index:* borderline group lower than fair and good groups.
> *Skeletal age:* borderline group lower than fair, good, and obese groups.
> *Chronological age:* none.
> *Wetzel developmental level and ratio:* borderline group lower than all other groups; fair group lower than stocky and obese groups; good group lower than obese group.

DEVELOPMENTAL LEVEL. Of the three Wetzel Grid criteria, developmental level had the highest zero-order correlations with the various structural, strength, and maturity variables. The high correlation of .984 with weight and high correlations, none below .896, with the other anthropometric variables indicates a close association of developmental level with gross body size. When chronological age was partialed from the correlations with developmental level, their magnitude generally declined appreciably, although in the case of weight, the partial correlation remained high at .963.

McCloy's arm strength score, Strength Index, and cable-tension strength average had correlations between .839 and .905 with developmental levels. The correlation with Rogers' arm strength score was .551; the correlation with Physical Fitness Index was insignificant.

The correlations between developmental level and skeletal age and chronological age were .841 and .825. When chronological age was partialed, the correlation with skeletal age dropped to .358.

In comparisons between the means of the advanced and retarded developmental groups, the advanced group had significantly higher means for all experimental variables except Rogers' arm strength score.

DEVELOPMENTAL RATIO. The highest correlations between developmental ratio and anthropometric measures were .552 for calf girth, .506 for chest girth, .505 for weight, and .480 for arm girth. The correlations with linear measures and strength tests were much lower; the correlations with the maturity indicators were not significant. A multiple correlation of .922 was obtained with this ratio; the independent variables were calf girth, chronological age, and weight.

Chapter Summary

This chapter concentrated on the physical structure of boys from 7 through 18 years of age. In factor analyses of the same boys at each age from 9 through 16, the following related rotated factors were identified: Body Bulk-Physique and Body Linearity, all ages; Relative Sitting Height, seven ages; and Relative Lung Capacity, five ages. Inter-age correlations for anthropometric measures and indices were high, mostly in the .80's and .90's.

Generally, body bulk measures correlated in the .80's and .90's with each other, as did linear measures. However, the correlations between bulk and linear measures were much lower, mostly in the .60's and .70's. The correlations between body size and strength were lower still and with motor tests they were largely insignificant; the highest such correlations were with Strength Index and cable-tension strength average, with a correlational range for weight from .326 to .641.

Mean growth curves were described and the extent of individual differences for structural measures was presented. The standard deviation of ages 7 and 18 respectively were: weight, 6.3 and 22.6 lbs.; arm girth, 1.4 and 2.5 cm.; hip width, 1.1 and 1.7 cm.; height, 2.0 and 2.5 in.; lung capacity, 11.9 and 40.6 cu. in. The growth patterns of heavy and light groups and tall and short groups formed at ages 9 and 12 were followed to ages 12 and 17 respectively; the differences between the means on anthropometric tests were significant at all ages.

With 12-year-old boys as subjects, the intercorrelations of skinfold measures taken at the back of the upper arm, the inferior angle of the scapula, and the lateral abdomen clustered between .797 and .810; with skinfold total, they correlated between .908 and .963. The ranges of correlations between the three skinfold tests and other measures were: .719 to .824 for endomorphy; −.587 and −.657 for ectomorphy; .269 to .379 for mesomorphy and skeletal age; .173 and .441 for Strength Index and cable-tension strength average; −.246 and −.346 for Physical Fitness Index, bar. push-ups, and standing broad jump.

Three aspects of the Wetzel Grid, physique channels, developmental levels, and developmental ratios, were studied for boys 9 through 15 years of age. The following multiple correlations will indicate the relationships obtained: physique channels, .901, with arm girth, standing height, and weight; developmental ratio, .922, with calf girth, chronological age, and weight. The zero-order correlation between developmental level and weight was .984; correlations between .839 and .905 were found for Strength Index and cable-tension strength average.

Chapter 5 / Muscular Strength and Endurance

The good condition of muscles, their strength and endurance, is essential to man. Volitional movements of the body or any of its parts are impossible without action by skeletal muscles. One cannot stand, walk, run, jump, climb, or swim without the contraction of muscles throughout the body. Smaller muscles perform intricate functions, including writing, playing musical instruments, singing, using hand tools, and the like. Muscles perform vital functions of the body. The heart is a muscle; death occurs when it ceases to contract. Breathing, digestion, and elimination would be impossible without muscular contractions. A sedentary society, in which the muscles are used only mildly, seldom if ever vigorously, is conducive to physical degeneration.

Hunsicker and Donnelly (57) have provided a brief historical account of the evolution of devices used to measure the strength of skeletal muscles as volitionally manifested by man. According to this account, the first person to use an instrument known as a dynamometer was an Englishman named Graham. The forerunner of the spring dynamometers in use today was produced in 1807 by Regnier. This device was used to measure grip strength, pulling power of the arm muscles, and lifting power of the back muscles. Sargent initiated strength testing in the United States at Harvard University in 1880. He utilized an instrument similar to Regnier's dynamometer for measuring back and leg strengths; for testing grip strength, he used a compact manuometer, small enough to fit inside the hand. The spring-type dynamometer was improved over the years and several types of grip dynamometers were devised.

Strength tests have not been commonly employed in longitudinal growth studies in this country. The work by Jones at the Institute of Child Welfare, University of California, Berkeley, is a noteworthy exception. His strength tests, however, were quite limited. They consisted only of right and left grips, arm pull and push, all performed with a manuometer, which had special attachments for the pull and push tests. However, Jones considered his results so significant that he published a monograph (60), in which he presented the results of his strength studies of the same children from 7 through 17 years of age.

An extensive use of strength tests was made in the Medford Boys' Growth Study. The strength tests consisted of the dynamometric measures contained in Rogers' Strength Index battery and eleven cable-tension tests. In addition, tests of the muscular endurance of the arm and shoulder girdle muscles were included. This chapter is devoted to significant findings for the study of growth resulting from the use of these tests.

Rogers' Strength Index Battery

In 1873, Sargent (88) proposed a battery of strength tests, which was popular at the time as a basis for conducting intercollegiate strength competition. In 1925, Rogers (84) made significant improvements in the tests and developed two battery scores, the Strength Index and the Physical Fitness Index, each of which has a distinctly different use. The Strength Index is a gross score obtained by adding all test items. The Physical Fitness Index is a relative strength score, derived from comparing the achieved

Strength Index to a norm for the individual's sex, age, and weight. Since its origin, improvements have been made in testing techniques, especially in 1938. The test items consist of four dynamometric tests (right and left grips, back and leg lifts), two muscular endurance tests (pull-ups and push-ups), and lung capacity. Detailed directions for administering these tests are provided by Clarke (12). Brief descriptions of the test items and the battery formations follow.

GRIP STRENGTH. A Narragansett manuometer, or grip dynamometer, was used to measure grip strength; right and left hands were tested separately. For each grip, the manuometer was squeezed as hard as possible; the elbow was slightly bent and the hand described a sweeping arc downward with the arm and hand free of the body. The measurement was recorded in pounds.

BACK AND LEG LIFTS. A dynamometer with a capacity of 2,500 pounds was used to measure back and leg lifting strengths. In both instances, the subject stood on a platform to which the dynamometer was attached. For the back lift, the knees were kept straight and the back was slightly bent. For the leg lift, the lifting bar was held firmly to the hips with a belt and the lift was performed with the knees slightly bent and the back straight. These tests are illustrated in Fig. 5.1.

PULL-UPS AND PUSH-UPS. Pull-ups is the well-known chinning test, performed with the hands grasping the bar with palms forward. Push-ups, or bar dips, consisted of the number of dips performed at one end of the parallel bars.

LUNG CAPACITY. The techniques for administering this test are described in Chapter 4, page 101.

ARM STRENGTH. The Rogers arm strength score was obtained from pull-ups and push-ups, using the following formula: (pull-ups + push-ups) $\left(\dfrac{W}{10} + H - 60\right)$, in which W represents the weight in pounds, and H the height in inches. If the boy was 60 inches or below in height, height was disregarded in the formula.

Fig. 5.1A Back lift
with dynamometer

STRENGTH INDEX. The Strength Index (SI) is the total score determined by adding right and left grips, back and leg lifts, arm strength score, and lung capacity.

PHYSICAL FITNESS INDEX. The Physical Fitness Index (PFI) is derived by dividing the achieved Strength Index by a norm for the individual's sex, age, and weight; this quotient is multiplied by 100.

Cable-Tension Strength Tests

Cable-tension strength testing was developed initially by Clarke and Peterson (18) during World War II while serving in the Army Air Force's convalescent hospital program to evaluate the strength of affected muscle groups involved in orthopedic disabilities. The instrument utilized, the tensiometer, was originally intended for testing the tension of aircraft control cables. Subsequently, Clarke and associates (15, 20) perfected 38 strength tests based on movements of the fingers, trunk, wrist, forearm, elbow, shoulder, neck, trunk, hip, knee, and ankle. More recently, these tests have been used widely for the measurement of the strength of the muscles of normal subjects. The most recent description of the equipment needed and the testing techniques for all tests are presented by Clarke and Clarke (24).* A review of much

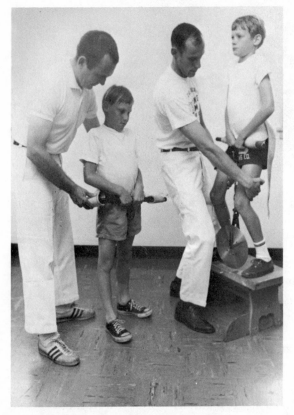

Fig. 5.1B   Leg lift with belt

* Tensiometers may be obtained from the Pacific Scientific Co., Inc., 6280 Chalet Drive, City of Commerce, California 90022.

of the research related to cable-tension strength testing is also provided by Clarke (16).

Initially, 12 cable-tension strength tests were included in the Medford Boys' Growth Project; after the first year, one test was dropped because of faulty testing techniques. The eleven tests retained and a brief description of each follow; illustrations of four cable-tension strength tests appear in Fig. 5.1A-B. All pulls were at right angles to the body part serving as lever. Strength was measured in pounds.

ELBOW FLEXION. Subject in supine lying position, hips and knees flexed, free hand resting on chest; left arm close to side, elbow in 115 degrees flexion, forearm in mid-prone-supine position; pulling strap placed around forearm midway between wrist and elbow joints.

SHOULDER FLEXION. Subject in supine lying position, hips and knees flexed, free hand resting on chest; left upper arm close to side, shoulder flexed to 180 degrees, elbow in 90 degrees flexion; pulling strap around arm midway between elbow and shoulder joints.

SHOULDER INWARD ROTATION. Subject in supine lying position, hips and knees flexed, free hand on chest; left arm close to side, elbow in 90 degrees flexion and supported by pad to bring arm into position parallel with body, forearm in mid-prone-supine position; pulling strap around forearm midway between wrist and elbow joints (pull is toward body).

TRUNK FLEXION. Subject in supine lying position with upper back over slit in testing table, legs straight and together, arms folded on chest; trunk strap around chest close under armpits.

TRUNK EXTENSION. Subject in same position as for trunk flexion, except in prone lying position with hands clasped behind back.

HIP FLEXION. Subject in supine lying position, hip and knee of right leg flexed, arms folded on chest; left hip and knee fully extended over slit in testing table; pulling strap around thigh, lower third between hip and knee joints.

Hip Extension. Subject in same position as for hip flexion, except in prone lying position with both legs extended and arms along sides.

Knee Flexion. Subject in prone position, patellas just at edge of testing table, head resting on folded arms; left knee flexed to 165 degrees; pulling strap placed around leg midway between knee and ankle joints.

Knee Extension. Subject in sitting, backward-leaning position, arms extended to rear without flexing at elbow, hands grasping sides of table, right leg hanging free; left knee in 115 degrees extension; pulling strap placed around leg midway between knee and ankle joints.

Ankle Dorsal Flexion. Subject in supine lying position with legs fully extended and arms folded on chest; left ankle in 125 degrees dorsal flexion; pulling strap around foot above metatarsal-phalangeal joint.

Ankle Plantar Flexion. Subject in same position as for ankle dorsal flexion, except left ankle in 90 degrees flexion and pulling strap around ball of foot.

Simplifications of the Strength Index

While the SI and PFI have been effectively used in school and college physical education programs, many users readily acknowledge that the following factors prevent more general use: (1) cost of testing equipment, (2) time required for giving the test to many students, and (3) necessity for well-trained testers. As a consequence, Carter (11, 22) undertook to simplify this battery for boys in upper elementary, junior high, and senior high schools.

The subjects were 356 Medford boys. The upper elementary school ages were restricted to 9, 10, and 11 years; the junior high school ages, to 12, 13, and 14 years; the senior high school ages, to 15, 16, and 17 years. Forty boys served as subjects at each age except 17 years, where the number was 36. Subsequently, these boys were found to be physically superior to normal populations, since their mean PFI's were 111 for upper elementary school, 120 for junior high school, and 108 for senior high school. The mean PFI for all subjects was 113.

Bases for Strength Index Norms

The first phase of this research was devoted to a restudy of the measures upon which norms for the Strength Index should be based. In the original research by Rogers, only age, height, and weight were considered. In addition to these three measures, the following six anthropometric tests were included in this study: sitting height, leg length, flexed-tensed upper arm girth, chest girth, calf girth, and hip width.

The multiple correlations obtained between the Strength Index and the two variables producing the highest coefficients at each school level were as follows:

Upper elementary school: .59 with standing height and flexed-tensed upper arm girth.
Junior high school: .79 with sitting height and flexed-tensed upper arm girth.
Senior high school: .68 with flexed-tensed upper arm girth and sitting height.

Since these correlations were quite low for predictive purposes, the selected test items at each school level were considered of questionable value as a basis for SI norms. Also, in determining the relationships, age in each instance was limited to three years, which had a partialing effect on the correlations; in the original research on the norms, age ranged over many years. As a consequence, the relationship of age, height, and weight to the Strength Index was studied for the combined ages, 9 to 17 years inclusive, using the scores of all 356 Medford boys. The resulting multiple correlation was .901 between the SI and weight and age; the addition of height to the computation did not increase this amount.

This correlation was .043 correlational points higher than the .858 obtained originally by Rogers (84). As a consequence of this evidence, the decision was made to continue the use of weight and age as the basis for Strength Index norms.

Multiple Correlations

Multiple correlations were computed at each of the three school levels with the SI and the PFI serving in turn as the dependent variable; the independent variables were the test items composing the SI battery. The multiple correlations obtained were as follows:

School Levels	Criteria	R	Independent Variables
Upper Elementary	PFI	.871	Leg lift, pull-ups, lung capacity
	SI	.977	Leg lift, back lift, push-ups
Junior High School	PFI	.849	Pull-ups, leg lift, push-ups, lung capacity
	SI	.987	Leg lift, Rogers' arm strength score
		.998	Leg lift, Rogers' arm strength score, right grip
Senior High School	PFI	.796	Push-ups, pull-ups, leg lift
	SI	.985	Leg lift, Rogers' arm strength score
		.996	Leg lift, Rogers' arm strength score, back lift

The multiple correlations with the SI as the criterion were found to be higher at all school levels than when the PFI was the dependent variable: .977 to .998 for the SI and .796 to .871 for the PFI. Leg lift appeared in all eight multiple correlations; it was the first variable in the five SI batteries and in one of the PFI batteries. In general, pull-ups and push-ups correlated better with the PFI than did the other tests; the Rogers arm strength score was an important variable in the SI multiple correlations.

Multiple Regression Equations

Since the multiple correlations with the Strength Index as criterion were all high, .977 and above, multiple regression equations were computed for them. Two equations are presented at both the junior and senior high school levels, so that the physical educator may choose whether he wishes to utilize only the leg lift and arm strength, thus limiting his testing to a minimum, or to add another test item at each school level, thus obtaining a closer approximation of each boy's actual SI. The multiple regression equations thus computed are as follows (the arm strength scores are by Rogers' formula):

Upper Elementary School Boys
$$R = .977$$
$$SI = 1.05 \text{ (leg lift)} + 1.35 \text{ (back lift)} + 10.92 \text{ (push-ups)} + 133$$
$$\sigma\text{est.} = 43$$

Junior High School Boys
$$A: R = .987$$
$$SI = 1.33 \text{ (leg lift)} + 1.20 \text{ (arm strength)} + 286$$
$$\sigma\text{est.} = 76$$

$$B: R = .998$$
$$SI = 1.12 \text{ (leg lift)} + .99 \text{ (arm strength)} + 5.19 \text{ (right grip)} + 129$$
$$\sigma\text{est.} = 30$$

Senior High School Boys
$$A: R = .985$$
$$SI = 1.22 \text{ (leg lift)} + 1.23 \text{ (arm strength)} + 499$$
$$\sigma\text{est.} = 86$$

$$B: R = .996$$
$$SI = 1.07 \text{ (leg lift)} + 1.06 \text{ (arm strength)} + 1.42 \text{ (back lift)} + 194$$
$$\sigma\text{est.} = 44$$

The second, or B, regression equations for the junior and senior high school boys, of course, approximate each boy's actual SI with a greater degree of accuracy than do the first, or A, equations. The degrees of accuracy are reflected in the standard errors of estimate: for the junior high school boys, the error is approximately 2.5 times greater for the A equation; for the senior high school boys, the error is about twice as large.

These regression equations were tested by comparing the actual PFI's with the PFI's predicted by the application of each of the regression equations. This tabulation is shown in Table 5.1.

Thus, the differences between the actual and predicted PFI means at the three levels and for all equations ranged from .3 to 1.0 PFI points. In all instances the predicted PFI means were

Table 5.1

COMPARISON OF ACTUAL AND PREDICTED PHYSICAL FITNESS INDICES
FOR ELEMENTARY, JUNIOR HIGH, AND SENIOR HIGH SCHOOL BOYS

	Equa-tion	Means		Mean Diff.	Std. Dev. of Diff.
School Level		*Actual*	*Predicted*		
Elementary School		110.8	111.9	+1.0	4.3
Junior High School	A	120.4	120.7	+ .3	6.3
	B	120.4	121.1	+ .7	4.0
Senior High School	A	108.2	109.9	+ .7	4.6
	B	108.2	109.2	+1.0	3.1

higher. The standard deviations of the differences between actual
and predicted PFI's ranged from 3.1 to 6.3. As would be expected
from the higher multiple correlations, the B equations resulted in
smaller standard deviations for both the junior and senior high
school boys.

Other Studies

Although not a part of the Medford Boys' Growth Study,
similar simplifications of the Strength Index were subsequently
accomplished at the University of Oregon separately for upper
elementary, junior high, and senior high school girls and college
men and women. The regression equations obtained appear in
Clarke's measurement text (12).

Cable-Tension Strength Battery

A cable-tension strength test battery was developed by
Schopf (35, 89) for boys 9 through 12 years of age in grades four,
five, and six. Two battery indices similar in function to the Strength
Index and Physical Fitness Index were constructed.

Selection of Test Items

In the selection of test items for the cable-tension
strength battery, the subjects were 128 Medford boys, distributed

by age as follows: 9 years, 37; 10 years, 28; 11 years, 27; and 12 years, 36. In addition to the 11 cable-tension tests included in the Medford Boys' Growth Study, the following seven were also administered to these boys: elbow extension, shoulder extension and abduction, neck extension, and hip abduction, abduction, and inward rotation.

The criterion for the selection of strength tests was the mean of the 18 cable-tension tests. Product-moment correlations were computed among all strength tests and between the strength tests and the criterion. The intercorrelations among the strength tests ranged from .223 between elbow extension and knee flexion to .809 between trunk extension and flexion; all correlations were significant near or beyond the .01 level (.227 necessary for significance at the .01 level). The strength tests with the highest correlations with other strength tests were shoulder extension, shoulder abduction, hip abduction, knee extension, and ankle plantar flexion; the strength tests with lowest correlations were elbow extension, hip inward rotation, and ankle dorsal flexion. The 18 correlation coefficients between the criterion and the individual tests ranged from .519 for elbow extension to .889 for shoulder extension.

A coefficient of multiple correlation was then computed by use of the Wherry-Doolittle method; the criterion was the dependent variable and the 18 individual strength tests were the independent variables. The development of the multiple correlation was as follows.

Strength Test	r with Criterion	Multiple Correlation
Shoulder Extension	.889	
Ankle Plantar Flexion	.844	.940
Trunk Extension	.795	.964
Knee Extension	.859	.976

These four tests, therefore, were selected to compose the strength test battery in this study. The selected tests represent almost equally strong movements; further, they all measure the strength of extension movements of the joints involved (ankle plantar flexion is, in fact, ankle extension).

Illustrations of the four tests selected for the cable-tension strength battery appear in Fig. 5.2. Descriptions of the trunk extension, knee extension, and ankle plantar flexion were given above. A similar description for shoulder extension strength is as follows: Subject in supine lying position, hips and knees flexed, right hand resting on chest; upper left arm adducted at shoulder to 180 degrees, shoulder flexed to 90 degrees, elbow flexed with wrist in prone position; pulling strap around arm midway between elbow and shoulder joints.

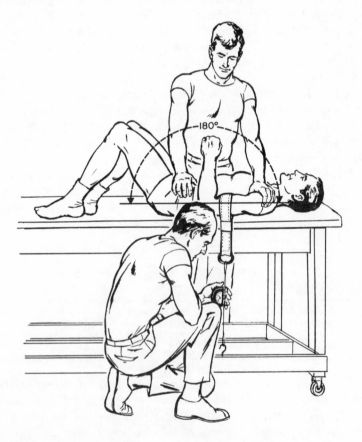

Fig. 5.2   Cable tension strengh tests A: Shoulder extension strength

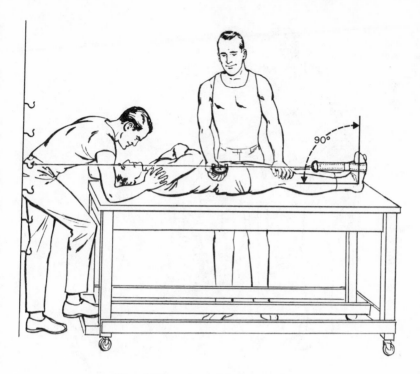

Fig. 5.2B   Ankle plantar flexion strength

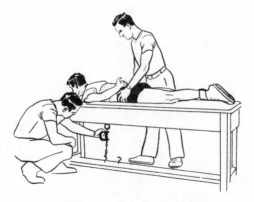

Fig. 5.2C   Trunk extension strength

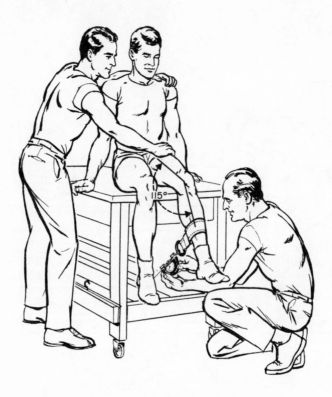

Fig. 5.2D Knee extension strength

Construction of Norms

The subjects used for the construction of norms in this study were 826 boys in grades four, five and six from ten public schools located in the state of Oregon. Schools were selected to represent various geographic sections of the state. Subjects were selected at random within each school. Separated into age groups of one-half year each, the number of subjects in each group follow.

The process adopted by Rogers (84) in the construction of Strength Index norms to obtain the Physical Fitness Index was adopted. The essential norm construction problem in this study, therefore, was the determination of the increase in strength associ-

Ages (years and months)	Number
9–0 to 9–5	105
9–6 to 9–11	147
10–0 to 10–5	135
10–6 to 10–11	117
11–0 to 11–5	101
11–6 to 11–11	110
12–0 to 12–5	68
12–6 to 12–11	44

ated with an increase in weight for a given age; a double-entry table containing the amounts of strength for various ages and weights was the final result.

Description of the steps taken in the establishment of the strength test norms follows. The strength of each boy was found as the sum of the four cable-tension strength tests in pounds. This gross strength score will be known herein as the strength composite.

1. The median weight and the median strength composite for the boys at each half-year in age were computed.

2. The median weights and strength composites were smoothed to reduce chance irregularities.

3. The amount of increase in the strength composite with weight increase for each half-year age was determined. In this process, cut-off points at the first and third quartiles were invoked. Thus, the procedure was as follows: (a) for each half-year in age, the first and third quartiles were determined for both weight and the strength composite; (b) the interquartile range for each of these was then computed at each age; (c) the interquartile range in strength composite was divided by the interquartile range in weight at each age. These quotients represent the increase in strength composite per increase in one pound of weight for the different ages and are designated as weight deviation multipliers.

4. The weight deviation multipliers were used to construct the norm chart. The median strength composite was entered for the median weight at each age. For each pound above the boy's weight at each age, the amount of the weight deviation multiplier was added to the corresponding median and was subtracted from this median for each pound below. The norm chart for this battery

appears in Table B.3 of Clarke's measurement text (12). Norms for heavier or lighter boys than those appearing on the norm chart may be obtained by use of the weight deviation multipliers.

Strength Quotient

The final procedure in this study was to propose a means of interpreting each boy's Strength Composite (SC). From the norm chart, a boy's SC can be compared with the normal expectation for his age and weight. In order to make this comparison, a Strength Quotient was proposed, derived from the following formula:

$$\text{Strength Quotient} = \frac{\text{Achieved Strength Composite}}{\text{Normal Strength Composite}} \times 100$$

A quotient of 100 is the median or normal SQ found in this study; SQ's of 85 and 115 correspond to the first and third quartiles.

Other Studies

Subsequent to Schopf's investigation, although not a part of the Medford Boys' Growth Study, research was undertaken at the University of Oregon to develop similar cable-tension strength test batteries for both boys and girls at the school levels of upper elementary, junior high, senior high, and college. In the test-selection phase, 25 cable-tension tests were administered to 24 boys and 24 girls from each public school grade, fourth through twelfth, and to 72 men and 72 women at the college level; thus, a total of 576 subjects were involved, 72 boys and 72 girls at each school level. At each school level, three strength tests were selected by multiple correlation procedures; in each instance, the average of the 25 cable tension tests was the criterion and the individual tests were the independent variables. The tests thus selected and the multiple correlations were:

R	Boys	R	Girls
	Upper Elementary school		
.963	Shoulder Extension	.936	Shoulder Extension
	Knee Extension		Hip Extension
	Ankle Plantar Flexion		Trunk Flexion

R	Boys	R	Girls
	Junior High School		
.965	Shoulder Extension Knee Extension Ankle Plantar Flexion	.941	Shoulder Extension Hip Extension Trunk Extension
	Senior High School		
.955	Shoulder Extension Knee Extension Ankle Plantar Flexion	.955	Shoulder Flexion Hip Flexion Ankle Plantar Flexion
	College		
.928	Shoulder Extension Knee Extension Ankle Plantar Flexion	.947	Shoulder Flexion Hip Flexion Ankle Plantar Flexion

At the upper elementary, junior high, and senior high school levels, norms for the three selected tests were constructed separately for boys and girls based on age and weight in the same manner as described above in Schopf's study. At the college level, the norm tables were based on arm and abdominal girths for men and arm girth and sitting height for women. Inasmuch as the highest multiple correlation between any two anthropometric tests and the criterion of 25 cable-tension strength tests was .59 at the college level, T scales were also constructed for the Strength Composites. The subjects tested for construction of SC norms for upper elementary, junior high, and senior high school levels were randomly drawn from schools in six Oregon communities. The numbers tested each for boys and for girls were 124 in each grade, 372 at each school level, and 1,116 in all for each sex, or 2,232 for both sexes. At the college level, the subjects were 372 men and 372 women.

A manual containing directions and illustrations for administering the cable-tension strength tests in the various batteries and the several norm charts constructed has been prepared by Clarke and Munroe (32).

Factor Analyses

Several factor analyses conducted in the Medford Boys' Growth Study in attempts to identify a general maturity factor were presented in Chapter 2; the rotated factors pertaining to body size were discussed in Chapter 4. This chapter will describe the rotated factors related to muscular strength and endurance obtained by Phillips (80) in his longitudinal analyses of 62 boys from 9 through 16 years of age.

Arm-Shoulder Endurance

Arm-Shoulder Endurance was the only muscular strength and endurance rotated factor to appear at all eight ages, as shown in Table 5.2. This factor was identified because of the highest loadings for the arm and shoulder endurance items. The ranges of the loadings of these endurance measures were as follows: arm strength score, −.780 to .855; bar push-ups, −.556 to .845; and pull-ups, .592 to .859. The negative loadings at ages 10, 11, 12, 13,

Table 5.2

ARM AND SHOULDER ENDURANCE ROTATED FACTOR
LOADINGS FOR BOYS AGED 9 THROUGH 16

Variables	Ages							
	9	10	11	12	13	14	15	16
Arm Strength Score	.781	−.796	−.780	−.850	−.877	.847	−.813	.855
Bar Push-Ups	.751	−.744	−.556	−.832	−.826	.845	−.822	.763
Pull-Ups	.592	−.640	−.792	−.655	−.719	.724	−.757	.859
Physical Fitness Index	.391	−.210	−.367	−.399	−.746	.737	−.619	.693

and 15 were interpreted as failure of arm and shoulder endurance of boys to keep pace with general development.

The loadings were most consistent and highest at the four older ages, 13 through 16. During these ages, the Physical Fitness Index loaded well on this factor, between −.619 and −.746. However, it did not load well at the younger four ages. Furthermore, these tests are intimately associated; the arm strength score is obtained from bar push-ups and pull-ups, and this score is a part of the Strength Index battery from which the PFI is derived. Also, bar push-ups, pull-ups, and PFI are relative measures since body weight is ruled out of consideration; the amount of weight is not included in push-up and pull-up scores and the SI norms are based in large part on weight. The arm strength score had been considered as a gross arm-shoulder endurance measure inasmuch as the weights and heights of the subjects are included in its scoring; however, this score loaded about the same as the other measures in this factor, which casts some doubt on its gross nature.*

Moderate loadings were obtained on the Arm-Shoulder Eudurance factor for several of the motor ability tests. The highest of these loadings were for standing broad jump and 60-yard shuttle run at ages 9, 13, and 14. The loadings for maturity, physique type, body size, and strength measures were low and mostly insignificant.

Arm-Shoulder Strength

Arm-Shoulder Strength was identified as a rotated factor at five ages due to high loadings of the three cable-tension strengths in the arm-shoulder area; the omitted ages were 10, 13, and 16. The loadings were:

Age	Elbow Flexion	Shoulder Flexion	Shoulder Inward Rotation
Nine Years	.825	.737	.810
Eleven Years	−.879	−.161	−.884
Twelve Years	.566	.756	.743
Fourteen Years	.691	.694	.832
Fifteen Years	−.557	−.502	−.449

The loadings of these strength tests were highest at the younger ages of 9 and 11, except for shoulder flexion at 11 years; the 15-year age was definitely lowest for all tests. Shoulder inward rotation had the most consistently high loadings, except for age 15. The negative loadings at ages 11 and 15 were interpreted as failure of arm and shoulder strength of boys to keep pace with general development.

Cable-tension strength average, of which these tests are a part, had significant but low loadings between −.242 and .455 on this factor. The loadings were nearly all insignificant for the other strength tests and for the maturity, physique type, body size, muscular endurance, and motor ability measures.

Leg-Back Lift Strength

Leg-Back Lift Strength was identified as a rotated factor at five ages because of high loadings of the back and leg lift tests;

---

* See the later section in this chapter on arm strength scores for a further treatment of this concept.

the omitted ages were 13, 15, and 16. High loadings on this factor were also obtained for the Strength and Physical Fitness Indices. As will be seen later, this factor was replaced by a General Strength factor at ages 15 and 16. The loadings were:

Age	Leg Lift	Back Lift	Strength Index	PFI
Nine Years	.881	.615	.771	.696
Ten Years	.866	.749	.908	.746
Eleven Years	−.293	−.557	−.755	−.567
Twelve Years	−.782	−.730	−.825	−.692
Fourteen Years	−.117	.663	.074	−.067

These loadings were not consistent at all five ages. Leg lift had high loadings at three ages, 9, 10, and 12, while back lift loaded moderately high at these ages. The identification of this factor was obscured somewhat by high loadings at four of the ages for Strength Index and Physical Fitness Index. However, the back and leg lifts constitute highly weighted tests in the test battery from which these indices are derived. Inasmuch as other tests in the battery, as well as the cable-tension strength tests, loaded low and mostly insignificantly on this factor, the designation of Leg-Back Lift Strength was made. The maturity, physique type, body size, and motor ability tests generally loaded insignificantly on this factor; the main exceptions were loadings of .516 for standing broad jump and .628 for athletic rating at age 11.

Lower-Leg Strength

Lower-Leg Strength was identified as a rotated factor at three ages, 9, 12, and 13 years, because of highest loadings of the lower-leg cable-tension strength tests. The loadings were:

Strength Tests	Nine Years	Twelve Years	Thirteen Years
Hip Flexion	.195	.765	.542
Hip Extension	.212	.753	.503
Knee Flexion	.640	.720	.761
Knee Extension	.789	.642	.720
Ankle Plantar Flexion	.731	.198	.697
Cable Tension Average	.170	.677	.657

Knee flexion and extension strengths loaded moderately high at all three ages, between .640 and .789; ankle plantar flexion strength had similar loadings except at age 12. In addition, hip flexion and extension strengths had loadings of comparable magnitude at age 12; the loadings were lower but significant at age 13. The maturity, physique type, body size, motor ability, muscular endurance, and other strength tests had low and mostly insignificant loadings on this factor, with exceptions of .567 for standing broad jump at age 12 and between .445 and .602 for left grip, leg lift, and back lift at age 13.

Grip Strength

Grip Strength was identified as a rotated factor at three ages, 9, 10, and 11, due to highest loadings of right and left grip strengths. The loadings were:

Strength Tests	Nine Years	Ten Years	Eleven Years
Right Grip	−.696	.762	−.686
Left Grip	−.776	.800	−.810

The grip strength loadings ranged from −.686 to −.810; the loadings were negative at ages 9 and 11 and positive at age 10. Nearly all other loadings on this factor were insignificant.

General Strength

The rotated factor of General Strength was identified at ages 15 and 16, because of highest loadings on most strength tests. The loadings appear in Table 5.3.

The strength loadings on this factor were highest and most consistent for all strength tests at age 15. The highest loading at this age was .878 for cable-tension average; with the exceptions of shoulder inward rotation, elbow flexion, and trunk extension, the loadings for the other strength tests ranged between .624 and .777. The loadings at age 16 were negative and lower than at 15 years; the highest of these correlations were −.745 for shoulder flexion, −.720 for leg lift, −.667 for cable-tension average, and −.649 for left grip. Other moderate loadings on the General Strength factor were .495 and −.419 for skeletal age and .656, .555, and −.498 for standing broad jump, Physical Fitness Index, and 60-yard shuttle run (positive connotation) at age 15.

The presence of the General Strength factor at the ages of 15

Table 5.3

GENERAL STRENGTH ROTATED FACTOR FOR BOYS
AT AGES 15 AND 16 YEARS

	Ages	
Variables	*15 Years*	*16 Years*
Shoulder Flexion	.625	−.745
Shoulder Inward Rotation	.496	−.525
Elbow Flexion	.492	−.347
Trunk Flexion	.721	−.092
Trunk Extension	.542	−.106
Hip Flexion	.748	−.450
Hip Extension	.661	−.586
Knee Flexion	.624	−.545
Knee Extension	.759	−.497
Ankle Plantar Flexion	.749	−.579
Cable-Tension Average	.878	−.667
Right Grip	.659	−.597
Left Grip	.696	−.649
Leg Lift	.777	−.720
Back Lift	.747	−.318
Strength Index	.746	−.634

and 16 was accompanied by the absence of other strength factors which were identified in the earlier ages. This situation was particularly true for the factors of Leg-Back Strength, Lower-Leg Strength, and Grip Strength. This result may indicate that general strength becomes more prominent in their developmental patterns as boys grow older.

Comparison with Other Studies

A rotated factor called Arm-Shoulder Endurance was found in Phillips' longitudinal factor analyses at all ages, 9 through 16. Of the other Medford factor analysis studies, Torpey (104) with 10-year-old boys was the only one to reveal a similar rotated factor.

Lower-Leg Strength was identified as a rotated factor in Phillips' analyses at ages 9, 12, and 13. A similar factor was found in Torpey's analysis of boys 16 years of age; the factor loadings were comparable to those obtained for 16-year-old boys in the Phillips study.

In Phillips' study, Grip Strength was obtained as a rotated factor at ages 9, 10, and 11. For boys 9 years of age, Willee (113) reported a similar rotated factor. The factor loadings were comparable at age 9 in both studies.

Leg-Back Lift Strength was found as a rotated factor at ages 9, 10, 11, 12, and 14 in Phillips' analyses. A similar rotated factor was reported by Willee for 9-year-old boys.

General Strength was identified as a rotated factor at ages 15 and 16 in Phillips' analyses. Among the other Medford factor analyses, only Burt (10) with 13-year-old boys reported a similar factor, which he interpreted as Maturity Lag because of negative strength loadings. Burt's factor for 13-year-old boys closely resembled Phillips' factor for 16-year-old boys, which also had negative loadings. At 15 years of age in Phillips' study, however, the factor loadings were positive.

The Arm-Shoulder Strength factor found by Phillips at 9, 11, 12, 14, and 15 years of age was not obtained in the other factor analytic studies.

Intercorrelations of Strength Tests

Due to the very large number of intercorrelations computed among muscular strength tests in the Medford Boys' Growth Study, only summaries of the individual strength tests are given here. These are followed by correlations of the individual tests with test batteries for the various ages. The correlations are from Phillips' longitudinal factor analyses (80) of 62 boys from 9 through 16 years of age. The tests are the same as those included above in the presentation of factor analyses.

Individual Strength Tests

DYNAMOMETRIC STRENGTH TESTS. The highest intercorrelations among the four dynamometric strength tests at all ages were between right and left grips; those correlations ranged from .614 at age 11 to .852 at age 15. The next highest correlations at most ages were between back and leg lifts, ranging from .367 at age 9 to .747 at age 15. Generally, the magnitude of these inter-correlations increased with age; the correlations were highest at age 15. Some of the intercorrelations were insignificant at the .05 level for ages 9 and 10.

CABLE-TENSION STRENGTH TESTS. Generally, the highest inter-correlations among the cable-tension strength tests were between antagonistic muscle groups. The correlations between hip flexion and extension were highest at four ages and among the highest at the other four ages; these correlations ranged from .582 at age 14 to .806 at age 9, with .806 being the highest intercorrelation among these tests. The correlations between trunk flexion and extension were also consistently among the highest intercorrelations at all ages; these correlations ranged from .582 at age 10 to .751 at age 9. The knee flexion-extension correlations were among the highest at three ages, between .663 and .722 at ages 12, 13, and 15.

Relatively high correlations were obtained at some ages be-tween nonantagonistic muscle groups, as follows: hip flexion vs. trunk flexion at 9 and 14 years; trunk extension vs. hip extension and hip flexion at 9 years; shoulder flexion vs. elbow flexion at 13 and 15 years; shoulder flexion vs. knee flexion at 14 and 15 years; and hip flexion vs. knee flexion at five of the ages. With one excep-tion, these intercorrelations were between adjacent muscle groups and, with two exceptions, the joint movements were the same, either flexion or extension.

All 45 intercorrelations among the cable-tension strength tests were significant at the .05 level and above for ages 13 to 16 inclu-sive. For the younger ages, the numbers of insignificant correlations were 16 at 9, 20 at 10, 16 at 11, and 8 at 12 years.

DYNAMOMETRIC VS. CABLE-TENSION STRENGTH TESTS. The high-est and largest numbers of significant correlations between dyna-mometric and cable-tension strength tests were obtained at the ages of 13, 14, and 15; of the 45 correlations at each age, all were significant at the .05 level at the ages of 13 and 14 and all but three were significant at age 14. The largest numbers of insignificant correlations were 18, 22, and 21 at ages 9, 10, and 11 respectively; at 12 and 16 years, the respective numbers were 9 and 6.

The highest such correlations were found at age 15; ten of these ranged between .667 and .732, all but two of which were higher than the highest at other ages. In this cluster, the correlations were between the following: leg lift and ankle plantar flexion, knee extension, knee flexion, hip flexion, and shoulder flexion; left grip and knee extension, knee flexion, and shoulder flexion; right grip and knee extension; back lift and hip flexion. Similar correlations, although lower, were obtained at ages 13 and 15; the clusters of highest correlations ranged between .571 and .678 at 13 years and between .601 and .660 at 14 years. The highest correlations at the other ages were: .570, right grip and hip flexion, 9 years; .561, back lift and shoulder flexion, 10 years; .526, leg lift and hip extension, 11 years; .588, right grip and ankle plantar flexion, 12 years; .687, leg lift and ankle plantar flexion, 16 years.

Correlations with Strength Test Batteries

The correlations between the individual dynamometric and cable-tension strength tests and the two gross test batteries of Strength Index and cable-tension strength average were computed for each of the eight ages. The results follow.

STRENGTH INDEX. The correlations between the Strength Index and the individual dynamometric and cable-tension strength tests appear in Table 5.4. The highest correlations were between .850 and .951 for leg lift. By ages, the highest correlations for all strength tests were at 13, 14, and 15 years. In addition to leg lift, the highest correlations at these ages were between .690 and .724 for right grip, .669 and .705 for left grip, .618 and .810 for back lift, .620 and .760 for shoulder flexion, and .662 to .729 for knee extension. In fact, the correlations at these ages were all significant and moderately high, the lowest being between .484 and .511 for trunk extension.

The correlations of the individual strength tests with Strength Index were lowest at ages 9, 10, and 11; with few exceptions, however, they were significant at the .05 level. Some increases in the magnitude of the correlations occurred at age 12, with a decrease to about the same level at age 16.

The correlations between Strength Index and cable-tension

Table 5.4

STRENGTH INDEX CORRELATIONS WITH OTHER STRENGTH TESTS
FOR THE SAME BOYS AGED 9 THROUGH 16

				Ages				
Variables	9	10	11	12	13	14	15	16
Dynamometric Tests								
Right Grip	.424	.288	.336	.542	.690	.704	.724	.542
Left Grip	.400	.260	.389	.612	.679	.705	.669	.543
Leg Lift	.850	.921	.939	.940	.951	.905	.928	.858
Back Lift	.504	.676	.575	.692	.618	.648	.810	.619
Cable-Tension Tests								
Shoulder Flexion	.259	.379	.424	.402	.760	.620	.736	.511
Shoulder Inward Rotation	.150*	.108*	.327	.421	.597	.514	.574	.487
Elbow Flexion	.332	.264	.282	.433	.650	.555	.562	.411
Trunk Flexion	.171*	.268	.267	.438	.485	.636	.525	.316
Trunk Extension	.262	.270	.312	.373	.484	.511	.463	.333
Hip Flexion	.383	.397	.517	.412	.510	.623	.726	.533
Hip Extension	.332	.362	.575	.383	.530	.604	.581	.488
Knee Flexion	.330	.341	.455	.534	.575	.619	.656	.560
Knee Extension	.348	.465	.491	.522	.686	.729	.662	.584
Ankle Plantar Flexion	.519	.376	.386	.549	.548	.588	.648	.660
C-T Strength Average	.471	.504	.655	.648	.805	.816	.820	.754

*Insignificant at .05 level.

Table 5.5

CABLE-TENSION STRENGTH AVERAGE CORRELATIONS WITH OTHER STRENGTH TESTS FOR THE SAME BOYS AGED 9 THROUGH 16

Variables	Ages							
	9	10	11	12	13	14	15	16
Dynamometric Tests								
Right Grip	.470	.409	.352	.488	.650	.709	.703	.548
Left Grip	.484	.451	.304	.473	.702	.783	.739	.500
Leg Lift	.359	.480	.574	.620	.761	.733	.788	.743
Back Lift	.441	.223*	.395	.458	.603	.552	.739	.572
Cable-Tension Tests								
Shoulder Flexion	.253	.302	.504	.513	.667	.678	.802	.560
Shoulder Inward Rotation	.413	.353	.573	.496	.610	.600	.749	.532
Elbow Flexion	.336	.491	.609	.561	.624	.647	.687	.547
Trunk Flexion	.655	.543	.542	.614	.701	.747	.746	.644
Trunk Extension	.652	.437	.631	.680	.713	.758	.683	.592
Hip Flexion	.751	.695	.767	.755	.668	.755	.779	.675
Hip Extension	.728	.649	.688	.666	.689	.805	.692	.665
Knee Flexion	.632	.569	.624	.736	.763	.640	.736	.558
Knee Extension	.725	.730	.675	.767	.822	.772	.737	.743
Ankle Plantar Flexion	.643	.721	.624	.687	.717	.701	.726	.790

*Insignificant at .05 level.

strength average were also highest at ages 13, 14, and 15, ranging between .805 and .820. At age 16, the correlation was .754; the lowest was .471 at age 9.

CABLE-TENSION STRENGTH AVERAGE. The correlations between cable-tension strength average and the individual strength tests are presented in Table 5.5. As for Strength Index, the highest of these correlations were obtained at ages 13, 14, and 15. Nearly all of these correlations were in the .60's and .70's, the highest reaching .802 for knee extension at age 13. The same magnitude of correlations generally prevailed at the eight ages for all cable-tension tests but shoulder flexion, shoulder inward rotation, and elbow flexion. With one exception, back lift at age 10, all correlations were significant at and above the .05 level.

Correlations with Body Size and Motor Ability Tests

Smith (99) studied the relationships between gross strength criteria and 17 maturity, physique type, body size, and motor ability measures of boys at each age 7, 9, 12, 15, and 17. The gross strength criteria were cable-tension strength average (11 tests), upper-body cable-tension strength average (5 tests), lower-body cable-tension strength average (6 tests), and Strength Index. For each strength criterion in turn, zero-order and multiple correlations were computed. The number of subjects and the zero-order correlation needed for significance at the .05 level for each of the ages were:

Age	Number	r at .05 level
7	113	.184
9	175	.148
12	278	.118
15	343	.107
17	272	.120

The age differences between zero-order correlations for each of the experimental variables were tested for significance by application of the t ratio to the differences between their z-coefficient equivalents.

Cable-Tension Strength Tests

The zero-order correlations between cable-tension strength average and the 17 experimental variables are shown in Table 5.6. All but six of the 81 correlations were significant at or beyond the .05 level. The insignificant correlations were with endomorphy at ages 7, 15, and 17, leg length at 17 years, and bar dips at 9 and 12 years. All correlations were positive or had positive connotations except for ectomorphy.

The highest correlations for the five ages with the range of correlations for each were: .338 to .536, arm girth; .391 to .591,

Table 5.6

CORRELATIONS BETWEEN CABLE-TENSION STRENGTH AVERAGE AND
MATURITY, PHYSIQUE, BODY SIZE, AND MOTOR ABILITY TESTS

Experimental Variables	Ages in Years				
	7	9	12	15	17
Skeletal Age	.341	.236	.403	.564	.146
Endomorphy	.013*	.154	.281	.030*	.070*
Mesomorphy	.366	.272	.326	.424	.351
Ectomorphy	−.202	−.178	−.306	−.216	−.394
Standing Height	.438	.336	.430	.486	.214
Sitting Height	.371	.339	.401	.543	.218
Leg Length	.407	.245	.345	.304	.111*
Arm Girth	.515	.338	.497	.536	.464
Weight	.484	.351	.533	.591	.462
Chest Girth x Height	.504	.309	.477	.578	.449
Rogers' Arm Strength Score		.232	.236	.471	.303
Bar Dips		.132*	.077*	.270	.178
Standing Broad Jump x Weight	.593	.521	.654	.704	.531
Standing Broad Jump Distance	.373	.376	.302	.444	.253
60-Yard Shuttle Run Time	−.485	−.512	−.292	−.312	−.289
10-Foot Run Time		−.304	−.281	−.218	−.218
Total Body Completion Time		−.367	−.272	−.261	−.291

*Insignificant at .05 level.

weight; .309 to .578, chest girth × standing height; .521 to .704, standing broad jump × weight. The lowest of these correlations were at age 9 and the highest at ages 12 and 15.

The correlations between lower-body and upper-body strengths with the experimental variables were similar to those for cable-tension strength average, except that they were a bit lower and had more insignificant correlations. The respective number of insignificant correlations were eight and seven. Insignificant correlations for both strength criteria were with endomorphy at all ages but 12 years, ectomorphy at 9 years, and bar dips at 9 and 12 years. In addition, insignificant correlations with upper-body strength were obtained for leg length at age 17 years.

Strength Index

The zero-order correlations between Strength Index and the 17 experimental variables appear in Table 5.7. All but five of

Table 5.7

CORRELATIONS BETWEEN STRENGTH INDEX AND
MATURITY, PHYSIQUE, BODY SIZE, AND MOTOR ABILITY TESTS

Experimental Variables	Ages in Years			
	9	12	15	17
Skeletal Age	.354	.470	.638	.292
Endomorphy	.109*	.123	−.164	−.169
Mesomorphy	.195	.145	.426	.329
Ectomorphy	−.135*	−.073*	−.063*	−.151
Standing Height	.365	.476	.545	.264
Sitting Height	.379	.484	.650	.248
Leg Length	.257	.358	.305	.095*
Arm Girth	.352	.443	.548	.385
Weight	.376	.444	.523	.294
Chest Girth x Height	.396	.477	.596	.351
Rogers' Arm Strength Score	.307	.492	.765	.721
Bar Dips	.209	.551	.551	.561
Standing Broad Jump x Height	.530	.627	.713	.504
Standing Broad Jump Distance	.362	.401	.562	.407
60-Yard Shuttle Run Time	−.344	−.342	−.342	−.431
10-Foot Run Time	−.185	−.230	−.383	−.332
Total Body Completion Time	−.242	−.237	−.378	−.354

*Insignificant at the .05 level.

68 correlations were significant at and beyond the .05 level. The insignificant correlations were with endomorphy at 9 years, ectomorphy at 9, 12, and 15 years, and leg length at 17 years. All correlations were positive or had positive connotations, except for ectomorphy at all ages and endomorphy at 15 and 17 years. The highest correlations for the four ages were for standing broad jump × weight; the range of these correlations was between .504 and .713. The lowest of these correlations were at age 9 and the highest at age 15.

Inter-Age Differences

In a number of comparisons, the magnitude of the correlations between each of the gross strength criteria and the experimental variables were not comparable from age to age. A summary of the significant differences between correlations follows. All comparisons for Strength Index were not possible since this test was not given at the age 7.

MATURITY. For *skeletal age,* the correlations at age 15 were higher than at the other ages on all four strength batteries, except for the upper-arm strength comparison between ages 12 and 15. The correlations at age 12 were higher than at 17 years on all strength criteria and at 9 years for upper-body strength.

PHYSIQUE TYPE. For *endomorphy,* the correlations at age 12 were higher than at 7, 15, and 17 years on cable-tension strength average and upper-body strength and at 15 years on lower-body strength. For *mesomorphy,* the correlations at age 15 were higher than at 9 years on upper-body and lower-body strengths and Strength Index and at 12 years on Strength Index; in addition, the 17-year-olds had a higher correlation than the 12-year-olds. For *ectomorphy,* the correlations at age 17 were higher than at 9 and 15 years on the three cable-tension strength batteries and at 7 years on upper-body strength; in addition, the correlation at age 12 was higher than at 9 years on upper-body strength.

LINEAR MEASURES. For *standing height,* the correlations at age 15 were higher than at 17 years on all strength criteria and at 9 years on cable-tension strength average and Strength Index; the correlations were lower at age 17 than at 12 years on all criteria but lower-body strength, at 7 years on cable-tension strength average, and at 9 years on upper-body strength. For *sitting height,* the correlations at age 15 were higher than at 9 and 12 years on all strength criteria, at 12 years on all criteria but upper-body strength, and at 7 years on upper-body strength; in addition, the 12-year-olds had higher correlations than the 17-year-olds on all criteria but lower-body strength. For *leg length,* the correlations at age 17 were lower than at 7 years on all criteria but Strength Index, at 12 and 15 years on all criteria but lower-body strength, and at 9 years on upper-body strength.

BODY BULK MEASURES. For *arm girth,* the correlations at age 9 were lower than at 15 years on all strength criteria, at 12 years on cable-tension strength average and upper-body strength, and at 17 years on upper body strength. In addition, the 15-year-olds had higher correlations than the 17-year-olds on Strength Index. For *weight,* the correlations at age 15 were higher than at 9 years on all strength criteria, at 15 years on cable-tension strength average and upper-body strength, and at 7 years on upper-body strength. In addition, the correlations at age 9 were lower than at 12 years on cable-tension strength average and upper-body strength and at 17 years on lower-body strength. The same correlational situation was found for *chest girth × height,* except that the 15-year-olds had a higher correlation than did the 12-year-olds.

MUSCULAR ENDURANCE. For *Rogers' arm strength score,* the correlations at age 15 were higher than at 9 and 12 years on all strength criteria and at 17 years on cable-tension strength average and upper-body strength; the correlations were also higher at age 17 than at 9 and 12 years on Strength Index and at 9 years on upper-body strength. In addition, the age 12 subjects had a higher correlation than those at age 9 on Strength Index. For *bar dips,* the correlations at age 15 were higher than at 9 and 12 years on upper body strength and Strength Index and at 12 years on cable-tension strength average. In addition, the correlations at age 17 were higher than at 9 and 12 years on Strength Index.

MOTOR ABILITY TESTS. For *standing broad jump* × *weight,* the correlations at age 15 were higher than at 9 years on all strength criteria, at 17 years on all criteria but lower-body strength, and at 7 years on upper-body strength; the correlations at age 12 were higher than at 9 and 17 years on cable-tension strength average and upper-body strength and at 15 and 17 years on Strength Index. For *standing broad jump distance,* the correlations at age 15 were higher than at 12 years on all strength criteria, at 15 years on all criteria but lower-leg strength, and at 9 years on Strength Index. For the *60-yard shuttle run,* the correlations at age 9 were higher than at 12 and 15 years on all strength criteria but Strength Index and at 17 years on cable-tension strength average and upper-body strength; the correlations at age 7 were higher than at 17 years on cable-tension strength average and upper-body strength and at ages 12 and 15 on upper-body strength. For *10-foot run,* the correlation at age 15 was higher than at 9 years on Strength Index. For *total-body completion time,* none of the differences between correlations was significant.

Multiple Correlations

CABLE-TENSION STRENGTH BATTERIES. The multiple correlations with cable-tension strength average as the dependent variable and the order of selection of the independent variables for the various ages appear in Table 5.8. These correlations ranged between .633 at age 9 to .742 at age 15. Standing broad jump × weight was the first selected variable at each of the five ages. The 60-yard shuttle run was the second selected variable at ages 7 and 9, the third selected variable at 12, and the fifth selected variable at 17. Rogers' arm strength score and ectomorphy each appeared in two multiple correlations; standing height, arm girth, and mesomorphy were each in one multiple battery.

The multiple correlations with upper-body strength as the criterion were: .734, 15 years; .708, 12 years; .688, 7 years; .567, 17 years; .544, 9 years. Standing broad jump × weight was the first selected variable at all ages but 7 years. The 60-yard shuttle run was the first selected variable at age 7 and the second at age 9. Ectomorphy was the second selected variable at age 17 and the

Table 5.8

SUMMARY OF MULTIPLE CORRELATIONS WITH CABLE-TENSION STRENGTH AVERAGE

Experimental variables	*Ages*				
	7	9	12	15	17
Standing Broad Jump x Weight	1	1	1	1	1
60-Yard Shuttle Run	2	2	3		5
Rogers' Arm Strength Score				2	3
Ectomorphy				3	2
Mesomorphy			2		
Arm Girth		3			
Standing Height					4
Multiple Correlations	.647	.633	.707	.742	.660

third at age 15. Other second selected variables were Rogers' arm strength score at 15, mesomorphy at 12, and weight at 7. Other third selected variables were chest girth × height at 9, standing height at 7, and total-body completion time at 12.

The multiple correlations with lower-body strength as the dependent variable were: .694, 17 years; .678, 15 years; .627, 12 years, .613, 7 years; and .564, 9 years. Standing broad jump × weight was the first selected variable at all ages but 9. The 60-yard shuttle run was the first selected variable at age 9, second at 12 and 17, and third at 7. Other second selected variables were arm girth at age 7, skeletal age at 15, and weight at 9. Other third selected variables were Rogers' arm strength score at age 9, chest girth × height at 15, and standing broad jump distance at 17.

STRENGTH INDEX. The multiple correlations with Strength Index as the dependent variable and the order of selection of the independent variables are shown in Table 5.9. These correlations ranged from .620 at age 9 to .887 at age 17. Rogers' arm strength score (an element in the SI battery) was the first selected variable at ages 15 and 17 and second at ages 9 and 12. Standing broad jump × weight was the first selected variable at ages 9 and 12 and second at age 15. The 60-yard shuttle run appeared in two multiple batteries;

Table 5.9

SUMMARY OF MULTIPLE CORRELATIONS
WITH STRENGTH INDEX

Experimental Variables	Ages			
	9	12	15	17
Rogers' Arm Strength Score	2	2	1	1
Standing Broad Jump x Weight	1	1	2	
60-Yard Shuttle Run	4			3
Weight				2
Chest Girth x Height	3		3	
Skeletal Age				
Multiple Correlations	*.620*	*.743*	*.887*	*.831*

chest girth × height, skeletal age, and weight were in one battery each.

Strength Criteria Intercorrelations

The intercorrelations between the various gross strength criteria at the five ages are given in Table 5.10. The highest of these correlations were between cable-tension strength average and lower-body strength, ranging from .873 to .949. The correlations between upper-body and lower-body strengths ranged between .611 and .694. The correlations of the Strength Index with the three cable-tension strength batteries were comparable, between .501 and .743.

Table 5.10

GROSS STRENGTH CRITERIA INTERCORRELATIONS

Strength Criteria	Ages				
	7	9	12	15	17
C-T Av. vs. Upper-Body	.861	.772	.859	.864	.777
C-T Av. vs. Lower Body	.902	.873	.949	.946	.869
Upper Body vs. Lower Body	.611	.694	.669	.674	.631
Strength Index vs. C-T Av.		.545	.656	.743	.589
Strength Index vs. Upper Body		.501	.643	.696	.538
Strength Index vs. Lower Body		.551	.568	.688	.659

Longitudinal Mean Growth Curves

Strength tests and batteries were included in the various cross-sectional, convergence, and longitudinal growth studies described in Chapter 4. Two dissertations concentrated on the longitudinal growth analyses of these measures: Jordan (61) followed 44 boys from ages 7 through 12 and Bailey (1) followed 111 boys from ages 12 through 17. For both analyses, the means of boys who dropped from the Medford study during the longitudinal periods were compared with those who remained on three strength and one motor ability measure. With one exception, the differences between means were not significant at the respective initial ages of 9 and 12.

In Jordan's study, the boys tested originally at age 7 and the boys tested originally at age 9 were to have been combined at age 9 to form one group if the groups were comparable at that age. However, the mean differences between the two on the Physical Fitness Index and cable-tension strength average were significant at and beyond the .01 level. Consequently, only the original 7-year-old boys were followed longitudinally in the growth curves presented.

Both Jordan and Bailey included the same nine gross strength tests and batteries in their longitudinal growth analyses. These tests were: cable-tension strength tests of shoulder flexion, shoulder inward rotation, hip flexion, knee extension, and ankle plantar flexion; dynamometric tests of left grip and back lift; and the batteries of cable-tension strength average and Strength Index. Descriptions of these longitudinal growth curves are presented in this section. When growth curves are illustrated, the mean curves from the two studies are joined at age 12.

Cable-Tension Strength Tests

CABLE-TENSION STRENGTH AVERAGE. The mean growth curve for cable-tension strength average is presented in Fig. 5.3; the means for the ages appear at the bottom of the figure. This curve has a straight-line rise from ages 7 to 10; the slope of the curve is

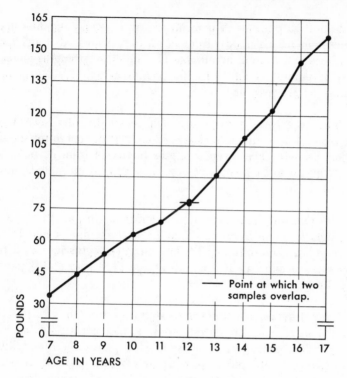

Fig. 5.3 Cable-tension strength average mean growth curve (Average of eleven strength tests)

MEAN STRENGTH IN POUNDS

Ages	Means	Ages	Means
7	34	12	78
8	44	13	91
9	54	14	109
10	63	15	122
11	69	16	145
12	79	17	157

steeper, increasing in a concave manner to age 16; the curve continues to rise at age 17 but is slightly decelerated. The strength means increased from 34 pounds at age 7 to 157 pounds at age 17, a gain of 123 pounds, or 362 percent.

SHOULDER FLEXION. The mean growth curve for shoulder flexion strength, increased slightly from ages 7 to 8, decreased at age 9, and, then, rose in a straight line to age 17. The mean strengths increased from 35 pounds at age 9 to 109 pounds at age 17, a gain of 74 pounds, or 211 percent.

SHOULDER INWARD ROTATION. The mean shoulder inward rotation strength growth curve closely resembled the curve for shoulder flexion strength. The mean strengths increased from 22 pounds at ages 7 and 9 to 71 pounds at age 17, a gain of 49 pounds, or 223 percent.

HIP FLEXION. The mean hip flexion strength growth curve had a straight-line rise from ages 7 to 10, a slight dip at age 11, and an irregular increase to age 17. The mean strengths increased from 33 pounds at age 7 to 164 pounds at age 17, a gain of 131 pounds, or 400 percent.

KNEE EXTENSION. The knee extension strength growth curve was the most irregular encountered: it had a concave rise from ages 7 to 9, a plateau at 10, a rise at 11, a plateau at 12, additional irregularities to 16, and a decrease at 17. The mean strengths increased from 47 pounds at age 7 to 197 pounds at age 16, a gain of 150 pounds, or 320 percent.

ANKLE PLANTAR FLEXION. The ankle plantar flexion strength growth curve had a straight-line rise from ages 7 to 8, another straight-line rise but steeper to age 11; the balance of the curve resembled the one for hip flexion strength. The mean strengths increased from 48 pounds at age 7 to 322 pounds at age 17, a gain of 274 pounds, or 569 percent.

Dynamometric Strength Tests

STRENGTH INDEX. The mean growth curve for Strength Index is presented in Fig. 5.4; the means for the ages appear at the bottom of the figure. This curve has a slow rise from ages 8 to 12; thereafter it is much steeper with annual increments over twice as large as for the younger ages. The Strength Index means in-

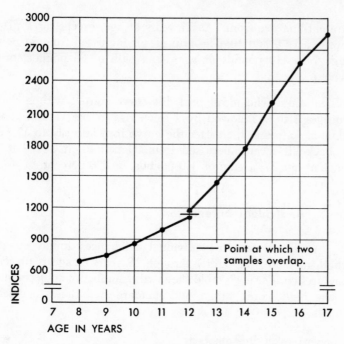

Fig. 5.4 Strength index mean growth curve

MEAN STRENGTH INDICES

Ages	Means	Ages	Means
8	690	12	1176
9	742	13	1434
10	861	14	1762
11	991	15	2196
12	1111	16	2566
		17	2842

creased from 690 at age 8 to 2,842 at age 17; the gain was 2,152, or 312 percent.*

LEFT GRIP. The mean growth curve for left grip strength was

---

* It should be remembered that the Strength Index battery contains more than dynamometric strength tests: right and left grips, back and leg lifts, lung capacity, and arm strength score derived from pull-ups and bar push-ups.

a straight-line rise from 7 to 17 years of age, except for a plateau between ages 9 and 10. The grip means increased from 24 pounds at age 7 to 110 pounds at age 17, a gain of 86 pounds, or 360 percent.

BACK LIFT. The mean back lift curve started with a decline from ages 8 to 9, followed by a steep rise to age 11 and another decline at 12 years; thereafter the curve rose linearily to 17 years. The back lift means increased from 90 pounds at age 9 to 430 pounds at age 17, a gain of 340 pounds, or 378 percent.

Individual Differences

The extent of individual differences found on gross strength measures for boys 7 through 18 years of age is presented in this section. For each table shown, the number of subjects, mean, low and high scores, range, and standard deviation are given at each age.

Cable-Tension Strength Tests

CABLE-TENSION AVERAGE. The individual differences in cable-tension strength test average (11 tests) are shown in Table 5.11. The standard deviations increased from 5.2 at age 7 to 27.2 at age 18. With some irregularities due to extreme scores, the ranges increased from 25 pounds at age 7 to 136 pounds at age 15; thereafter, they were of comparable magnitude, between 134 and 136 pounds. At each of the twelve ages, the strongest boy was two to three times stronger than the weakest boy. At most ages, the ranges nearly reached or exceeded their respective means.

ANKLE PLANTAR FLEXION. The individual differences for ankle plantar flexion strength are presented in Table 5.12. This test produced the strongest of the cable-tension measures; the mean at 18 years of age was 314.4 pounds, produced from attempting to "point the toes" of the left foot only. The standard deviations increased steadily from 6.8 pounds at age 7 to 70.0 pounds at age 16 years; thereafter, they were comparable in magnitude, between 66.0 and 71.6 pounds. The ranges increased in a similar manner;

Table 5.11

CABLE-TENSION STRENGTH AVERAGE INDIVIDUAL DIFFERENCES
(Pounds)

Age	N	Mean	Low	High	Range	S.D.
7	113	34.2	23	48	25	5.2
8	91	44.9	32	70	38	6.6
9	175	50.5	30	85	55	10.7
10	220	64.6	38	87	49	10.0
11	183	70.3	35	112	77	11.9
12	296	76.6	45	136	91	14.3
13	231	90.3	58	170	112	16.8
14	220	109.0	65	166	101	20.1
15	342	119.0	51	187	136	23.0
16	308	139.7	67	204	137	22.5
17	282	152.9	61	232	171	25.2
18	152	161.6	94	228	134	27.2

Table 5.12

ANKLE PLANTAR FLEXION STRENGTH INDIVIDUAL DIFFERENCES
(Pounds)

Age	N	Mean	Low	High	Range	S.D.
7	113	33.8	15	52	37	6.8
8	91	60.5	33	98	65	14.1
9	174	72.0	37	168	131	19.8
10	220	100.3	36	166	130	26.4
11	184	124.1	26	203	177	33.1
12	297	139.1	56	250	194	37.3
13	233	161.1	65	319	254	41.9
14	220	205.1	64	360	296	52.5
15	343	211.4	73	377	304	58.8
16	310	263.9	103	514	411	70.0
17	284	302.3	150	551	401	66.0
18	153	314.4	139	491	352	71.6

the amounts were 37 pounds at age 7 and 411 pounds at age 16. At the various ages, the strongest boys were two to four times stronger than the weakest boys. At nearly all ages, the ranges reached or exceeded their respective means.

Dynamometric Strength Tests

STRENGTH INDEX. The individual differences in Strength Index are given in Table 5.13. The standard deviations increased

Table 5.13

STRENGTH INDEX INDIVIDUAL DIFFERENCES

Age	N	Mean	Low	High	Range	S.D.
8	92	687.7	408	995	587	117.6
9	176	735.8	419	1162	743	149.7
10	223	886.2	442	1415	973	176.1
11	183	1010.5	651	1521	870	183.1
12	299	1163.9	680	1996	1316	237.1
13	239	1425.9	795	2454	1659	308.7
14	222	1758.7	982	3126	2144	413.7
15	352	2165.6	818	3700	2882	490.7
16	319	2571.5	984	3828	2844	473.2
17	283	2826.2	1534	4142	2608	470.8
18	153	2986.8	1562	4318	2756	506.9

steadily from 117.6 at age 7 to 490.0 at age 15; thereafter, they were comparable in magnitude, between 473.2 and 506.9. The ranges increased in a similar manner; the amounts were 587 at age 7 and 2882 at age 15. At all ages, the strongest boys had Strength Indices that were two to four times greater than the weakest boys. At all ages but 8, 11, 17, and 18, the ranges exceeded their respective means.

LEG LIFT. The individual differences in leg lift are presented in Table 5.14. This test is by far the strongest measure in the Strength Index battery; as shown above, it correlates between .85

Table 5.14

LEG LIFT INDIVIDUAL DIFFERENCES
(Pounds)

Age	N	Mean	Low	High	Range	S.D.
8	92	316.8	150	520	370	81.5
9	176	360.5	180	710	530	106.1
10	223	434.4	165	855	690	124.6
11	184	505.7	300	900	600	137.8
12	300	621.8	250	1180	930	169.1
13	243	763.8	320	2250	1930	215.2
14	224	911.9	225	1600	1375	244.7
15	354	1101.9	380	2000	1620	274.9
16	318	1274.8	520	2070	1550	268.0
17	286	1372.7	825	2180	1355	274.0
18	154	1453.1	800	2280	1480	304.8

and .95 with Strength Index at the various ages. As for Strength Index, the standard deviations increased steadily from 81.5 pounds at age 7 to 274.9 pounds at age 15; thereafter, they were comparable in magnitude, between 274.0 and 304.8 pounds. The ranges from age to age were somewhat erratic due to the presence of extreme leg lifts at some of the ages; the lowest and highest ranges were 370 and 1,930 pounds at 7 and 13 years of age respectively. The highest leg lifts equaled or exceeded one ton, a feat that was accomplished at the ages of 13, 15, 16, 17, and 18. At all ages, the ranges nearly reached or exceeded their respective means.

RIGHT GRIP. Inasmuch as grip strength testing has been included in other growth studies, especially by Jones (60), the individual differences for right grip are shown in Table 5.15; the individual differences for left grip were comparable, but the amounts are lower throughout. The standard deviations increased from 7.0 pounds at age 7 to 19.3 and 19.0 at ages 16 and 18. The ranges from age to age were somewhat erratic due to the presence of extreme high and low scores at some of the ages; the lowest and highest ranges were 24 and 160 pounds at 8 and 16 years of age respectively. At all ages, the strongest boys had right grips that were two to five times greater than the weakest boys; at age 7, this differential was seven times. At most ages, the ranges nearly reached or exceeded their respective means.

Table 5.15

RIGHT GRIP INDIVIDUAL DIFFERENCES
(Pounds)

Age	N	Mean	Low	High	Range	S.D.
7	113	25.5	6	42	36	7.0
8	92	36.5	24	48	24	5.9
9	174	40.0	22	62	40	8.3
10	223	45.8	20	68	48	8.9
11	185	53.6	36	76	40	8.0
12	299	59.0	20	90	70	11.0
13	242	70.5	40	131	91	14.1
14	223	84.1	42	141	99	17.7
15	353	95.2	48	152	104	18.4
16	322	109.9	28	188	160	19.3
17	298	119.4	64	170	106	17.4
18	156	125.7	68	183	115	19.0

Table 5.16

INTER-AGE CORRELATIONS FOR STRENGTH TESTS AND BATTERIES

Strength Tests	Adjacent Ages Medians		5-Year Span Correlations	
	7–12 Group	12–17 Group	7–12 Group	12–17 Group
Cable-Tension Tests				
Shoulder Flexion	.374	.448	.217**	.181**
Shoulder Inward Rotation	.343	.413	.226**	.238
Hip Flexion	.446	.585	.363	.013**
Knee Extension	.550	.644	.400	.508
Ankle Plantar Flexion	.195**	.544	.582	.465
Av. 11 Tests	.507	.787	.723	.432
Dynamometric Tests				
Left Grip	.348	.725	.397	.336
Back Lift*	.180**	.543	.169**	.364
Strength Index*	.553	.831	.529	.395

*Only four years intervened for 7-12 age group on these tests.
**Insignificant at the .05 level.

Inter-Age Correlations

Inter-age correlations were obtained for the various strength tests and batteries for boys aged 7 through 12 and 12 through 17 years in the longitudinal growth studies by Jordan (61) and Bailey (1). The median correlations obtained for adjacent ages and the correlation found when a span of five years intervened between tests* are presented in Table 5.16.

Generally, the inter-age correlations were low, both for adjacent ages and when five years intervened. The highest correlations were for adjacent ages of the 12 to 17 group for all tests; the lowest of these correlations were .413 and .448 for shoulder inward rotation and shoulder flexion, and the highest were .725, .787, and .831 for left grip, cable-tension strength average, and Strength Index. With

* Only four ages intervened for back lift and Strength Index in the 7–12 age group.

two exceptions, the correlations were lower for adjacent ages than when separated by five years; the exceptions were correlations of .582 and .723 for ankle plantar flexion and cable-tension strength average for the 7 to 12 age group. Several of the correlations were insignificant as indicated by the double asterisks in the table.

The generally low inter-age correlations for the strength tests and batteries demonstrate considerable inconsistency in the strength scores of the subjects from age to age, 7 to 12 and 12 to 17. Two reasons are suggested for this phenomenon: (a) As growth takes place, strength scores increase with age; the subject-to-subject increases may not be sufficiently consistent to maintain each boy's position in the group. (b) Strength is a developmental trait, affected by participation and lack of participation in vigorous physical activities; the amount of such participation may not be consistent from subject to subject.

Physical Fitness Index

As indicated earlier in this chapter, the Physical Fitness Index is a relative strength score, derived from dividing the achieved Strength Index by a norm for the individual's sex, age, and weight. Based on the Strength Index norms, a PFI of 100 is the median score and PFI's of 85 and 115 are the first and third quartile. Because of its relative nature, this index provides a significant contrast with the gross strength measures presented above. Generally low correlations would be expected due to the norming effect which cancels the effect of weight on the score.

Correlations

STRENGTH TESTS. Correlations between the Physical Fitness Index and dynamometric and cable-tension strength tests and batteries for each age 9 through 16 were obtained by Phillips (80). For the dynamometric strength tests, the highest correlations were with Strength Index; these correlations ranged from .608 to .798. The correlations with leg lift ranged between .393 and .546. Most of the correlations with right and left grips were not significant at the .05 level; the highest such correlation was .389 for left grip at age 12.

For the cable-tension strength tests, the correlations with Physical Fitness Index were mostly insignificant at ages 9, 10, 11, 12, and 16. However, all but one of these correlations were significant at ages 13, 14, and 15. The highest correlations were found for cable-tension strength average, although they ranged widely between .239 and .527 for the eight ages. Two other strength tests, hip extension and ankle plantar flexion, had significant correlations at six ages.

MATURITY, PHYSIQUE, AND BODY SIZE. In the study by Smith (99) reported above, the relationship between the Physical Fitness Index and skeletal age, somatotype components, and body size measures of boys 9, 12, 15, and 17 years of age were reported. The number of subjects and the correlations necessary for significance at the .05 level were the same as given on page 180.

The only significant correlation with skeletal age was .213 at age 15. All correlations with endomorphy were negative and significant; the correlations in order of age were −.248, −.392, −.514, and −.550. Mesomorphy had only one significant correlation, .119 at age 15. All correlations with ectomorphy but one at age 9 were significant, with the highest being .297 at 12 years. All significant correlations with body size measures were negative, although 11 of the 24 correlations were insignificant. Weight was the only body size measure to have significant correlations at all ages; these correlations ranged from −.176 at age 9 to .524 at age 17. All of the body size correlations were significant at age 17 and all but one were insignificant at age 9.

MOTOR ABILITY TESTS. All but two of the 20 correlations between Physical Fitness Index and motor ability tests were significant; with one exception, the relationships were positive or had positive connotations, as for timed events. The ranges of these correlations were: .363 to .555 for standing broad jump distance, −.376 to −.491 for 60-yard shuttle run, −.286 to −.461 for total-body completion time, −.184 to −.430 for 10-foot run, and .021 to −.182 for reaction time.

Table 5.17

SUMMARY OF MULTIPLE CORRELATIONS WITH
PHYSICAL FITNESS INDEX

Experimental Variables	Ages			
	9	12	15	17
Rogers' Arm Strength Score	1	1		3
Bar Dips			1	1
Weight		3		2
60-Yard Shuttle Run	2			
Total-Body Completion Time		2		
Endomorphy			2	
Standing Broad Jump Distance			3	
Multiple Correlations	.537	.697	.812	.855

MULTIPLE CORRELATIONS. The multiple correlations with Physical Fitness Index as the dependent variable and the order of selection of independent variables for the various ages in Smith's study appear in Table 5.17. These correlations ranged from .537 to .855, increasing progressively with age. Rogers' arm strength score was the first selected variable at ages 9 and 12 and the third at age 17. Bar dips was the first selected variable at ages 15 and 17. The second selected variable differed at each age: 60-yard shuttle run at 9, total-body completion time at 12, endomorphy at 15, and weight at 17. Other third selected variables were weight at age 12 and standing broad jump distance at age 15.

Individual Differences

The extent of individual differences for the Physical Fitness Indices of boys 7 through 18 years of age is presented in Table 5.18. The means for all ages were higher than the expectation of 100 from the norms. The lowest means were 105.2 and 108.8 at ages 9 and 8 respectively. For ages 10 to 17 inclusive, the means nearly reached, reached, or exceeded the normal third quartile of 115. Thus, the Medford boys generally had exceptionally high Physical Fitness Indices.

Although the standard deviations were lower at ages 8 and 18, they clustered mostly between 19.9 and 21.7. The ranges were

Table 5.18

PHYSICAL FITNESS INDEX INDIVIDUAL DIFFERENCES

Age	N	Mean	Low	High	Range	S.D.
8	92	108.8	74	153	79	16.9
9	176	105.2	71	170	99	20.2
10	223	114.5	57	179	122	21.7
11	183	116.9	65	178	113	19.9
12	299	114.6	52	184	132	21.0
13	239	117.8	59	183	124	20.3
14	222	118.2	68	199	131	21.4
15	350	113.8	52	191	139	21.3
16	318	115.9	48	185	137	20.1
17	283	115.1	58	190	132	21.6
18	153	111.3	54	161	107	18.2

erratic, due to the presence of extreme high or low scores at some ages and not at others; in general they followed a pattern similar to the standard deviations, ranging between 79 and 139 with most clustering between 122 and 139. At the various ages, the relative strength of the strongest boys was two to three times the relative strength of the weakest boys. At seven of the ages, the ranges exceeded their respective means.

High and Low Strength Groups

Borms (5, 21) contrasted the maturity, physique, body size, and motor performances of boys 10, 13, and 16 years of age divided into high, average, and low gross and relative strength groups. These ages were chosen because they cover the growth period in the following respects, as demonstrated by Degutis (25, 41): at age 10, most boys are prepubescent; at age 13, most boys are early pubescent; and at age 16, the pubescent development of most boys is well advanced.

The subjects were 722 Medford boys, distributed by age as follows: 224, 10 years; 249 each at 13 and 16 years. The gross strength measures were the Strength Index and cable-tension strength average; the relative strength measure was the Physical

Fitness Index. The experimental variables were skeletal age, somato-type components, standing height, weight, arm girth, thigh girth, chest girth X height, standing broad jump, 60-yard shuttle run, and total-body reaction time.

For each of the strength criteria at each of the three ages, three strength groups, high, average, and low, were formed. As shown in the following tabulation for cable-tension strength average and Physical Fitness Index, these groups were arranged so as to provide definite gaps between groups.

Age	Strength Level	Cable-Tension Strength Average	No.	Physical Fitness Index	No.
10	High	Above 70	42	Above 138	39
	Average	60-63	45	108-119	44
	Low	Below 53	46	Below 97	49
13	High	Above 104	48	Above 136	49
	Average	80-93	47	113-121	46
	Low	Below 76	49	Below 100	49
16	High	Above 160	46	Above 132	47
	Average	134-143	44	113-120	47
	Low	Below 119	37	Below 99	47

For the various strength groups, the means of the subjects were computed for each of the 12 experimental variables. At each age, the differences between the means of the three strength groups were tested for significance by application of the t ratio. Since analysis of variance was not used in this study, the .01 level of significance was applied. Unless otherwise stated in the presentation of results, the high strength groups had the high means.

Gross Strength

Only one of the gross strength batteries, cable-tension strength average (C-TS), will be presented here, since the results for both batteries were comparable. The differences between the means on the experimental variables for boys 10, 13, and 16 years of age classified into high, average, and low C-TS scores are summarized in Table 5.19 in the form of t ratios. In these comparisons, generally, the highest t ratios were found for differences between high-low groups; and the lowest, between average-low groups.

Table 5.19

Variables	Age	High-Average	High-Low	Average-Low
Skeletal Age	10	2.98*	5.15*	1.90
	13	5.04*	7.13*	2.58
	16	4.11*	5.39*	1.67
Endomorphy	10	5.14*	7.41*	2.75*
	13	1.36	2.54	1.05
	16	1.47	1.56	.14
Mesomorphy	10	.55	2.50	1.97
	13	2.43	5.80*	3.03*
	16	3.68*	5.89*	2.51
Ectomorphy	10	−1.44	−1.34	− .10
	13	−2.33	−4.98*	−2.06
	16	−3.63*	−4.30*	− .67
Standing Height	10	4.56*	5.68*	1.85
	13	4.69*	7.32*	3.14*
	16	1.46	5.39*	4.06*
Body Weight	10	5.22*	8.42*	3.43*
	13	6.30*	10.10*	4.85*
	16	4.67*	10.37*	5.37*
Upper Arm Girth	10	3.85*	7.05*	2.73*
	13	5.12*	9.94*	4.59*
	16	4.08*	8.37*	4.35*
Thigh Girth	10	3.83*	7.38*	2.85*
	13	5.15*	7.61*	3.05*
	16	2.73*	7.47*	3.74*
Chest Girth Height	10	5.14*	7.41*	2.75*
	13	6.02*	9.61*	4.68*
	16	3.43*	8.86*	4.93*
Standing Broad Jump	10	1.37	2.79*	1.47
	13	3.04*	5.45*	2.40
	16	.31	4.46*	3.68*
Sixty-Yard Shuttle Run	10	− .50	−2.11	−1.71
	13	−1.40	−3.91*	−2.32
	16	− .24	−2.00	−1.70
Total-Body Reaction Time	10	−1.09	−2.99*	−1.89
	13	−2.77*	−5.36*	−2.00
	16	−1.18	−4.27*	−3.08*

Significant at the 0.1 level.
NOTE: *A negative sign before a t ratio indicates that the lower C-TS groups had the highest mean; the reverse is true for timed events.*

MATURITY. The differences between skeletal age means for high-average and high-low C-TS groups were significant at and beyond the .01 level; the t ratios ranged between 2.98 and 5.04 and between 5.15 and 5.73 respectively. For average-low groups, the difference between the means was approximately significant at 13 years of age. In all instances, the higher C-TS group had the highest means—were most mature.

PHYSIQUE TYPE. The differences between the endomorphy means were significant for all groups at age 10: the t ratios ranged between 2.75 and 5.14. For mesomorphy, the high-average and high-low groups at age 16 and the high-low and average-low groups at age 13 had significantly different means. The ectomorphy means of the low CS-T groups were higher than the means of the high groups for all comparisons; however, the only significant mean differences were for the high-low groups at ages 13 and 16 and the high-average group at age 16.

BODY SIZE. With the exceptions of the comparisons for the high-average and the average-low groups at age 10, the differences between the body size means of the C-TS groups at the three ages were significant; in all instances, the higher C-TS groups had the highest means. The highest t ratios were 10.10 and 10.37 in the comparisons of the weight means between the high-average groups at ages 13 and 16. Mostly, higher t ratios were obtained when the C-TS groups were contrasted at age 13. Generally, lower t ratios were found for standing height than for the body bulk measures and for the index, chest girth $\times$ height.

MOTOR ABILITY. For motor ability elements, the greatest differences between means of the C-TS groups were obtained for the comparisons of high-low groups; the differences were significant at all ages on standing broad jump and total-body reaction time and at age 13 on 60-yard shuttle run. The only other significant mean differences were for the high-average groups at age 13 and the average-low groups at age 16 on the standing broad jump, and the high-average groups at age 13 and the average-low groups at age 16 on total-body reaction time.

Relative Strength

A summarization of the differences between means on the comparison variables for boys 10, 13, and 16 years of age classified into high, average, and low Physical Fitness Index groups is presented in Table 5.20 in the form of *t* ratios. In these comparisons, generally, the highest *t* ratios were found for the mean differences between high-low and average-low groups; and the lowest, between high-average groups.

MATURITY. None of the differences between skeletal age means was significant at the .01 level.

PHYSIQUE TYPE. With the exception of the high-average group comparison at age 10, the low PFI group had significantly higher endomorphy means than did the high PFI groups; the *t* ratios ranged between −3.21 and −6.43. The differences between ectomorphy means for high-low and average-low PFI groups were significant or nearly so at the three ages; in all instances higher PFI groups had highest means. The differences between mesomorphy means for all comparisons were not significant.

BODY SIZE. For the linear measure of standing height, only one difference between the means of the PFI groups was significant; the low exceeded the high group at 16 years. For the body bulk measures, the low groups had higher means than other groups as follows: thigh girth at all three ages, body weight at ages 10 and 16, and arm girth at age 10. For chest girth × height, the low group had higher means than the high and average groups at age 10 and the high group at age 16.

MOTOR ABILITY. The differences between the means of the high-low PFI group comparisons on the three motor ability elements were significant at all ages; the *t* ratios ranged from 3.17 to 9.15. All differences between standing broad jump and 60-yard shuttle run means of the average-low groups were significant. For high-average groups, the differences between the means on all three tests were significant at age 13; in addition, the mean difference in

Table 5.20

Variables	Age	High-Average	High-Low	Average-Low
Skeletal Age	10	.39	−1.76	−2.16
	13	.44	1.40	.92
	16	1.68	.59	−1.02
Endomorphy	10	−1.52	−5.62*	−3.88*
	13	−3.21*	−6.43*	−3.33*
	16	−3.57*	−6.15*	−3.73*
Mesomorphy	10	.91	.09	− .83
	13	.48	.15	− .31
	16	2.12	.68	−1.40
Ectomorphy	10	− .16	3.30*	3.36*
	13	.57	4.33*	3.39*
	16	− .74	2.57	3.12*
Standing Height	10	−1.00	−2.30	−1.56
	13	.77	1.60	.76
	16	−2.60	−3.29*	− .75
Body Weight	10	−1.85	−4.75*	−3.21*
	13	− .18	−2.02	−1.86
	16	−2.16	−5.84*	−4.06*
Upper Arm Girth	10	−1.03	−3.66*	−2.71*
	13	.41	−1.69	−1.90
	16	.99	−1.44	−2.25
Thigh Girth	10	−1.72	−5.19*	−3.54*
	13	−1.07	−3.91*	−2.67*
	16	−1.62	−4.82*	−4.12*
Chest Girth x Height	10	−1.12	−3.65*	−2.75*
	13	.61	− .43	−1.06
	16	−1.48	−4.11*	−2.55
Standing Broad Jump	10	2.22	6.75*	4.05*
	13	5.20*	9.12*	4.68*
	16	.51	5.22*	4.76*
Sixty-Yard Shuttle Run	10	−2.38	−5.55*	−3.84*
	13	−4.79*	−9.15*	−4.33*
	16	− .60	−5.17*	−4.82*
Total-Body Reaction Time	10	−2.85*	−4.34*	−1.75
	13	−4.40*	−6.02*	−2.09
	16	−1.35	−3.17*	−2.11

Significant at the .01 level.
NOTE: A negative sign before a *t* ratio indicates that the lower C-TS group had the highest mean; the reverse is true for timed events.

total-body reaction time was significant at age 10. In all comparisons, higher PFI groups had superior performances.

Arm-Shoulder Endurance

Muscular Endurance Measures

In the Medford Boys' Growth Study, two arm and shoulder muscular endurance tests, pull-ups and bar push-ups, were given. The techniques for administering these tests follow.

PULL-UPS. As shown in Fig. 5.5, pull-ups, or chins, were performed from a horizontal bar, placed high enough so that the tallest subject's feet could not touch the floor when he was in an extended hanging position. The subject grasped the bar with a forward hand grip and then chinned himself as many times as possible. The chinning effort was a straight pull-up with no kicking, jerking, or kipping motion permitted. Half-counts were recorded when the subject did not pull his body high enough the bring his chin above the bar or did not extend his arms completely when lowering his body; the maximum number of half-counts allowed was four.

PUSH-UPS. As shown in Fig. 5.6, the push-up test was administered on gymnasium parallel bars adjusted to the shoulder height of each subject. The subject grasped one end of the bars and jumped to a straight-arm position (count one). The body was lowered until the angle of the upper arm and forearm was less than a right angle; the arm was then extended so that the subject was again in straight-arm position (count two). This movement was repeated as many times as possible without jerking or kicking to aid the performance and without pause for rest between push-ups. The tester indicated the distance the body should be lowered by holding his hand so that the subject could touch it with his shoulder on each dip. If the subject did not go down to the proper bent-arm angle or all the way up to a straight-arm position, only half-credit was given, up to four half-counts.

In addition to the pull-up and push-up tests, two "arm strength" scores have been used in the Medford growth project; these scores

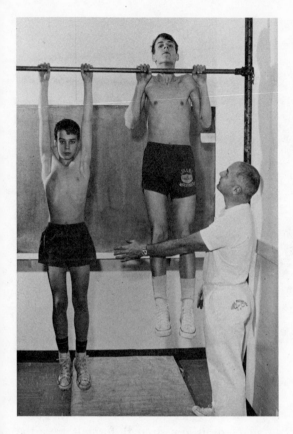

Fig. 5.5 **Pull-up test**

were proposed by McCloy and Rogers. Although commonly known as arm strength scores, they should correctly be called muscular endurance scores, for they are derived from the muscular endurance tests of pull-ups and push-ups.

Pull-ups and push-ups may be considered as measures of relative muscular endurance since only the number of repetitions is counted. The weight of the subject and the distance his weight is pulled or lifted are not considered in the score; heavy-tall and light-short persons receive the same credit for each pull-up or push-up. As a consequence, arm-strength scores, which credited these factors in the performances, were developed as gross muscular endurance measures.

Fig. 5.6 Bar push-up test

Rogers' Score

Rogers (84) adapted his arm strength formula from the earlier work by Sargent and included it in his Strength Index battery described above. The formula is:

AS = (Pull-ups + Push-ups) (.1 Weight + Height − 60)

If the subject is 60 inches tall or shorter, height is disregarded in the formula. In this formula, heavier and taller persons receive more credit for pull-ups and push-ups than do lighter and shorter persons, since they pull and push more weight and for greater distances on each repetition.

With 217 boys 16 years of age, Santa Maria (87) proposed the following new arm and shoulder strength and endurance formulae:

F1 = (Pull-ups + Push-ups) (Elbow Flexion + Shoulder Inward Rotation Strengths) × Weight/1000
F2 = Pull-ups × Elbow Flexion Strength × Weight/1000
F3 = Push-ups × Shoulder Inward Rotation Strength ×Weight
/1000

The correlations between Rogers' arm strength score and the three
formulae were .918 for F1, .812 for F2, and .837 for F3. The ranges
of correlations between strength formulae and strength tests were
.127 to .383 for Rogers' score, .206 to .595 for F1, .154 to .594 for
F2, and .206 to .703 for F3. The strength measures with the highest
correlations were elbow flexion for Rogers' score, F1, and F2 and
shoulder inward rotation for F3.

The highest correlations with all formulae were obtained with
the relative endurance tests of pull-ups and push-ups and the relative strength measure of Physical Fitness Index. These correlations
were as follows:

	Pull-ups	*Push-ups*	*PFI*
Rogers' Score	.756	.911	.774
F1	.690	.862	.688
F2	.829	.688	.621
F3	.531	.848	.661

Generally, the correlations with Rogers' arm strength score were
the highest. This score also correlated higher with 60-yard shuttle
run and standing broad jump; the respective correlations were
−.550 and .587 for Rogers' score, −.474 and .466 for F1, −.460
and .427 for F2, and −.442 and .441 for F3.

McCloy's Score

McCloy (70) contended that Rogers' arm strength score
penalized individuals who could chin only a few times and unduly
rewarded those who could chin many times. In developing his
method of chinning and dipping, his subjects chinned as many
times as possible on each of the first two days; on succeeding days,
they did the same but with five pounds of weight added each day
until a single chin could not be accomplished. The following multiple regression equation resulted: 1.77 Weight + 3.42 Chins − 46.

This equation was also applied to push-ups; all weightings in the equation were doubled when chins and dips were combined.

In several studies, body weight had high correlations, high enough for prediction purposes, with McCloy's equations. With junior high school boys, for example, Tomaras (103) obtained correlations of .96 and .95 between weight and McCloy's pull-up and push-up formulae respectively. These results are supported logically when it is realized that weight is nearly doubled (1.77 weight) in the equation and the K constant deducted (-46) usually equals or is more than the amount included from chinning or dipping (3.42 chins or dips). As a consequence of the high correlations with weight, the McCloy arm strength criteria were not included as experimental variables in subsequent Medford analyses.

Relationships

FACTOR ANALYSES. In Phillips' factor analyses (80) of boys 9 through 16 years of age, a rotated factor named Arm and Shoulder Endurance was found at all eight ages. The ranges of the highest loadings on this factor were: Rogers' arm strength score, $-.780$ to .855; push-ups, $-.556$ to .845; pull-ups, .592 to .859; and Physical Fitness Index, $-.210$ to $-.746$. Negative loadings resulted at ages 10, 12, 13, and 15. Moderate loadings were obtained for motor ability measures. The highest loadings were at 13 and 14 years for standing broad jump ($-.641$ and .638), 60-yard shuttle run (.628 and $-.659$), and athletic rating ($-.624$ and .404). The loadings may indicate that these motor ability elements are more affected by arm and shoulder endurance at ages 13 and 14 than at the other ages.

INTERCORRELATIONS. The ranges of intercorrelations among the arm-shoulder endurance measures in Phillips' study were: .844 and .949, Rogers' arm strength score and push-ups; .636 to .829, Rogers' arm strength score and pull-ups; and .518 to .720, push-ups and pull-ups.

RELATIVE STRENGTH. The magnitude of the correlations between the Physical Fitness Index, a test of relative strength (relative to age and weight), and Rogers' arm strength score and push-ups were comparable; these correlations ranged between .538 and .844 for the eight ages. A similar situation existed for correlations between Physical Fitness Index and pull-ups except for ages 9 and 10, when the correlations were .341 and .262 respectively.

GROSS STRENGTH. The three arm-shoulder endurance measures were correlated with 14 cable-tension and dynamometric strength tests and with the two gross strength batteries of cable-tension average and Strength Index for each age 9 through 16 in Phillips' study. Of the 172 such correlations for the ages 9 through 12, 33, or 19 percent, were significant at the .05 level; the highest of these correlations were low, all but one in the upper .20's and .30's. The same situation prevailed for the correlations between the gross strength measures and pull-ups for ages 13 through 16. All but five of the 64 correlations between Rogers' arm strength score and the gross strength measures for ages 13 through 16 were significant; the highest correlation at each age was with Strength Index, ranging between .727 and .825 for the four ages. For the correlations with push-ups for ages 13 through 16, 38 percent were significant; the highest of these correlations at the four ages ranged between .372 and .594.

MATURITY. Of the 24 correlations between skeletal age and the three arm-shoulder endurance measures, eight, or 25 percent, reached significance at the .05 level. The significant correlations were: for Rogers' arm strength score, .316 at 13, .431 at 14, and .440 at 15 years of age; for pull-ups, −.278 at 13 and −.255 at 16 years of age; and for push-ups, −.284 at age 10.

PHYSIQUE TYPE. All 24 correlations between endomorphy and the arm-shoulder endurance measures were negative and significant. With one exception, these correlations ranged between −.315 and −.571; the exception was the high of −.705 with pull-ups at age 14. Significant positive correlations between ectomorphy and pull-ups were obtained at five ages, 10 through 14; these correlations ranged between .261 and .393. Only two correlations with mesomorphy were significant: .320 for Roger's arm strength score at 16 and .279 for push-ups at 10 years of age.

LINEARITY. Three linearity tests were included in Phillips' study: standing height, sitting height, and leg length. Of the 72 correlations between these tests and the three arm-shoulder endurance measures, 51, or 71 percent, were significant. All significant correlations were negative, except for positive correlations for Rogers' arm strength score at age 13 and over. Numbers of significant correlations by endurance measures were 20 for pull-ups, 17 for Rogers' arm strength score, and 14 for push-ups; by linear tests, the numbers were 20 for leg length, 17 for standing height, and 15 for sitting height. The highest correlations obtained were −.540 and −.520 between standing height and push-ups respectively at age 11 and −.514 and −.512 between push-ups and standing height and leg lift respectively.

BODY BULK. The body bulk measures in Phillips' study were arm, abdominal, buttock, thigh, calf, and chest girths, weight, hip width, and lung capacity. All nine tests were given at all ages, except at 9 years when abdominal, buttock, and thigh girths were omitted; thus, 207 correlations were computed between these tests and the three arm-shoulder endurance measures at the eight ages. Of this number, 146, or 71 percent, were significant. As for the linear measures all significant correlations were negative, except positive correlations for Rogers' arm strength score at 13 years of age and over. Numbers of significant correlations by endurance measures were 59 for pull-ups, 41 for push-ups, and 36 for Rogers' arm strength score. The smallest number of significant correlations was for lung capacity, only four out of 24, or 25 percent. Lung capacity, however, had the highest correlations of any bulk measure with Rogers' arm strength score, as follows: .375 at 13, .410 at 14, and .352 at 15 years of age. The highest correlations obtained were with pull-ups; the range of highest correlations for the eight ages for this measure was between −.413 and −.614.

INDICES. The following seven indices were included in Phillips' study: sitting height/standing height, lung capacity/standing height, standing height/cube root of weight, weight/standing height squared, chest girth/standing height, weight/standing height, and chest girth × standing height. For the eight ages, 168 correlations were computed between these indices and the three arm-shoulder endurance measures; 95 of these correlations, or 57 percent, were significant. Numbers of significant correlations by endurance measures were 39 for pull-ups, 30 for Rogers' arm strength score, and 26 for push-ups. The correlations between the arm strength score and sitting height/standing height were positive and significant, except at ages 14 and 16; the significant correlations ranged between .250 and .331. The correlations of the endurance measures and weight/standing height were negative and significant at nearly all ages, except for Rogers' arm strength score at ages 13, 14, and 15 and push-ups at 15; the range of significant correlations was from −.250 to −.578. Chest girth × height had significant correlations, mostly negative, with the endurance measures at all ages, except push-ups at ages 13, 14, and 15 and the arm strength score at 13 and 16; the significant correlations ranged from −.276 to −.547.

MULTIPLE CORRELATIONS. In his study of arm-shoulder endurance measures of 217 16-year-old boys, Santa Maria (87) computed multiple correlations with Rogers' arm strength score as the dependent variable and muscular strength, relative muscular endurance, and motor ability elements as the independent variables. The following coefficients were obtained.

R	Independent Variables
.962	Push-ups, right grip, pull-ups, right grip/weight
.927	Push-ups, standing broad jump
.544	Shoulder flexion/weight, back lift/weight, and elbow flexion/weight.
.464	Elbow flexion, back lift, and shoulder inward rotation strengths

High multiple correlations were obtained with Rogers' arm strength score when push-ups was an independent variable; the zero-order correlations between the score and push-ups was .911. Similar results were obtained by Phillips for each of the ages 9 through 16. By contrast, in Phillips' study, the correlations between the arm strength score and pull-ups were mostly in the .70's for the eight ages; and push-ups and pull-ups correlated between .518 and .720, half of them in the .60's.

INTER-AGE CORRELATIONS. Inter-age correlations were obtained for push-ups for boys aged 8 through 12 and 12 through 17 in the longitudinal growth studies by Jordan (61) and Bailey (1). The respective median correlations for adjacent ages were .85 and .84. When four and five years intervened between tests, the respective inter-age correlations were .73 and .67.

Growth Curve

Data from the longitudinal growth studies by Jordan (61) and Bailey (1) permitted the construction of a mean growth curve for push-ups; the curve for the two samples 8 to 12 and 12

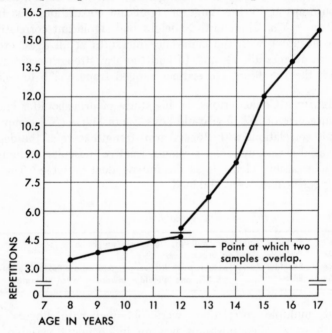

Fig. 5.7   Bar push-up mean growth curves
MEAN PUSH-UPS

Ages	Means	Ages	Means
8	3.4	12	5.1
9	3.8	13	6.7
10	4.0	14	8.5
11	4.4	15	12.0
12	4.6	16	13.8
		17	15.9

to 17 years of age appears in Fig. 5.7. This curve shows a slow rise from ages 8 to 12; the means increased from 3.4 to 4.6 times, a gain of 1.2 push-ups, or 33 percent. Starting at age 12, however, the curve rose sharply with sizable increases each year, especially between the ages of 14 and 15 years; the means increased from 5.1 to 15.9 times, a gain of 10.8 push-ups, or 201 percent.

Individual Differences

The extent of individual differences for the three arm-shoulder endurance measures is presented here. For each table shown, the number of subjects, mean, low and high scores, range, and standard deviation are given at each age.

BAR PUSH-UPS. The individual differences for bar push-ups are shown in Table 5.21. The standard deviations started at 2.5 repetitions at age 8, varied between 3.3 and 3.9 times for ages 9 through 12, and then increased consistently to 7.3 times at 17 years. The

Table 5.21

BAR PUSH-UPS INDIVIDUAL DIFFERENCES
(Repetitions)

Age	N	Mean	Low	High	Range	S.D.
8	93	3.2	0.5	11.0	10.5	2.5
9	160	4.0	0.0	19.0	19.0	3.3
10	221	4.1	0.0	17.0	17.0	3.7
11	179	4.0	0.0	20.0	20.0	3.6
12	297	4.5	0.0	20.0	20.0	3.9
13	243	6.2	0.5	24.5	24.0	4.9
14	215	8.4	0.0	27.5	27.5	5.4
15	343	10.9	0.0	43.5	43.5	6.4
16	320	13.3	1.0	39.0	38.0	6.4
17	292	15.0	0.0	44.0	44.0	7.3
18	164	16.0	0.0	45.0	45.0	7.0

ranges were erratic due to the presence of extremely high scores at some ages; the lowest was 10.5 at age 8; the highest were 43.5, 44.0, and 45.0 at ages 15, 17, and 18. Truncation was found at eleven ages, as shown by zero scores. Skewness of distributions may be inferred from the fact that the highest scores at the various ages were from three to five times their respective means.

PULL-UPS. The individual differences for pull-ups appear in Table 5.22. The standard deviations were fairly consistent for the eleven ages, varying between 2.8 and 3.7 repetitions. The ranges were erratic due to the presence of extremely high scores at some ages; the lowest was 13.0 at ages 8 and 13 and the highest were 25.0 and 25.5 at ages 15 and 18. At all ages, the lowest scores were zero pull-ups, showing distribution truncations throughout. Skew-

Table 5.22

PULL-UPS INDIVIDUAL DIFFERENCES
(Repetitions)

Age	N	Mean	Low	High	Range	S.D.
8	93	4.5	0.0	13.0	13.0	3.0
9	176	3.3	0.0	16.0	16.0	3.0
10	221	3.6	0.0	17.0	17.0	3.3
11	184	3.1	0.0	15.0	15.0	2.9
12	296	3.0	0.0	18.5	18.5	3.0
13	243	3.4	0.0	13.0	13.0	2.8
14	222	4.4	0.0	14.5	14.5	3.2
15	343	5.3	0.0	18.5	18.5	3.3
16	319	6.6	0.0	25.0	25.0	3.7
17	292	7.1	0.0	21.0	21.0	3.7
18	164	7.4	0.0	25.5	25.5	3.5

Table 5.23

ROGERS' ARM STRENGTH SCORE INDIVIDUAL DIFFERENCES
(Scores)

Age	N	Mean	Low	High	Range	S.D.
8	93	44.8	6.0	111.0	105.0	27.5
9	176	45.1	0.0	162.0	162.0	33.1
10	221	54.2	4.0	172.0	168.0	39.8
11	184	52.8	0.0	198.0	198.0	41.0
12	296	68.9	0.0	335.0	335.0	54.6
13	243	114.5	9.0	525.0	516.0	90.4
14	222	197.0	0.0	632.0	632.0	133.5
15	343	327.2	0.0	1007.0	1007.0	184.1
16	319	453.2	20.0	1103.0	1083.0	198.5
17	292	539.0	10.0	1218.0	1208.0	226.0
18	164	596.9	31.0	1334.0	1303.0	219.5

ness of distributions may be inferred, since the highest scores at the various ages were from three to six times their respective means.

ROGERS' ARM STRENGTH SCORE. The individual differences for Rogers' arm strength scores are given in Table 5.23. The standard deviations began at 27.5 at age 8, were between 33.1 and 49.0 for 9 to 12 years, and then increased consistently to 226.0 at 17 years. The ranges showed a fairly consistent rise from 105.0 at age 8 to 1303 at age 18. Some truncation of distributions was found with zero scores at five ages. The highest scores at the various ages were 2.5 to 4.8 times greater than their respective means, again, as for pull-ups and push-ups, inferring the presence of skewness.

Chapter Summary

The focus of this chapter was on the muscular strength and endurance of boys from 7 through 18 years of age. The strength tests consisted of dynamometric measures contained in Rogers' Strength Index battery and eleven cable-tension strength tests. The muscular endurance tests were confined to the arm-shoulder area.

Studies of strength test batteries were included. The number of test items to obtain the Strength Index was reduced separately for upper elementary, junior high, and senior high school boys. Through regression equations, the Strength Index can be predicted and the norms used to predict Physical Fitness Indices. A cable-tension strength battery of four tests was constructed for upper elementary school boys with norms based on age and weight.

Factor analysis studies of the muscular strength and endurance tests conducted at each age 9 through 16 produced the following rotated factors: Arm-Shoulder Endurance, all ages; Arm-Shoulder Strength and Leg-Back Lift Strength, five ages each; Lower-Leg Strength and Grip Strength, three ages each; and General Strength, two ages. Intercorrelations among strength tests and correlations between strength tests and maturity, physique type, body size, and motor ability tests were reported.

Mean connecting growth curves for muscular strength and

endurance tests were constructed for boys from 7 to 12 and from 12 to 17 years of age. The ranges and standard deviations of these tests were presented to show the extent of individual differences. Inter-age correlations among these tests were also obtained.

High, average, and low strength groups were formed at each age 10, 13, and 16 based separately on Strength Index, cable-tension strength average, and Physical Fitness Index. Significant differences between these gross strength batteries were generally obtained for body size measures, standing broad jump, and total-body reaction time. By contrast, the lower Physical Fitness Index groups had higher means on the tests.

Chapter 6 / **Motor and Athletic Abilities**

Materials from the Medford Boys' Growth Study pertaining to the motor and athletic abilities of boys are presented in this chapter. A number of motor ability test items were included, as follows: standing broad jump, 60-yard shuttle run, hand-arm and total-body reaction times, and 10-foot run. In the first part of the chapter, these motor tests are considered separately. In the Medford school system, interschool athletics begin in the fifth grade and continue through high school. The latter part of the chapter contrasts the traits of boys who qualify for and have varying degrees of success on interscholastic athletic teams, and contrasts these athletes with nonparticipants.

Standing Broad Jump

The standing broad jump was included in this growth study as a measure of the explosive power of the leg extension muscles. It has been widely used for this purpose, and has frequently been included in motor ability and motor fitness test batteries. Power in the jump is displayed by combining muscular strength with speed of movement; thus, strength and velocity work together in projecting the body forward in space. In this performance, strength is necessary, speed of reaction and movement is required, and these elements are integrated.

Test Description

A take-off line was drawn at one end of a gymnasium mat, allowing space enough for the subjects to toe this line. At a distance the shortest distance any subject could jump, parallel lines were drawn 2 inches apart; the distance of each of these lines from the take-off line was marked along the side.

In taking the test, the subject stood with his feet several inches apart with toes back of the take-off line. Taking off from both feet simultaneously, he jumped as far as possible, landing on both feet. In jumping, he crouched by bending his knees, bringing his body weight forward on his toes, and swung his arms vigorously forward and upward to aid the jump. Scoring was the distance to the nearest inch from the take-off line to the closest heel position. The best of three trials was recorded.

Scoring Methods

The common method of scoring standing broad jump performance is simply by the distance jumped. This method is used in motor ability and motor fitness testing when the jump is included in the test battery. Distance jumped should be considered a relative power test, as the amount of body weight projected is not considered in the score. A distance of 60 inches jumped by 100-pound and 150-pound boys is scored the same for both boys; yet, one boy projected 50 percent more weight than did the other.

Other investigators have recognized this situation in connection with the vertical jump, another power test of the extensor muscles of the legs. By combining the vertical jump with the right combination of age, height, and weight, McCloy (73) found that power-type athletic ability was predicted quite accurately. He reported an increase in multiple correlation from .75 to .89, when height and weight were included in the correlation between the vertical jump and a battery of four track and field events. Gray, Start, and Glencross (48) developed a "vertical power test" based on principles of physics and mathematical logic; the score was composed of work done and time taken in a vertical jump, expressed in horsepower units. For practical use in physical education, this complicated method correlated .989 with scoring by distance jumped × weight.

In the Medford series, with 203 12-year-old boys, Flynn (42) studied the following four methods of scoring standing broad jump performance: distance jumped, distance × weight, weight/distance, and leg length/distance. The highest correlations among these methods were −.848 and .753 between leg length/distance and distance jumped and weight/distance, respectively. The other intercorrelations ranged from .429 to −.549, except between distance × weight and leg length/distance.

Flynn also studied the relationships between his four methods of scoring standing broad jump performance and strength, speed, body size, and physique measures with 12-year-old boys as subjects. A summarization of the results follow.

Distance × weight had the highest correlations with strength tests. With the exception of the Physical Fitness Index, a relative strength measure, the correlations were significant and ranged from .406 to .750; the highest correlation was with cable-tension strength average. With the exception of skinfold total (.436), the correlations with body size measures ranged between .589 for leg length and .836 for weight. The correlations with somatotype components and 10-foot run were low and insignificant. A multiple correlation of .902 was obtained with this method as the dependent variable and weight, Strength Index, and skinfold total as the independent variables.

Weight/distance correlated low but significantly with six of eight strength measures; the highest correlation was −.441 with Physical Fitness Index. With the exceptions of sitting height (.429) and leg length (.462), the correlations with body size measures ranged from .793 for skinfold total to .872 for abdominal girth. This method correlated −.537 and .774 with ectomorphy and endomorphy, respectively. A multiple correlation of .908 was obtained between this method and the independent variables of abdominal girth, Physical Fitness Index, and skinfold total.

Leg length/distance correlated insignificantly with all but two strength measures and with sitting height, mesomorphy, and ectomorphy. The highest correlation was −.503 with Physical Fitness Index. A multiple correlation of .717 was obtained with this method; the independent variables were Physical Fitness Index, leg length, 10-foot run, and skinfold total.

Distance jumped correlated significantly with all strength tests but back lift; the significant correlations ranged between .260 for hip flexion strength and .474 for Physical Fitness Index. The only significant correlations with body size measures were .224 for sitting height, −.260 for abdominal girth, and −.327 for skinfold total. Of the four methods, distance jumped had the highest correlation with 10-foot run, −.416 (positive connotation). A multiple correlation of .690 was obtained with this method; the independent variables were Physical Fitness Index, 10-foot run, sitting height, skinfold total, and cable-tension strength average.

In an earlier study, Degutis (26, 40) studied standing broad jump distance with 12-year-old boys; 16 maturational, anthropometric, and strength tests were administered to 81 subjects. Of the 16 correlations between distance jumped and these tests, only seven, or 44 percent, were significant at the .05 level. The significant correlations were with strength measures, as follows: .47, elbow flexion; .40, cable-tension strength average; .39, hip extension; .34, Strength Index; .32, ankle plantar flexion; .28, knee extension; and .26, back lift. The highest multiple correlation obtained was .694; the independent variables were elbow flexion strength, weight, hip extension strength, ankle plantar flexion strength, and back lift. A multiple coefficient of .520 was obtained with only elbow flexion and hip extension strengths.

Ward (106) related body size, strength and motor ability tests to three standing broad jump scoring methods, distance × weight, distance/weight, and distance jumped. For the scoring methods and tests in common with Flynn's and Degutis' studies, comparable results were obtained at both ages. Ward included some experimental variables that were not present in the other investigations. The significant correlations are shown in the following tabulation.

The significant correlations for distance × weight and distance/weight were comparable at both ages, between .184 and .460. The

	Dist. × Wt.		Dist./ Wt.		Distance Jumped	
	12	15	12	15	12	15
Rogers' Arm Strength Score	.282	.460	.338	.184	.557	.638
60-Yard Shuttle Run	−.352	−.353	−.252	−.352	−.574	−.616
Total-Body Reaction Time	−.291	−.270		−.306	−.469	−.525

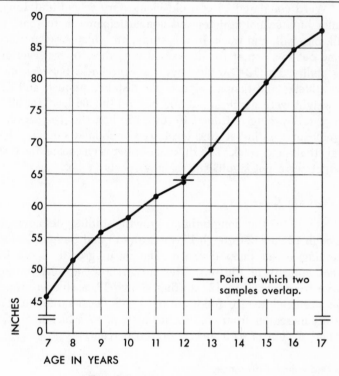

Fig. 6.1 Standing broad jump mean growth curve

MEAN STANDING BROAD JUMPS IN INCHES

Ages	Means	Ages	Means
7	45.8	12	64.4
8	51.5	13	68.9
9	55.9	14	74.7
10	58.1	15	79.4
11	61.5	16	84.7
12	63.9	17	87.7

correlations with distance jumped for the arm-shoulder endurance, speed-agility, and reaction-time measures were higher, between −.469 and .638; the negative correlations with the timed events, of course, have positive connotations for distance-speed relationships.

Ward compared 12-year-old elementary school and 15-year-old junior high school athletes and nonparticipants in football, basketball, baseball, and track. In this study, an athlete was any boy who came out for a sport for the season regardless of his level of playing ability. For 12-year-old boys, the differences between means of the athletes and nonparticipants for distance jumped and distance × weight were significant at and beyond the .05 level for all sports; the *t* ratios ranged from 2.07 to 3.25. For the 15-year-old boys, significant *t* ratios at this level were obtained only for football, basketball, and track. The differences between means for distance/ weight were not significant for any sports at both ages.

Growth Curve

In the longitudinal growth studies of boys ages 7 through 12 and 12 through 17, Jordan (61) and Bailey (1) included standing broad jump distance. The mean growth curve for this event appears in Fig. 6.1. The curve shows a steep but convex curve from ages 7 to 12; starting at age 12, a steeper straightline rise occurred to 16, followed by some deceleration at 17. The means increased from 45.8 inches at 7 to 87.7 inches at 17 years of age, a gain of 41.9 inches, or 109 percent.

Individual Differences

The extent of individual differences for standing broad jump distance for boys ages 7 through 18 appears in Table 6.1. The standard deviations started at 5.0 and 5.2 inches at ages 7 and 8, increased erratically to 7.9 inches at 14, and remained fairly constant to 18 years. The ranges followed a somewhat similar pattern, increasing from 27 and 26 inches at ages 7 and 8 to 45 and 47 inches at ages 13 and 14. At the various ages, the boys with greatest muscular leg power jumped approximately twice as far as those with the least power.

Table 6.1

STANDING BROAD JUMP INDIVIDUAL DIFFERENCES
(Inches)

Age	N	Mean	Low	High	Range	S.D.
7	113	45.6	32	59	27	5.0
8	90	51.7	38	64	26	5.2
9	174	53.5	38	71	33	6.3
10	214	57.4	36	72	36	6.0
11	182	60.6	35	73	38	6.1
12	286	63.8	42	83	41	6.8
13	234	68.6	42	87	45	6.9
14	215	74.3	45	92	47	7.9
15	333	78.7	52	100	48	7.9
16	305	83.4	56	101	45	7.7
17	258	87.1	59	105	46	7.4
18	150	88.1	62	106	44	7.9

Sixty-Yard Shuttle Run

The 60-yard shuttle run was utilized in the Medford Boys' Growth Study as a measure of speed and agility in a running situation; the shuttle distance was 10 yards. The selection of this test was based on research by Gates and Sheffield (45), who experimented with 18 tests, 15 of which involved change of direction when running and three of which were other motor ability elements. A criterion measure was established consisting of the total T scores of the subjects on all tests. For boys in the seventh, eighth, and ninth grades, a 60-yard shuttle run correlated .805, .810, and .813 with the criterion. The reliability coefficient was .932. Lawson (68) obtained similar results with a 40-yard shuttle run for girls ages 7 through 12; her criterion consisted of Hull-scale totals on 12 obstacle and shuttle runs.

Test Description

In order to provide a common running surface no matter where the test was performed and to insure tight turns, two strips of rubberized matting, each 38 feet by 3 feet, were utilized; thus, this surface was 38 feet long and 6 feet wide. The strips were secured to the floor with adhesive tape. Four feet from each end and at the junction of the two mats, thus 30 feet apart, an upright wand was located; this wand was held erect by use of a "plumber's helper." A diagram of this running surface appears in Fig. 6.2.

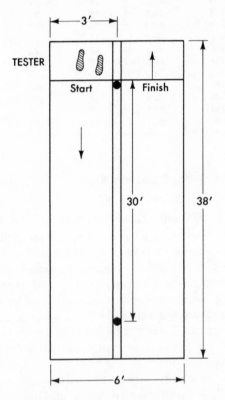

Fig. 6.2   Sixty-yard shuttle run diagram

The subject was instructed to stay on the mats while running; he was urged not to slow down at the end of the run until he had passed the finish line. The test was repeated if the subject ran off the mats, knocked over a wand, or slowed before reaching the finish line. Time was recorded to the nearest tenth of a second.

Relationships

Radcliff (82) studied relationships between the 60-yard shuttle run and 15 maturity, physique, body size, strength, and motor measures. The subjects were 179 boys 14 years of age. Twelve of the 15 correlations with this run, or 80 percent, were significant at the .05 level and beyond. The significant correlations* were as follows:

−.15 Skeletal age	−.23 Lung capacity
.44 Endomorphy	−.23 Hip extension strength
−.19 Ectomorphy	−.53 Physical Fitness Index
.36 Skinfold total	−.23 Cable-tension strength average
.28 Abdominal girth	−.57 Standing broad jump
−.34 Standing height	.40 Total-body reaction time

The highest of these correlations were −.57 and −.53 with standing broad jump and Physical Fitness Index respectively. A multiple correlation of .650 was obtained; the independent variables were standing broad jump, Physical Fitness Index, and total-body reaction time.

GROWTH CURVE. In the longitudinal growth studies of boys ages 7 through 12 and 12 through 17, Jordan (61) and Bailey (1) included 60-yard shuttle run; the mean growth curve for this event appears in Fig. 6.3. This curve shows a straightline rise from ages 8 to 14, although slightly steeper from 12 to 14 years; a plateau occurred from ages 14 to 15, after which the curve continued to rise but in a decelerated manner.

Individual Differences

The extent of individual differences for 60-yard shuttle run for boys ages 7 through 18 appears in Table 6.2. The standard deviations were quite constant at most ages, between .9 and 1.1 seconds; the exceptions were at ages 7, 9, and 18, when the standard deviations were 1.4 to 1.5 seconds. The ranges were quite erratic

---

* The negative correlations have positive connotations and vice versa, except when the correlation is with another timed event, as with total-body reaction time.

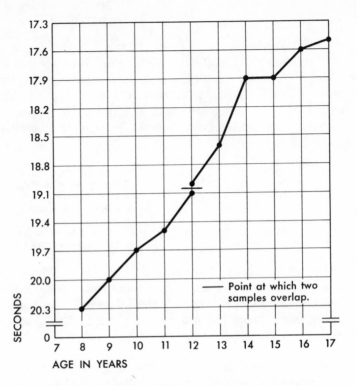

Fig. 6.3 Sixty-yard shuttle run mean growth curve

MEAN 60-YARD SHUTTLE RUNS IN SECONDS

Ages	Means	Ages	Means
8	20.3	12	19.0
9	20.0	13	18.6
10	19.7	14	17.9
11	19.5	15	17.9
12	19.1	16	17.6
		17	17.5

Table 6.2

60-YARD SHUTTLE RUN INDIVIDUAL DIFFERENCES
(Seconds)

Age	N	Mean	Low	High	Range	S.D.
7	113	22.6	26.6	19.0	7.6	1.5
8	90	20.1	23.3	18.4	4.9	1.0
9	174	20.6	25.6	17.9	7.7	1.4

Age	N	Mean	Low	High	Range	S.D.
10	214	19.7	24.6	17.4	7.2	1.1
11	182	19.4	24.7	17.3	7.4	1.1
12	285	19.1	23.0	16.8	6.2	1.1
13	234	18.5	23.0	16.4	6.6	1.1
14	215	18.0	22.4	15.9	6.5	1.0
15	332	18.0	21.8	16.0	5.8	1.1
16	304	17.5	21.6	15.6	6.0	0.9
17	257	17.5	20.5	15.8	4.7	0.9
18	153	17.5	31.8	15.8	16.0	1.4

due to extreme scores, varying with one exception between 4.7 and 7.7 seconds. An extremely slow time of 31.8 seconds at age 18 resulted in a high range of 16.0 seconds.

Reaction and Movement Times

Considerable research has been conducted in the area of reaction time in psychology since the end of the nineteenth century; since 1930, both reaction and movement times have been studied in physical education. Investigations of interest to the physical educator have dealt with relationships between reaction time, movement time, athletic ability, and motor performances. In general, the studies in physical education resulted in low to insignificant correlations between reaction time and speed of movement, little if any correlation between speed of arm and leg movements and reaction time involved in a modified baseball throw and football kick, and low correlations in neuromuscular ability for movements and tasks of considerable similarity. Studies have shown that reaction time is related to chronological age and that little or no relationship exists between reaction time and anthropometric measures. Generally, athletes, especially at the higher levels of ability, have faster reactions and speed of movement than do non-participants.

In the Medford Boys' Growth Study, two reaction and movement time measures were included in the second year of the project and continued annually through the twelfth. The tests were for total body and arm and hand.

Test Descriptions

TIMER. The Hale Reaction Timer* was used in this study. This timer has two .01 second clocks. One of these clocks measures reaction time, or the time elapsed between appearance of the stimulus and the moment the subject can initiate discernible movement. The other clock indicates the completion, or overall, time for a given motor performance; this measure includes the reaction time as well as the time required to complete the movement. A third measure, movement time, was obtained by subtracting reaction time from completion time. Thus, in this study, three times were used for each motor performance employed; they are known herein as reaction time, movement time, and completion time.

The subject's reaction is transmitted through switch and target mats. The switch mat consists of two pieces of metal screening with a rubber cover. Releasing pressure on the mat separates the screen pieces and closes the electric circuit wired to the reaction time clock on the instrument. The target mats have the same metal screens. However, they are electrically wired to the second timer so as to produce a closed circuit when sufficient pressure is applied to unite them. For all tests, a light stimulus was used.

TOTAL BODY MOVEMENT TEST. Two switch mats large enough to stand upon, one for each foot, were taped securely to the floor. The subject stood erect on these mats facing the target mat and the light stimulus; his hands were clasped lightly behind his back. He was instructed to "get ready" and "watch the light." When the light appeared, he left the switch mats and ran as fast as possible past the target mat located on a table 10 feet away; he hit this mat with his right hand as he ran past. The subject was given several trials, continuing long enough to produce a cluster of three trials close together; the middle time of these three trials was recorded in hundredths of a second. Two practice trials were allowed before the test was given. A diagrammatic plan for this test is shown in Fig. 6.4.

ARM MOVEMENT TEST. Switch and target mats were fastened

---

* Custom-made by Creighton J. Hale, Little League Baseball, Williamsport, Penn.

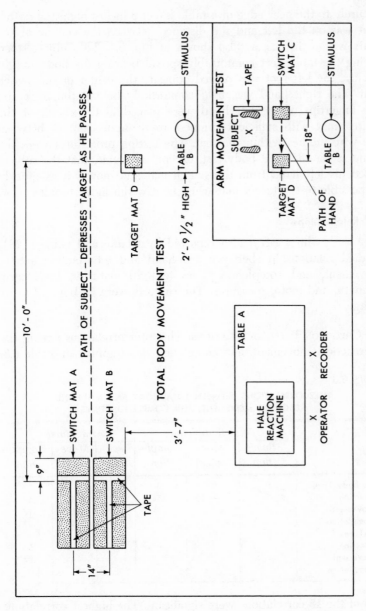

Fig. 6.4 Diagram of total body and arm reaction time tests

securely to the near edge of a table 2 feet 9 inches high; the switch mat was on the left and the distance between the centers of the mats was 18 inches, as also shown in Fig. 6.4. The subject stood facing the table, feet comfortably spread bearing the body weight evenly; the left foot was placed opposite the center of the switch mat. The right hand was held comfortably behind the back and the fingertips of the left hand were placed in the center of the switch mat with sufficient firmness to maintain contact between the wire meshes within the mat. The testing procedures were the same as for the total body test, except, of course, that the subject lifted his left hand from the switch mat and moved it as quickly as possible to the target mat when he saw the light stimulus.

Relationships

Glines (47), also reported by Clarke and Glines (28), studied relationships between arm-hand and total-body reaction, movement, and completion times and 26 maturity, body size, strength, and motor measures. The subjects were 65 boys 13 years of age.

CRITERION INTERCORRELATIONS. The intercorrelations among the six reaction, movement, and completion times appear in Table 6.3.

Table 6.3

INTERCORRELATIONS BETWEEN TOTAL-BODY AND ARM-HAND
REACTION, MOVEMENT, AND COMPLETION TIMES

	Total Body Times			Arm Times		
	Reac-tion	Move-ment	Comple-tion	Reac-tion	Move-ment	Comple-tion
Total Body Time						
Reaction		−.20	.54	.44	.36	.53
Movement			.73	.04	.18	.17
Completion				.34	.41	.51
Arm Times						
Reaction					.10	.53
Movement						.84
Completion						

Ten of the 15 correlations were significant. The highest correlations were between the movement and completion times, .84 for the arm performance and .73 for the total body performance. Following these in magnitude are the correlations between reaction and completion times, .54 for the total body performance and .53 for the arm performance.

The correlation between the two reaction time measures was .44, which, while low, was significant well beyond the .05 level. For the cross correlations between body and arm times, body completion time correlated .53 with arm reaction time and .51 with arm completion time; body movement time correlated significantly with these same times, .41 with arm completion and .36 with arm reaction. The only other significant correlation was .34 between arm completion time and body reaction time. Arm movement time did not correlate significantly with any of the total body times.

CORRELATIONS WITH EXPERIMENTAL VARIABLES. The correlations between total-body and arm-shoulder reaction, movement, and completion time and the 26 experimental variables are shown in Table 6.4. A summary of this table follows.

1. *Reaction times.* None of the correlations between either body or arm-hand reaction times and the experimental variables were significant at the .05 level of .25. Three body reaction time correlations, however, approximated this significance: the shuttle run, arm strength, and standing height.

2. *Body movement time.* The correlations between body movement time and the experimental variables that reached significance at the .05 level were as follows: −.58 with Physical Fitness Index, .48 with shuttle run, −.42 with standing broad jump, −.39 with arm strength, −.36 with Strength Index, −.32 with leg lift, and .26 with thigh girth. The following multiple correlations were obtained with body movement time as the criterion: .64 with Physical Fitness Index and back lift; .63, with shuttle run and standing broad jump.

3. *Body completion time.* Body completion time had correlations significant at the .05 level with the following experimental variables: .58 for shuttle run, −.49 for standing broad jump, −.48 for Physical Fitness Index, −.37 for back lift, and .25 for buttocks girth. The following multiple correlations were obtained with body completion time as the criterion: .76, with shuttle run and standing broad jump; .63, with Physical Fitness Index, arm strength, back lift, Strength Index, and leg lift.

4. *Arm-hand movement time.* Four correlations between arm-hand movement time and experimental variables were significant at the .05 level; these were .42 with shuttle run, −.35 with standing broad jump, −.29 with shoulder inward rotation strength, and −.25 with hip extension strength. The multiple correlations obtained for this criterion were: .54, with shuttle run and standing broad

Table 6.4

CORRELATIONS BETWEEN TOTAL-BODY AND ARM-HAND REACTION, MOVEMENT, AND COMPLETION TIMES AND MOTOR, STRENGTH, BODY SIZE, AND MATURITY TESTS

Experimental Variables	Total Body Times			Arm Times		
	Reaction	Movement	Completion	Reaction	Movement	Completion
Motor						
Shuttle run (60 yds.)	.24	.48*	.58*	.14	.42*	.40*
Standing broad jump	−.18	−.42*	−.49*	.01	−.35*	−.26*
Strength						
Ankle plantar flexion	−.06	−.11	−.13	−.09	−.18	−.19
Knee extension	−.11	−.12	−.18	−.09	−.21	−.21
Knee flexion	−.05	−.24	−.24	−.02	−.20	−.16
Hip extension	−.08	−.22	−.24	−.21	−.25*	−.31*
Hip flexion	−.02	−.18	−.17	.13	.05	−.11
Shoulder flexion	−.19	−.06	−.19	−.18	−.08	−.16
Shoulder inward rotation	.01	−.09	.07	.10	−.27*	−.14
Cable-tension mean	−.07	−.19	−.22	−.11	−.16	−.18
Leg lift	.09	−.32*	−.22	−.11	.00	−.07
Back lift	.02	−.11	−.37*	−.11	−.14	−.17
Arm strength	.24	−.39*	−.17	.09	−.06	.00
Strength Index	.12	−.36*	−.23	−.06	−.03	−.06
Physical Fitness Index	.03	−.58*	−.48*	−.08	−.14	−.15
Body Size						
Standing height	.22	−.05	.11	−.02	.18	.13
Body weight	.11	.15	.21	.00	.12	.09
Calf girth	.06	.13	.15	−.04	−.02	.01
Thigh girth	−.01	.26*	.22	.01	.00	.01
Buttocks girth	.08	.23	.25*	.02	.13	.11
Hip width	.15	.06	.15	.00	.21	.16
Abdominal girth	−.03	.20	.15	−.06	.14	.07
Chest girth	.05	.21	.21	−.04	.12	.07
Upper arm girth	.03	.18	.16	.04	−.04	.06
Wetzel Physique Channel	.07	.23	.15	.00	−.03	.03
Maturity						
Pubescent Assessment	.14	.06	.04	.00	.00	.01

*Significant at .05 level (.25).

jump; .37, with shoulder inward rotation, hip flexion, and hip extension strengths.

5. *Arm-hand completion time.* Only three experimental variables were significantly correlated with arm-hand movement time; these were .40 for shuttle run, −.31 for hip extension strength, and −.26 for standing broad jump. The multiple correlations obtained for this criterion were .47, with shuttle run and standing broad jump; .43, with hip extension and flexion strengths, shoulder flexion strength, and mean of 12 cable-tension strength tests.

Longitudinal Relationships

Sandstrom (85) investigated longitudinally the differences in total-body reaction and movement times associated with age, maturity, physique type, and athletic ability of 165 junior high school boys ages 13 through 15. The reaction and movement time tests were given with the Hale Reaction Timer as described above; the movement test, therefore, was for 10 feet minus the reaction time. The experimental variables used in the study were skeletal age, somatotype categories, and athletic ability.

GROUPINGS. Groupings based on the experimental variables were formed as described below.

1. *Maturity.* Based upon skeletal age, three groups were formed at age 13: *advanced,* 168 to 182 months, 23 subjects; *normal,* 151 to 162 months, 77 subjects; *retarded,* 133 to 145 months, 28 subjects.

2. *Physique.* Based upon somatotype designations, five physique categories were formed at age 13: *endomorphs,* endomorph component of 4^2 or over with no other component over 4, 14 subjects; *mesomorphs,* mesomorph component of 4^2 or over with no other component over 4, 33 subjects; *ectomorphs,* ectomorph component of 4^2 or over with no other component over 4, 34 subjects; *endomesomorphs,* mesomorph component of 4^2 or over, endomorph component of 4 or over, and ectomorph component below 4, 22 subjects; *mid-types,* all components 4 or below, 62 subjects.

3. *Athletic Ability.* The athletic abilities of the subjects were rated each year by the coaches of the various junior high school athletic teams as described in the next section of this chapter, "Characteristics of Athletes." Two groups were formed for this study: *Athletes,* boys with athletic ratings of 2

or 3 for two or more years in junior high school interscholastic athletics, 34 subjects; *nonparticipants,* boys who did not participate on junior high school athletic teams during any of the three years, 82 subjects.

RESULTS. Among the results of this longitudinal study of the reaction and movement times of junior high school boys were the following:

1. The mean total-body reaction times of all groups decreased slightly with age; the year-to-year differences were not significant. The changes in mean movement time were more marked; significant improvement occurred from ages 13 to 15 for the normal and advanced skeletal age groups, for the mesomorph and mid-type groups, and for the athletes and nonparticipants.

2. Comparisons of the reaction time means showed differences as follows: the advance maturity group was significantly slower than the normal and retarded groups (probably because the subjects were larger); the endomorphs and endomesomorphs had slower times than other somatotype categories at all ages, although the mean differences were not always significant; the athletes had significantly faster times than the nonparticipants at all ages.

3. Generally low correlations were obtained between total-body reaction and 10-foot movement times; for the entire sample, these correlations were −.013, −.098, and .200 at ages 13, 14, and 15 respectively. Significant correlations of .625 and .609 for the endomorphs at ages 13 and 15 indicate that those subjects who reacted slowly also moved slowly and vice versa.

Characteristics of Athletes

The study of athletes is a unique phase of the Medford project, since interschool competitive athletics are conducted in the fifth and sixth grades of the elementary schools and in junior and senior high schools. Thus, the characteristics of boys as young as 11 and 12 years of age who are able to make and are successful on such teams can be examined; various fundamental traits and abilities found among these young athletes may be identified; and these charateristics and patterns may be investigated longitudinally from the age of seven years through their high school tenure.

At the close of a competitive season, coaches rated each member of their athletic squads on the following scale:

3 *Outstanding:* exceptional athletic ability.
2 *Regular player:* average athlete; played regularly.
1 *Substitute:* played occasionally as a substitute.
NP: did not complete the season; did not go out for the team.

Sports included in the Medford schools' interscholastic athletic program are:

Fifth and sixth grades: football, basketball, baseball, track
Junior high school: football, basketball, track, wrestling
Senior high school: football, basketball, track, baseball, wrestling, tennis, golf

In the Medford series, a number of studies were conducted in which the maturity, physique, body size, strength, and motor characteristics of athletes were contrasted for the different levels of athletic ability and with nonparticipants. Petersen (79) cross-sectionally investigated upper elementary school and junior high school athletes. Wiley (112), Mitchell (75), and Kelly (63) studied upper elementary school, junior high school, and senior high school athletes, respectively, at single ages and longitudinally. In the latter three studies, athletic ratings were determined at ages 12, 15, and 17; longitudinally, the 12-year-old athletes were traced back to 9 years, the 15-year-old athletes to 12 years, and the 17-year-old athletes to 15 years. In the studies by Petersen, Wiley, and Mitchell, the *t* ratio was used to test the significance between means of the various groups; Kelly utilized analysis of variance for this purpose with application of the Scheffé test for post-hoc comparison of means when significant F ratios were obtained. Significance between means throughout was accepted at the .05 level. In addition, profiles of outstanding athletes were developed by Shelly (95) and Howe (56). Former reports on studies of Medford athletes are contained in references 13, 14, 33, 34, and 36.

In this section of the monograph, data are assembled in support of basic conclusions that may be drawn from studies of upper elementary school, junior high school, and senior high school athletes. To report in detail on the studies of athletes would be too voluminous for this monograph.

First Conclusion

Boys who make and are successful on interscholastic athletic teams are definitely superior to their peers in maturity, physique, body size, and muscular strength, endurance, power, and motor ability. Thus, the decision as to whether boys are physically ready for such participation, especially in elementary and junior high schools, should be determined by factors other than chronological age, or grade in school. Actually, within close age limitations, natural selection takes place, based in part at least on the factors listed.

Petersen (34, 79) contrasted maturational, structural, and motor traits of upper elementary and junior high school boys with the different levels of athletic ability and compared boys with the various athletic ratings with nonparticipants. Such results as the following were obtained: The outstanding athletes at both school levels had significantly higher mean skeletal ages than did the other groups; in studying maturity relative to chronological age, the outstanding elementary school athletes only were advanced. In general, the size of athletes as compared with nonparticipants was more significant at the junior high school than at the elementary school level; this was particularly true for the outstanding athletes. A higher proportion of mesomorphs was found among the junior high school athletes. Strength and muscular power were consistent differentiators of athletic ability.

Illustrations of the contrasting characteristics of athletes and nonparticipants follow. Differences between means were tested for significance by application of the *t* ratio. The *t* ratios necessary for significance ranged from 1.99 to 2.04 at the .05 level, depending upon the degrees of freedom for the various comparisons.

SKELETAL AGE. In Fig. 6.5, *t* ratios representing the differences between the skeletal age means of the three athletic groups and nonparticipants are illustrated. Considerable similarity was found for the upper elementary and junior high school boys. The outstanding athletes were significantly more mature than all other groups at both school levels; the other mean differences were not significant. These results are logical, since more of the older boys, chronologically, won positions on the athletic teams and achieved the highest athletic ratings.

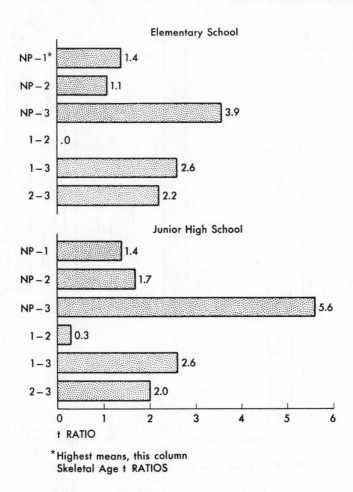

Elementary School

NP – 1*   1.4
NP – 2   1.1
NP – 3   3.9
1 – 2   .0
1 – 3   2.6
2 – 3   2.2

Junior High School

NP – 1   1.4
NP – 2   1.7
NP – 3   5.6
1 – 2   0.3
1 – 3   2.6
2 – 3   2.0

0   1   2   3   4   5   6
t RATIO

*Highest means, this column
Skeletal Age t RATIOS

Fig. 6.5 Skeletal age *t* ratios mean differences

Consequently, the relative maturity of the athletic and non-participant groups was compared. The mean deviations of the groups from the chronological ages of the respective members are presented in Fig. 6.6. The outstanding elementary school, but not the junior high school, athletes were significantly more mature for their ages than were the other groups. However, the mean relative maturity of the 3-rated athletes was similar at both school levels, 7.7 to 7.9 months advanced. The difference in significance

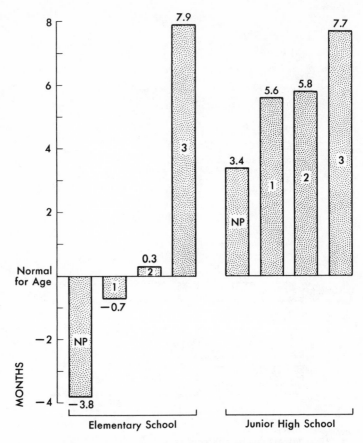

Fig. 6.6 Relative skeletal age *t* ratios mean differences

at the two school levels was due to the immaturity of the non-participants and the average maturity of 1- and 2-rated elementary school athletes as contrasted with the advanced maturity of these same groups in junior high school. No reason can be supported from the study for these differences in maturity.

STRENGTH INDEX. Rogers' Strength Index illustrates the gross strength characteristics of the young athletes. This index is the sum of the following tests: right and left grips, back and leg lifts, lung capacity, and arm strength (derived from chins and bar dips). The Strength Index means for all elementary and junior high school groups are portrayed in Fig. 6.7. The means increased with athletic ratings at both school levels; and, the mean of the junior high school nonparticipants was higher than the mean of the outstanding elementary school athletes. The significant differences between

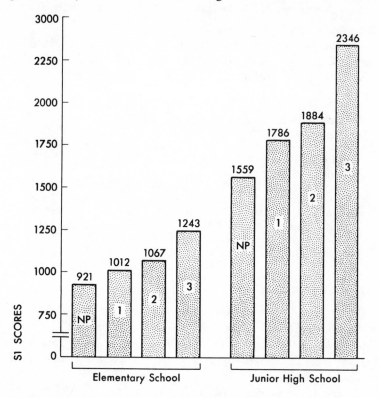

Fig. 6.7 Mean strength indices for elementary and junior high school athletes

the means were: outstanding athletes superior to all groups at both school levels, regular players superior to nonparticipants at both school levels, and substitutes superior to nonparticipants in junior high school.

SOMATOTYPE. The somatotype distribution of junior high school boys differed from elementary school boys in the following respects: a greater percentage of mesomorphs among all three groups of athletes, a much greater percentage of mid-types among the nonparticipants and a smaller percentage among the 3-rated group (23 percent vs. 36 percent), and a greater percentage of endomesomorphs among the outstanding athletes and regular players.

OTHER SIGNIFICANT DIFFERENCES. To record other significant mean differences found among the elementary and junior high school athletes, the following notations are made:

> *Elementary school:* 2 and 3 over NP and 3 over 1 for standing height, Rogers' arm strength score, and cable-tension strength average; 2 and 3 over NP for lung capacity and Rogers' Physical Fitness Index; all groups over NP and 3 over 1 for standing broad jump; 3 over NP and 1 for sitting height; 3 over NP for weight; none for arm, chest, and calf girths.
>
> *Junior high school:* 3 over all groups for weight, standing height, sitting height, and Rogers' arm strength score; 3 over all groups and 2 over NP for lung capacity and cable-tension strength average; 3 over NP and 1 for arm and chest girths; 3 over NP and 1 and 2 over NP for calf girth; 2 and 3 over NP for Physical Fitness Index.

Second Conclusion

Some fundamental characteristics of 12-year-old elementary school athletes, 15-year-old junior high school athletes, and 17-year-old senior high school athletes are clearly evident at younger ages, although differences in characteristics exist at the three school levels.

In the three longitudinal studies of athletes by Wiley (112), Mitchell (75), and Kelly (63), the abilities of athletes were judged at age 12 and traced back to 9 years in elementary school, at age 15 and traced back to 12 years in junior high school, and at age 17 and traced back to 15 years in senior high school. In this section, the longitudinal look is limited to contrasting the highest-rated athletes with nonparticipants. In all instances, the 3-rated athletes were superior unless otherwise indicated.

ELEMENTARY AND JUNIOR HIGH SCHOOLS. A summary of the significant differences between means of 3-rated athletes and nonparticipants for upper elementary and junior high school boys, expressed as *t* ratios, appears in Table 6.5. An athlete was included as a 3 in these analyses if he attained that rating in at least one sport.

Significant mean differences for only one test, 60-yard shuttle run, were obtained at all ages for both school levels; the *t* ratios ranged from 2.72 to 4.24. The standing broad jump mean differences were significant at all ages but 12 years for the elementary school boys. The differences between Physical Fitness Index means were significant at three ages for each of the school levels. Only one test, ectomorphy, failed to produce significant mean differences.

The number of significant mean differences was much less for the elementary than for the junior high school boys. Notable differences between the school levels were the complete absence of significant mean differences for all maturity, physique, and body size measures at the elementary school ages, and the presence of significant differences for total-body reaction time at these same ages. Thus, the traits with longitudinal significance for outstanding elementary school athletes were not those of maturity, physique, and body size, all nondevelopmental characteristics.

The junior high school 3-rated athletes were superior to nonparticipants at all ages for skeletal age, weight, standing height, Strength Index, Rogers' arm strength score, standing broad jump, and 60-yard shuttle run. In addition, they were superior at three ages for arm girth and Physical Fitness Index. The highest *t* ratios were obtained for Strength Index (3.36 to 6.20) and Rogers' arm strength score (3.80 to 7.58). Ectomorphy and total-body reaction time were the only tests without significant mean differences at any age. For endomorphy, the 3-rated athletes had lower means; the reverse was true for ectomorphy. Thus, nearly all traits studied had longitudinal significance for outstanding junior high school athletes.

SENIOR HIGH SCHOOL. By analysis of variance with post hoc Scheffé tests of the significance of differences between paired means, the following differences between the means of senior high school 3-rated athletes and nonparticipants were significant:

Table 6.5

SUMMARY OF SIGNIFICANT MEAN DIFFERENCES EXPRESSED AS *t* RATIOS LONGITUDINAL SERIES FOR 3-RATED ATHLETES VERSUS NONPARTICIPANTS

Tests	Upper Elementary School				Junior High School			
	12	11	10	9	15	14	13	12
Maturity								
Skeletal Age					4.36	4.62	3.42	2.50
Physique								
Endomorphy					−2.78	−2.22		
Mesomorphy					3.37	2.25		
Ectomorphy								
Body Size								
Weight					2.11	2.85	2.75	2.08
Arm Girth					2.85	2.63	2.50	
Calf Girth						2.25	2.05	
Standing Height					2.41	3.38	3.78	2.79
Strength								
Strength Index	2.12	2.89			6.20	6.02	6.06	3.36
Physical Fitness Index		2.33		2.22	4.93	4.25	4.51	
Endurance								
Rogers' Arm Strength Score	2.45			2.22	7.36	7.58	7.50	3.80
Pull-ups					2.86		2.12	
Motor								
Standing Broad Jump	2.96	2.67	3.39	2.93	3.87	4.41	4.66	3.37
60-Yard Shuttle Run	2.93	3.23	4.24	2.35	2.72	2.97	3.16	2.90
Total-Body Reaction Time		1.98	2.29	3.55				

All ages: Strength Index
Ages 17 and 15: standing broad jump, 60-yard shuttle run
Ages 16 and 15: height, upper-body cable-tension strength
average
Ages 17 and 16: lower-body cable-tension strength average
Age 15: endomorphy and skinfold total (nonparticipants
highest), total-body reaction time.

As for the elementary school boys, the traits favoring the 3-rated athletes were developmental in nature. The Strength Index was the most significant of these measures, clearly evident at age 15. Other strength tests were of importance, as were the standing broad jump and the 60-yard shuttle run.

Third Conclusion

The longitudinal significance of the physical character-istics of athletes may be extended to specific sports, and some varia-tions in these characteristics exist for the different sports and at different school levels.

In the three longitudinal studies by Wiley (112), Mitchell (75), and Kelly (63), traits were also contrasted for the four sports, football, basketball, track, and baseball. As before, the athletic abilities of the boys were rated by their coaches at ages 12, 15, and 17 respectively for the elementary, junior high, and senior high school levels; and, as in the preceding conclusion, the longi-tudinal look reported here was limited to comparing the highest rated athletes with nonparticipants. In some instances, the number of boys with 3 ratings was too small to justify statistical inference; in these cases, 2- and 3-rated athletes were combined. On such occasions, it should be observed that direct comparison of 3-rated athletes at one school level with 2 + 3-rated athletes at another is not equitable. In all of the following comparisons, the higher rated athletes were superior unless otherwise stated.

FOOTBALL. A summary of the significant differences between nonparticipants and 2 + 3-rated elementary school and 3-rated junior high school football athletes expressed as *t* ratios appears in Table 6.6 Significant mean differences were obtained at all ages for both school levels for Strength Index, standing broad jump, and 60-yard shuttle run and at all ages but one (9 years) for

Table 6.6

SUMMARY OF SIGNIFICANT MEAN DIFFERENCES EXPRESSED AS *t* RATIOS LONGITUDINAL SERIES FOR HIGHLY RATED FOOTBALL ATHLETES VERSUS NONPARTICIPANTS

Tests	Upper Elementary School 2 + 3 Ratings				Junior High School 3 Ratings			
	12	11	10	9	15	14	13	12
Maturity								
Skeletal Age	2.47	2.22	1.96		4.23	4.29	3.28	2.55
Physique								
Endomorphy					−2.39			
Mesomorphy					3.36	2.48		
Ectomorphy								
Body Size								
Weight	2.11				1.96	2.56	2.41	
Arm Girth					2.63	2.35	2.04	
Calf Girth		2.19				2.19		
Standing Height						2.81	3.26	2.23
Strength								
Strength Index	3.33	3.78	2.10	3.15	5.51	5.66	5.68	3.79
Physical Fitness Index	2.37			2.16	4.22	4.03	4.31	2.30
Endurance								
Rogers' Arm Strength Score					6.20	6.64	7.22	4.64
Pull-ups					2.20		2.16	
Motor								
Standing Broad Jump	2.11	2.35	2.77	2.77	4.01	4.45	5.23	3.66
60-Yard Shuttle Run	2.54	2.97	4.15	2.22	2.82	3.25	3.17	3.11
Total-Body Reaction Time				2.34				

skeletal age. The other mean differences for the elementary school boys were scattered and fewer in number than those for the junior high school boys. At the junior high school level, the Physical Fitness Index and Rogers' arm strength score were significant differentiations at all ages. Tests that differentiated significantly at three ages were weight, arm girth, and standing height.

By analysis of variance with post hoc Sheffé tests of the significance of differences between paired means, the following differences between the means of senior high school 3-rated football players and nonparticipants were significant:

All ages: Strength Index
Ages 17 and 16: 60-yard shuttle run
Age 17: standing broad jump, lower-body cable-tension strength average.
Age 16: standing height, upper-body cable-tension strength average.
Age 15: endomorphy (nonparticipants highest), mesomorphy.

The traits favoring the 3-rated senior high school football players were mostly developmental in nature. The Strength Index was the most significant of these measures, evident at 15 years of age.

BASKETBALL. A summary of the significant differences between nonparticipants and 2 + 3-rated elementary school and 3-rated junior high school basketball athletes, expressed as *t* ratios, is given in Table 6.7. Significant mean differences were obtained for both school levels at all ages for standing broad jump and at three ages each for Physical Fitness Index. The mean differences for the 60-yard shuttle run were significant at three elementary school ages but only one junior high school age. For the elementary school boys, other significant mean differences were for Strength Index at two ages and Rogers' arm strength score and total-body reaction time at one age each; none of the maturity, physique, and body size mean differences were significant. At the junior high school level, standing height and Rogers' arm strength score were also significant differentiations at all ages. Tests that differentiated significantly at three ages were skeletal age, weight, and Physical Fitness Index; for all three measures, significance was not obtained at the youngest age of 12. Endomorphy was a hindrance at ages 15 and 14.

Table 6.7

SUMMARY OF SIGNIFICANT MEAN DIFFERENCES EXPRESSED AS *t* RATIOS LONGITUDINAL SERIES FOR HIGHLY RATED BASKETBALL ATHLETES VERSUS NONPARTICIPANTS

Tests	Upper Elementary School 2 + 3 Ratings				Junior High School 3 Ratings			
	12	11	10	9	15	14	13	12
Maturity								
Skeletal Age					3.93	4.25	2.83	
Physique								
Endomorphy					-2.76	-2.17		
Mesomorphy					2.28			
Ectomorphy								
Body Size								
Weight					2.14		2.47	
Arm Girth					2.23			
Calf Girth								
Standing Height					3.02	3.79	4.14	3.00
Strength								
Strength Index	1.97	2.78			5.37	5.54	5.72	3.49
Physical Fitness Index	2.72	3.53		1.97	3.84	3.62	4.22	
Endurance								
Rogers' Arm Strength Score	2.22				5.98	6.11	6.75	3.14
Pull-ups								
Motor								
Standing Broad Jump	2.81		3.90	2.95	3.74	3.93	4.19	2.72
60-Yard Shuttle Run	2.60		4.19			2.05		
Total-Body Reaction Time				3.25				

For the comparisons of senior high school 3-rated basketball athletes and nonparticipants, analysis of variance with post hoc Scheffé tests of differences between paired means revealed the following significant mean differences:

All ages: standing height, Rogers' arm strength score, 60-yard shuttle run
Ages 17 and 15: standing broad jump
Age 17: mesomorphy
Age 15: weight, calf girth, Strength Index, Physical Fitness Index

The traits most consistently favoring the senior high school basketball athletes were standing height, Rogers' arm strength score, and 60-yard shuttle run. Standing broad jump and mesomorphy were assets at age 17. Four traits were significant differentiations at age 15 but not at the other ages.

TRACK. A summary of the significant differences between nonparticipants and 2 + 3-rated elementary school and 3-rated junior high school track athletes, expressed as *t* ratios, are presented in Table 6.8. Significant mean differences were obtained for both school levels at all ages for standing broad jump, at three ages for Physical Fitness Index, and at all junior high and three elementary school ages for 60-yard shuttle run. The mean differences for Strength Index, Rogers' arm strength score, and total-body reaction time were significant at two elementary school ages each. At the junior high school level, skeletal age, Strength Index, and Rogers' arm strength score were also significant differentiations at all ages. Other tests that differentiated significantly were: standing height at three ages; endomorphy (nonparticipants highest), mesomorphy, and pull-ups at two ages each; and weight and arm girth at one age each (13 years).

For the comparisons of senior high school 2 + 3-rated track athletes and nonparticipants, the following significant mean differences were obtained from analysis of variance with post hoc Scheffé tests of differences between paired means:

All ages: weight, 60-yard shuttle run
Ages 17 and 15: mesomorphy, standing broad jump
Ages 16 and 15: calf girth
Age 15: standing height

Table 6.8

SUMMARY OF SIGNIFICANT MEAN DIFFERENCES EXPRESSED AS *t* RATIOS LONGITUDINAL SERIES FOR HIGHLY RATED TRACK ATHLETES VERSUS NONPARTICIPANTS

Tests	*Upper Elementary School* 2 + 3 *Ratings*				*Junior High School* 3 *Ratings*			
	12	11	10	9	15	14	13	12
Maturity								
Skeletal Age					3.78	4.47	3.30	2.69
Physique								
Endomorphy					−2.36	−2.03		
Mesomorphy					3.00	2.17		
Ectomorphy								
Body Size								
Weight							2.30	
Arm Girth							2.14	
Calf Girth								
Standing Height						2.28	2.90	2.07
Strength								
Strength Index	2.10	2.97			4.85	4.73	5.33	3.07
Physical Fitness Index	2.95	4.00		2.03	4.22	3.69	3.99	
Endurance								
Rogers' Arm Strength Score	3.06		1.99		5.67	6.19	6.48	3.45
Pull-Ups					2.13		2.27	
Motor								
Standing Broad Jump	3.69	2.88	3.95	2.79	3.49	3.92	4.50	2.93
60-Yard Shuttle Run	4.09	3.13	6.43		3.41	3.83	3.95	3.41
Total-Body Reaction Time			2.25	3.26				

The differentiating traits at the senior high school level were mostly physique and body size measures, although the two motor traits of 60-yard shuttle run and standing broad jump, events closely related to some track events, had significant differentiating value. None of the strength measures produced significant mean differences.

BASEBALL. In Medford, baseball was only conducted as an interscholastic sport in the upper elementary and senior high schools. The highest classification for this sport for both school levels was the combination of 2 + 3-rated athletes. Of all comparisons made with nonparticipants at the senior high school level, only one significant mean difference was found; this difference was for endomorphy at age 15 with the athletes having the lowest mean.

For the elementary school 2 + 3-rated baseball athletes and nonparticipants, the following mean differences were obtained:

All ages: standing broad jump
Ages 12, 11, and 9: Physical Fitness Index
Ages 12 and 11: Strength Index
Ages 11 and 10: 60-yard shuttle run
Age 9: total-body reaction time.

The traits showing significant differentiation between elementary school baseball athletes and nonparticipants were all strength and motor measures. None of the mean differences for the maturity, physique, body size, and endurance tests was significant.

Fourth Conclusion

The general physical fitness of all boys, as reflected in their relative strength, is an indirect contributing factor to a higher physical fitness level of the athletes, especially in elementary and junior high schools. The logic is that athletes will be superior to nonathletes; as the fitness level of nonathletes is raised, the fitness level of the athletes also rises, thus maintaining their superiority.

The Physical Fitness Index is used in the Medford Boys' Growth Study as a measure of relative strength, since it is derived by relating the Strength Index, a gross strength measure, to norms based on sex, age, and weight. This measure has been widely used as a measure of physical fitness, inasmuch as two generally recognized fitness components, muscular strength and muscular endurance, are measured by this test. An index of 100 is considered average; 85 and 115, the first and third quartiles.

The PFI means of nonparticipants and highest rated groups of athletes in the various interscholastic sports are shown in Table 6.9 for the elementary, junior high, and senior high school boys. These means were obtained respectively at ages 12, 15, and 17. An exact comparison of school levels is not justified, since 2 + 3-rated athletes were combined in elementary and senior high schools and the 3-rated athletes only were grouped in junior high school.

Table 6.9

CONTRASTING PHYSICAL FITNESS INDEX MEANS FOR NONPARTICIPANTS
AND ATHLETES IN VARIOUS ELEMENTARY, JUNIOR HIGH,
AND SENIOR HIGH SCHOOL SPORTS

Groups	School Levels*		
	Elementary	*Junior High*	*Senior High*
Nonparticipants	106	111	115
Football	121	138	121
Basketball	127	133	116
Track	127	130	118
Baseball	127		99

*Athletic ratings: 2 + 3, elementary and senior high school; 3, junior high school.

The general physical fitness level of all boys was high for all school levels, as indicated by the PFI means of 106, 111, and 115 for the nonparticipants; the mean of the senior high school nonparticipants reached the normal third quartile. In elementary and junior high schools, the PFI means of the athletes were exceptionally high, ranging between 121 and 127 for the 2 + 3-rated elementary school athletes and between 129 and 138 for the 3-rated junior high school athletes. Although the degree of superiority was not maintained by the senior high school 2 + 3-rated athletes, except for baseball, the PFI means exceeded the mean of the nonparticipants.

The PFI means of the football athletes were lowest in elementary and senior high schools and highest in junior high school; the respective means were 121 and 138. The only sport group to produce a low PFI mean was baseball; the mean of 99 was not only much lower than the nonparticipants but was slightly below the normal expectation of 100.

Further substantiation of this conclusion is contained in Whittle's study (110) of 12-year-old elementary school boys who had participated for three years in good and poor physical education programs. The Physical Fitness Index mean of the athletes in the poor program (116) was actually lower than the mean of all boys in the good program (121); and, the mean of the athletes in the good program was much higher (132).

Fifth Conclusion

The gross strength of athletes participating in all interscholastic sports is consistently high at all school levels.

The Strength Index will demonstrate this conclusion. The SI means of nonparticipants and highest rated athletes in the various interscholastic sports are shown in Table 6.10 for the elementary, junior high, and senior high school boys. As for the fourth conclusion, these means were obtained at ages 12, 15, and 17; and 2 + 3-rated athletes were combined for elementary and senior high school boys, while the 3-rated athletes were separate for junior high school boys.

Table 6.10

CONTRASTING STRENGTH INDEX MEANS FOR NONPARTICIPANTS
AND ATHLETES IN VARIOUS ELEMENTARY, JUNIOR HIGH,
AND SENIOR HIGH SCHOOL SPORTS

	School Levels*		
Groups	Elementary	Junior High	Senior High
Nonparticipants	1080	2043	2723
Football	1266	2903	3338
Basketball	1195	2761	3123
Track	1232	2768	3190
Baseball	1227		3123

Athletic ratings: 2 + 3, elementary and senior high schools; 3, junior high school.

The Strength Index means of the athletes in all sports were higher than the means of the nonparticipants at the three school levels. The football athletes had the highest means throughout;

these means were 1,266, 2,903, and 3,338. For junior high school boys, the mean of the 3-rated football athletes was 42 percent higher than the mean of the nonparticipants (2,903 and 2,043 respectively).

Sixth Conclusion

The explosive muscular power of athletes participating in all interscholastic sports is consistently high at all school levels.

The standing broad jump was utilized in the Medford Boys' Growth Study as a measure of explosive muscular power. The means on this test for nonparticipants and highest rated athletes in the various interscholastic sports are shown in Table 6.11 for the elementary, junior high, and senior high school boys. As for conclusions four and five, the means were obtained at ages 12, 15, and 17; and 2 + 3-rated athletes were combined for elementary and senior high school boys, while the 3-rated athletes only were grouped at the junior high school level.

Table 6.11

CONTRASTING STANDING BROAD JUMP MEANS IN INCHES FOR
NONPARTICIPANTS AND ATHLETES IN VARIOUS ELEMENTARY,
JUNIOR HIGH, AND SENIOR HIGH SCHOOLS SPORTS

	*School Levels**		
Groups	*Elementary*	*Junior High*	*Senior High*
Nonparticipants	62.1	77.5	77.7
Football	65.8	88.5	91.6
Basketball	68.1	88.1	94.0
Track	68.3	89.4	92.9
Baseball	67.0		88.0

*Athletic ratings : 2 + 3, elementary and senior high schools ; 3, junior high school.

The standing broad jump means of the athletes in all sports were higher than the means of the nonparticipants at the three school levels. The basketball and track athletes had higher means than for the other sports, with the exception of the junior high school football athletes. The means of the junior and senior high school athletes were between 10.6 and 16.3 inches higher than the means of the nonparticipants.*

Seventh Conclusion

Although successful athletes generally have common characteristics, the pattern of these characteristics varies from athlete to athlete; where a successful athlete is low in such a trait, he compensates by strength in another.

From the Medford study, Shelley (36, 95) constructed a Hull-scale (seven sigma) profile chart for each of 38 boys rated as outstanding athletes by their coaches in elementary and junior high school interscholastic athletics. The profiles were based on 23 measures of maturity, body-size, strength, motor ability, and intelligence. The profile for each athlete was based on H-scales constructed from test scores of other boys his age in the Medford study.

Fig. 6.8 presents the profile of one outstanding junior high school athlete 14 years of age. For his age group, this athlete was below average in skeletal age (43); was near the average in all body size scores except calf girth (59), lung capacity (58), and one low score in height (43); was high on the 60-yard shuttle run (84) and standing broad jump (71); was as strong as the larger boys in Strength Index (67); was especially high in relative strength (PFI, 73) and in arm-shoulder endurance (arm score, 75; push-ups, 83); and was superior in intelligence. His somatotype designation was 1^2 6 3.

As contrasted with his age group, this athlete was physically immature and was about average in body size, thus these factors were not advantages in his athletic competition. However, his speed and agility, muscular power, muscular endurance, and relative strength were superior; he was well above average on most muscular strength tests; his physique was strongly mesomorphic; and he

---

* Conclusions four, five, and six were centered around three measures reflecting relative and gross muscular strength and endurance and explosive muscular power of nonparticipants and highest-rated athletes in the different interscholastic sports. Other tests could also be used for this purpose, but the ones selected had the greatest discriminatory significance between nonparticipants and athletes at all school levels.

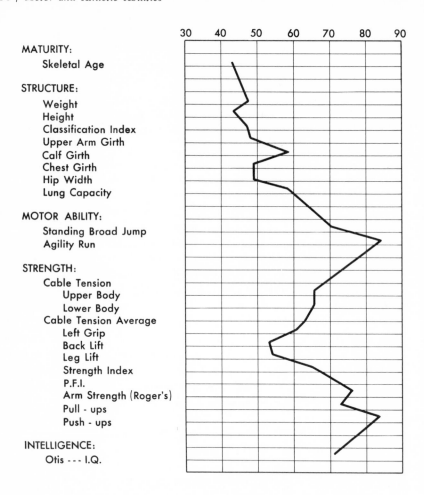

Fig. 6.8 Profile chart of an outstanding 14-year-old athlete

possessed high intelligence. Thus, this profile demonstrates weaknesses in some traits that are advantageous in interscholastic athletic competition for which compensation is made by great strengths in others. Actually, under these circumstances, this athlete's physical immaturity could well be an advantage for future athletic participation, since he still has ahead the advantages associated with increased maturity.

The 14-year-old athlete portrayed in the profile was outstanding in three sports: football, quarterback and defensive halfback, outstanding leader, easy to coach; basketball, guard and play maker, excellent leader; track, hurdler. He played summer baseball, leading in batting average and base stealing. Three years later, when this athlete was 17 years old, Medford High School won three state championships in football, basketball, and baseball; he was on all three of these teams and was selected on all-state teams in football and basketball. As a senior at age 18 he was selected the outstanding scholar-athlete in the state of Oregon. The football team that year only punted twice all season. As a collegian, he played football for Stanford University; in his senior year, he was chosen as the most valuable player on the Stanford team.

For all profile tests, the H-score means of the 38 outstanding athletes were above the means for all boys of their respective ages. The most distinctive characteristics of these athletes were their high H-score means on tests of explosive power, speed and agility, gross strength, and arm strength. Of less importance, but still with high means, were skeletal age, height, and all measures of muscular strength but back lift. The standing broad jump, shuttle run, Strength Index, and Rogers' arm strength score were most frequently observed as compensating variables for apparent deficiencies when found among the outstanding athletes.

Eighth Conclusion

Outstanding elementary school athletes may not be outstanding in junior high school and outstanding junior high school athletes may not have been outstanding in elementary school; longitudinal test profiles reveal distinguishing differences between athletes in these categories.

Howe (56) contrasted T-scale (10 sigma) test profiles based on physical and mental tests for elementary school boys 12 years of age and junior high school boys 15 years of age who were rated by their coaches as outstanding athletes. Each athlete's chart contained three profiles, when he was 9, 12, and 15 years old. In the construction of the T scales, the number of subjects varied at each age, as follows: 9 years, 176; 12 years, 256; 15 years, 340. Thus, some changes in positions at the different ages may be due to differences in the samples upon which the T scales were based; however, the profiles do reveal the athlete's position in his age group.

Three groups of outstanding athletes were identified as follows: A, athletes who were outstanding at both 12 and 15 years; B, athletes who were outstanding at 12 but not at 15 years; C, athletes who were outstanding at 15 but not at 12 years. Of the 20 outstanding athletes, only five, or 25 percent, were outstanding in both elementary and junior high school; nine, or 45 percent, were outstanding in elementary but not in junior high school; and six, or 30 percent, were outstanding in junior high but not in elementary school.

While profiles were prepared for each athlete, average profiles, to be known as the average athlete, were also constructed for each group at the three ages. These profiles reveal typical longitudinal differences between the groups and so are presented here.

GROUP A. The profile chart for the average group A athlete (outstanding, both ages) is shown in Fig. 6.9. The distinguishing features of this chart are:

1. Profile positions on all tests were average and above at all three ages.
2. Skeletal age and body size profile positions clustered between T scores of 50 and 55; were generally more advanced at 15 years. The 9- and 12-year profiles paralleled fairly well.
3. Strength profile positions were definitely higher at 15 years; with the exception of lower body strength (high at 9 years), profile lines coincided closely at 9 and 12 years. High T scores at 15 years were 57 for upper body strength, 64 for Strength Index, and 65 for Physical Fitness Index.
4. Arm-shoulder endurance profile positions were much higher at 15 years; higher at 12 years than at 9 years. Similar results were obtained for the motor ability items, except for the 60-yard shuttle run.
5. Mental test profile positions improved with age. At all ages, the T scores were average and above.

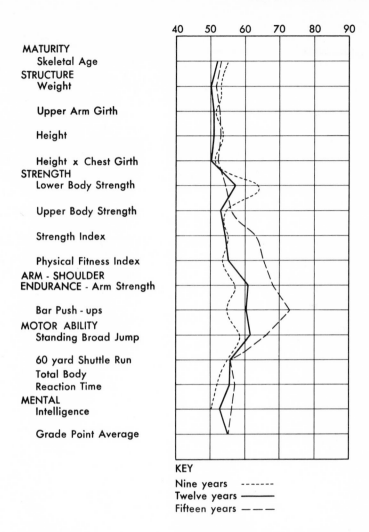

Fig. 6.9 Mean profile chart of outstanding athletes age 12 and 15 years

GROUP B. The profile chart for the average Group B athlete (outstanding, 12 years only) appears in Fig. 6.10. Contrasting features of this chart are:

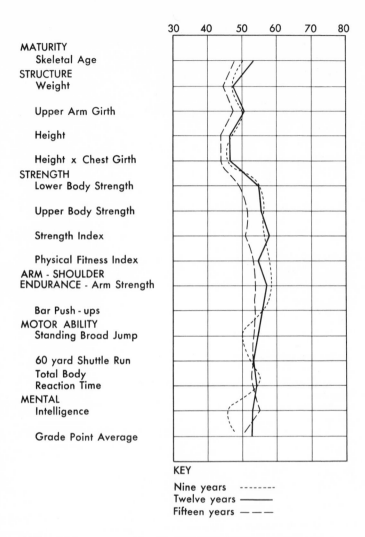

Fig. 6.10 Mean profiles of outstanding athletes age 12 years only

1. Skeletal age and body size profile positions were mostly average and below; 9 and 12 year lines coincided; decrease on all tests at 15 years. Compared with other boys his age, this athlete was small at 15 years.

2. Strength profile positions were mostly above average; coincided well at 9 and 12 years; decreased on all tests at 15 years. Similar results were obtained for the arm-shoulder endurance and motor ability tests.
3. Mental test profile positions were above average at 12 and 15 years; decreased in grade-point-average position at 15 years.

GROUP C. The profile chart for the average group C athlete (outstanding, 15 years only) appears in Fig. 6.11. Comparisons from this chart are:

1. Profile positions on most tests were above average at all three ages.
2. Skeletal age profile positions improved steadily for the three years. The T score at 15 years was 59.
3. Body size profile positions were above average for the three years; 12 and 15 profile lines coincided, but lower than at 9 years. The same T score of 58 was obtained for height at all ages.
4. Strength and arm-shoulder endurance profile positions improved greatly at 15 years; 12-year positions were superior to 9-year positions in strength tests but not in arm-shoulder endurance tests. The highest T scores at 15 years were 66 for arm strength, 64 for bar push-ups, upper body strength, and Strength Index, and 63 for Physical Fitness Index.
5. Motor ability test profile positions were above average in standing broad jump and 60-yard shuttle run at all ages and below average in total-body reaction time at 12 and 15 years. At 15 years, there were losses in shuttle run and reaction time profile positions and a gain in standing broad jump profile position.
6. Mental test profile positions were above average and about equal at 12 and 15 years and below average at 9 years.

SUMMARIZATION. A summarization of the distinctive longitudinal profile patterns of the three groups of outstanding elementary and junior high school athletes follows.

1. The test profiles of athletes rated outstanding at both 12 and 15 years showed increases in nearly every profile position at 15 years. These increases were especially marked for strength tests, arm-shoulder endurance, and standing broad jump; smaller in-

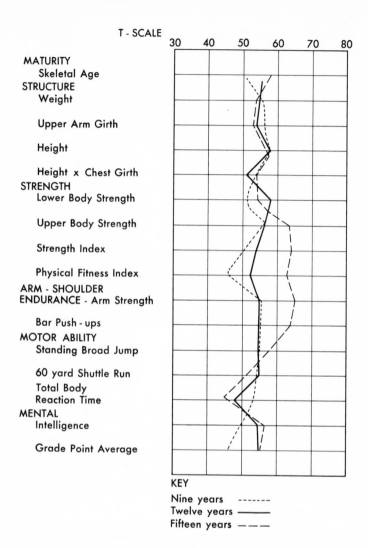

T - SCALE

MATURITY
  Skeletal Age
STRUCTURE
  Weight

  Upper Arm Girth

  Height

  Height x Chest Girth
STRENGTH
  Lower Body Strength

  Upper Body Strength

  Strength Index

  Physical Fitness Index
ARM - SHOULDER
ENDURANCE - Arm Strength

  Bar Push - ups
MOTOR ABILITY
  Standing Broad Jump

  60 yard Shuttle Run
  Total Body
  Reaction Time
MENTAL
  Intelligence

  Grade Point Average

KEY

Nine years ------
Twelve years ————
Fifteen years — — —

Fig. 6.11 Mean profiles of outstanding athletes age 15 years only

creases occurred for skeletal age, body size, and mental test. The mean profiles were average or above average on all tests for the three years.

2. The test profiles of athletes who were outstanding at 12 but not at 15 years were similar at 9 and 12 years, generally average or below in skeletal age and body size measures and above average on the other tests. At 15 years, losses in profile position occurred on nearly all tests.

3. The test profiles of athletes who were outstanding at 15 but not at 12 years improved markedly in strength and arm-shoulder endurance tests at 15 years. They were mostly above average on the profile tests at the three ages.

Reaction and Movement Times of Athletes

The total-body and arm-hand reaction, movement, and completion times of nonparticipants and boys classified into three levels of success in interscholastic athletics were studied separately at three ages by Smith (98). The subjects were 214 boys at 12, 141 boys at 14, and 151 boys at 17 years of age. The athletic ratings of 3, 2, and 1 by coaches were explained in the preceding section. The reaction, movement, and completion times were tested with the Hale Reaction Timer as described earlier in this chapter. Thus, the movement and completion times were over distances of 10 feet for the total-body and 18 inches for hand-arm tests. A summary of the significant results of this study is given below.

1. Athletes in general were faster in total-body and hand-arm measures of reaction, movement, and completion times than nonparticipants at ages 12 and 17. At age 14, they were superior only in total-body movement and completion times.

2. In comparing athletes according to their highest ratings, the most significant results were as follows: (a) At age 17, the 1- and 2-rated athletes were faster than the nonparticipants on all six tests; the 3-rated athletes were also superior to the nonparticipants in total-body movement and completion times. (b) At age 12, the 2- and 3-rated athletes were superior to the nonparticipants in total-body movement and completion times and hand-arm reaction and completion times; in addition, the 3-rated athletes exceeded in total-body reaction time. (c) At age 14, the 3-rated athletes were faster than the nonparticipants and 1- and 2-rated athletes

in hand-arm reaction time, than the nonparticipants and 2-rated athletes in total-body completion time, and than the nonparticipants in total-body and hand-arm completion times.

3. Football athletes of all ratings as a group had faster times than nonparticipants on all six measures at ages 12 and 17, except for hand-arm movement time at age 17. Track athletes as a total group were superior to nonparticipants in total-body completion time at the three ages and in total-body reaction and movement and hand-arm reaction times at age 17.

4. In comparing athletes by their ratings in different sports, the most significant results were as follows: (a) With only an occasional exception, the 3-rated football and track, the 2-rated football, and the 1-rated track athletes had faster times than the nonparticipants on all six tests. (b) The 3-rated were superior to the 1-rated football athletes on all tests but total-body reaction time; and the 2-rated football players were faster than nonparticipants on all tests but arm-hand movement time. (c) The 1-rated track athletes exceeded the nonparticipants on all six tests; and those rated 3 were better than those rated 2 on all tests but total-body reaction and hand-arm movement times. (d) The 3-rated basketball players had faster total-body reaction time than did the nonparticipants and the 1- and 2-rated athletes in this sport; the 3's were also superior to the 2's in total-body reaction time. (e) In baseball, the 3- and 2-rated athletes showed some advantage over the nonparticipants in total-body reaction and completion times.

5. The intercorrelations between total-body and hand-arm reaction times were .385 at 12, .188 at 15, and .271 at 17 years of age. These results support the concept expressed by others that "a" reaction time for a given individual does not exist, but, rather, there are several reaction times depending on the parts of the body involved.

Election of Physical Education

As has also happened elsewhere, physical education in grades eleven and twelve of public schools of Oregon is optional with local school districts. As a consequence, few schools in the state require physical education in these grades. In Medford, physical education is the option of individual boys and girls. Under these circumstances, empirical observations have led many physical educators to believe that those who choose physical education are usually the ones who need it least. With the availability of longitudinal growth and development data on Medford boys, Ragsdale (83) designed a study to check on this belief, at least in part. He investigated the significance of mean differences in maturity, physique, body size, strength, endurance, motor, and scholastic measures existing between boys who elected and boys who did not elect physical education in grade eleven, and then followed up on their respective effects a year later.

The subjects were 93 boys in Medford High School. Four groups were formed among the subjects in the tenth grade based on the eleventh grade election of physical education, as follows:

AP: Boys who elected physical education and also participated in interscholastic athletics (N = 17).
P: Boys who elected physical education, but did not participate in interscholastic athletics (N = 17).
A: Boys who did not elect physical education, but who participated in interscholastic athletics (N = 15).
N: Boys who did not elect physical education and did not participate in interscholastic athletics (N = 44).

The differences between the means of the four groups were tested for significance by application of the *t* ratio for 22 tests at both grades ten and eleven and for changes occurring between grades. Formulae used were appropriate for uncorrelated groups for the intra-grade comparisons and for correlated groups for inter-grade comparisons. Inasmuch as analysis of variance was not used in this study, the .01 level of significance was adopted; however, in the tables presented, significant mean differences at the .05 level are reported. The *t* ratios necessary for significance at the .01 level range from 2.66 to 3.00.

Comparisons at Grade Ten

The *t* ratios for significant differences between the means on the 22 tests at grade ten between the four groups are shown in Table 6.12; these differences contrast the status of the subjects

Table 6.12

SUMMARY OF SIGNIFICANT DIFFERENCES BETWEEN MEANS EXPRESSED
AS *t* RATIOS FOR ALL VARIABLES AT GRADE TEN

Variable	AP vs. P	AP vs. A	AP vs. N	P vs. A	P vs. N	A vs. N
1. Skeletal Age						
2. Endomorphy						
3. Mesomorphy			2.04*			
4. Ectomorphy						
5. Weight						
6. Thigh girth						
7. Upper arm girth			2.34*			
8. Skinfold						
9. Standing height			2.44*			
10. Sitting height	2.05*		2.63*			
11. Strength Index	2.55*		3.59**			3.07**
12. Physical Fitness Index						2.45*
13. Arm Strength Score			4.04**		2.70**	3.39**
14. Pull-ups						
15. Bar dips			3.38**		2.55*	3.95**
16. Standing broad jump			2.79**		2.23*	
17. 60-yard shuttle run		2.13*	2.84**	2.35*	3.07**	
18. 10-foot run			2.83**			2.14*
19. Reaction time			2.32*		2.08*	
20. Intelligence Quotient				−2.36*		
21. Grade point average	2.50*	−2.56*		−4.62**		3.62**
22. Physical activities			2.80**		2.48*	2.27*

*Significant at the .05 level.
**Significant at the .01 level.
Code : AP, Athletics and Physical Education.
    A, Athletics, No Physical Education.
    P, Physical Education, No Athletics.
    N, Neither Athletics nor Physical Education.

at the time of their decision to take or not to take physical education in grade eleven.

Among the nonathletes, the physical education group had tenth grade means significantly superior to the nonphysical education group on two tests (P vs. N). These measures and their *t* ratios were: 60-yard shuttle run, 3.07; Rogers' arm strength score, 3.07. The means of the physical education group were significantly higher at the .05 level on four other tests: bar dips, standing broad jump, total-body reaction time, and participation in physical activities.*

The athletes who elected physical education had significantly higher means on most tests than did the boys who neither elected physical education nor participated in interscholastic athletics (AP vs. N). Significance at the .01 level was obtained for Strength Index, Rogers' arm strength score, bar dips, standing broad jump, 60-yard shuttle run, 10-foot run, and participation in physical activities. In addition, significant differences at the .05 level were obtained for mesomorphy, upper arm girth, standing height, sitting height, and total-body reaction time.

For all comparisons in which significant differences were found at the .05 level and above, group AP had the higher mean on 16 of 17 tests. Group N, on the other hand, had the lower mean on all 25 of its comparisons resulting in significant differences. Group A had higher means on 10 of 12 comparisons with other groups which yielded significant differences; seven of these were with group N. Group P had the superior mean on seven of 12 significant mean differences, six being with group N.

Comparisons at Grade Eleven

The *t* ratios for significant differences between the means on the 22 tests at grade eleven for the four groups appear in Table 6.13. At this time, the boys who did not participate in physical education or interscholastic athletics were inferior to all other groups on three developmental tests, Strength Index, Rogers' arm strength score, and bar dips. In all instances, mean differences were significant at the .01 level and above; the nine *t* ratios ranged from 2.75 to 5.00.

Discussion

The investigator, who was physical education teacher and director of health, physical education, and athletics in the

* The number of different physical activities during grades ten and eleven were obtained from the Medford Boys' Growth Study Activity Questionnaire. Physical education class and interscholastic athletic activities were excluded in Ragsdale's study.

Table 6.13

SUMMARY OF SIGNIFICANT DIFFERENCES BETWEEN MEANS EXPRESSED
As *t* RATIOS FOR ALL VARIABLES AT GRADE ELEVEN

Variable	AP vs. P	AP vs. A	AP vs. N	P vs. A	P vs. N	A vs. N
1. Skeletal Age						
2. Endomorphy						−3.00**
3. Mesomorphy						
4. Ectomorphy						
5. Weight			2.52*			
6. Thigh girth						
7. Upper arm girth	2.09*	2.11*				
8. Skinfold						
9. Standing height						
10. Sitting height						
11. Strength Index			4.12**		2.75**	3.42**
12. Physical Fitness Index						2.42*
13. Arm Strength score			5.00**		3.63**	4.79**
14. Pull-ups						
15. Bar dips			4.05**		3.40**	4.90**
16. Standing broad jump						
17. 60-yard shuttle run						
18. 10-foot run						
19. Reaction time						
20. ITED Composite				−3.70**		2.17*
21. Grade point average	2.81**			−2.99**		2.01*
22. Physical activities					3.02**	

*Significant at the .05 level.
**Significant at the .01 level.
Code : AP, Athletics and Physical Education.
     A, Athletics, no Physical Education.
     P, Physical Education, No Athletics.
     N, Neither Athletics nor Physical Education.

Medford schools from 1948 to 1966, was acquainted with the school system over this period and personally knew the boys serving as subjects for his study. From this broad understanding of the Medford situation, he made a number of observations relative to the results. His comments are reported here as observations only.

First, the classification of boys into groups of athletes and nonathletes did not adequately reflect their physical abilities. Many subjects of good athletic ability were included in the two groups of nonparticipants in interscholastic athletics. Conversely, some boys of just average physical ability chose to participate in interscholastic athletics. These two circumstances could logically result in smaller group differences on many measures than the names of the groups might suggest.

Second, in assessing the group which did not participate in either physical education or interscholastic athletics at grade eleven, it should be recognized that this was not a misfit group. Many individuals in the group were poor on many of the measures, but the group as a whole was average or better on tests having norms, such as the Physical Fitness Index, Iowa Test of Educational Development, Otis Quick-Scoring Mental Ability Test, and skeletal age. However, this group was not superior to any other group on any of the 132 comparisons at grades ten and eleven, which indicates its general inferiority to the other groups.

Third, the physical and social environment in which the subjects lived was conducive to achievement on both physical and scholastic measures. Scholarship was regarded highly in the community. General public interest plus the honoring of scholastic achievement resulted in an atmosphere encouraging to academic effort. The existence of mountains, forests, streams, and lakes within a short distance of town resulted in much out-of-door recreation. In and near Medford, numerous playgrounds, fields, parks, swimming pools, tennis courts, and gymnasia were easily accessible. The city and the schools conducted cooperative recreation programs on a year-round basis with qualified personnel in charge. Community interest in athletics was high. Even the N group participated in an average of 6.27 out-of-school physical activities during the eleventh grade. Nearly all of the subjects had taken ten years of physical education in the public schools. The physical education program was designed fundamentally to develop strength, stamina, and motor skills. The unusually high Physical Fitness Index means of the four groups in this study (112 to 126) attest, in part at least, to the success of this effort. Any effects of lack of participation in physical education at grade eleven should be evaluated with this background in mind.

Chapter Summary

This chapter presented materials related to the motor and athletic abilities of boys in the Medford Boys' Growth Study. The first part of the chapter considered studies pertaining to the standing broad jump, 60-yard shuttle run, and total-body and arm-hand reaction, movement, and completion times; the latter part was devoted to contrasting the traits of boys who made and had varying degrees of success on interscholastic athletic teams with nonparticipants.

Four methods of scoring the standing broad jump were investigated. The following multiple correlations were obtained for 12-year-old boys: Distance × weight, .902, with weight, Strength Index, and skinfold total. Weight/distance, .908, with abdominal girth, Physical Fitness Index, and skinfold total. Leg length/distance, .717, with Physical Fitness Index, leg length, and 10-foot run. Distance jumped, .690, with Physical Fitness Index, 10-foot run, and others. A multiple correlation of .650 was obtained for 14-year-old boys with the 60-yard shuttle run; the independent variables were standing broad jump, Physical Fitness Index, and total-body reaction time.

In the study of athletes, data were assembled in support of the following eight basic conclusions regarding their characteristics:

1. Boys who make and are successful on athletic teams are definitely superior to their peers in maturity, physique, body size, muscular strength, endurance, and power, and motor ability.
2. Some fundamental characteristics of 12-year-old elementary school, 15-year-old junior high school, and 17-year-old senior high school athletes are clearly evident at younger ages, although differences in characteristics exist at the three school levels.
3. The longitudinal significance of the physical characteristics of athletes may be extended to specific sports, and some variations in these characteristics exist for the various sports and at different school levels.
4. The general physical fitness of all boys, as reflected in their relative strength, is an indirect contributing factor to a higher

physical fitness level of the athletes, especially in elementary and junior high schools.

5. The gross strength of athletes participating in all interscholastic sports is consistently high at all school levels.

6. The explosive muscular power of athletes participating in all interscholastic sports is consistently high at all school levels.

7. Although successful athletes generally have common characteristics, the pattern of these characteristics varies from athlete to athlete; where a successful athlete is low in such a trait, he compensates in another.

8. Outstanding elementary school athletes may not be outstanding in junior high school and outstanding junior high school athletes may not have been outstanding in elementary school; longitudinal test profiles reveal distinguishing differences between athletes in these categories.

This chapter concluded with a report of differences obtained between boys who elected and did not elect physical education in the eleventh grade; for each category, differentiation was made between those who participated and did not participate in interscholastic athletics. Although the differences were not always significant, those boys who did not elect physical education and did not participate in interscholastic athletics were inferior to all other groups on 22 tests of maturity, physique, body size, muscular strength and endurance, motor performances, and scholastic achievement. The tests showing generally significant differences were 60-yard shuttle run, Rogers' arm strength score, bar push-ups, total-body reaction time, and amount of participation in out-of-school physical activities at the time of physical education election in the tenth grade. One year later, these same boys had not gained as much as physical education electees in tests of muscular strength and endurance.

Chapter 7

Summary and Implications

This monograph presents the significance of maturity, physique type, body size, muscular strength and endurance, and motor ability tests in studying the growth of boys 7 through 18 years of age, as shown in the Medford Boys' Growth Study. This growth study extended over a period of twelve years, 1955–56 to 1967–68. At the time this manuscript was written, 76 graduate theses had been completed, two-thirds of which were doctoral dissertations. It is anticipated that a second monograph will be prepared, which will deal with the scholastic aptitude and achievement, personal-social adjustment, and interests of the Medford subjects.

During the first year of the Medford growth study, approximately 100 boys were tested at each age, 7, 9, 12, and 15; these boys were tested annually until graduation from high school. In addition, to provide cross-sectional samples from 9 through 15 years, 40 boys were tested at each of the intervening ages of 10, 11, 13, and 14. Each year, all boys were tested within two months of their birthdays in order to provide reasonable homogeneity in respect to chronological age. Four types of growth analyses were made: longitudinal, cross-sectional, convergence, and single year.

Summary

Maturity

In the Medford Boys' Growth Study, two physiological maturity measures were given annually. These measures were: skeletal age, as determined from X rays of the wrist and hand, assessed by use of the Greulich-Pyle atlas (49); pubescent assessment, utilizing the five-category scale proposed by Greulich and associates (50).

In the evaluation of skeletal age from X rays in the atlas, some 30 bones must be assessed, the exact number for each boy depending on his age. In a study to determine the minimum number of bones necessary for such an assessment, a multiple correlation of .9989 was obtained between all wrist-hand sites and the following four bones: capitate, metacarpal III, proximal phalanx III, and middle phalanx III.

Skeletal age was found to be definitely superior to pubescent assessment as a physical maturity measure at ages 10, 13, and 16. Pubescent assessment was most valuable at age 13, of no value at age 10, and of limited value at age 16. Considerable overlapping in skeletal age occurred for the pubescent categories at the different ages.

Inter-age skeletal age correlations were determined for boys ages 7 to 12 and ages 12 to 17. The median correlations between adjacent ages were .879 for the 7 to 12 boys and .915 for the 12 to 17 boys. The inter-age correlations decreased in magnitude with the number of intervening ages. The attempt to locate a general maturity factor through factor analysis with skeletal age included as a maturity criterion was unsuccessful; the independent variables were measures of physique type, body size, muscular strength and endurance, and motor ability elements.

At the ages of 7 and 8, when only a small number of subjects were tested, the skeletal age means of the boys were retarded by

8.6 and 7.8 months respectively. For the ages 9 through 17, these means corresponded reasonably well to their chronological age expectations. The standard deviations at each age from 7 through 17 ranged from 11.9 to 15.1 months; the ranges varied from 58 to 85 months.

Advanced, normal, and retarded maturity groups, based on skeletal age, were formed at each age 9, 12, 15, and 17; the differences between means of the maturity groups at each age were tested for significance on physique type, body size, strength, and motor tests. For all variables, except ectomorphy, when the differences between paired means were significant, the more advanced maturity group had the superior mean. Significant mean differences were obtained most frequently at 15 years of age. Except for age 17 and for the advanced-normal comparison at age 9, the differences between all other standing height means were significant. Other test variables with many significant mean differences were body weight, chest girth × height, and cable-tension strength average.

Physique Type

The Sheldonian somatotype was the principal physique measure used in the Medford Boys' Growth Study; the three somatotype components are endomorphy, mesomorphy, and ectomorphy. The somatotype photographs were taken in accordance with Sheldon's specifications (92). The assessment followed Sheldon's anthroposcopic process, except that Heath's table (54) of possible components from the ratio of height-over-cube-root-of-weight was utilized in determining the somatotype; this table is a slight modification of Sheldon's, providing open ends on the component rating scales and a more linear relationship between changes in component ratings and the ratio.

A comparison of Sheldon's original phenotype assessment through the trunk index (91, 93) was made. Generally, the trunk index produced higher somatotype designations than did the anthroposcopic method. The correlations between the two assessment methods for boys 9 through 16 years ranged from .394 to .758; the endomorphy and ectomorphy correlations were higher than those for mesomorphy. Generally, more subjects were identified as endomorphs, endo-mesomorphs, and ectomorphs by the trunk-index method and as mid-types by the anthroposcopic method. The correlations between somatotype components and body size measures were much higher from age to age by anthroposcopic than by trunk-index assessments.

In studying the stability of somatotype components from ages 9 through 12 and 12 through 17, the highest inter-age correlations were obtained between adjacent ages, .79 to .93. The lowest such correlations were for a four-year gap, the largest gap studied: .50, .60, and .67 for the three components in customary order. Various fluctuations in component designations occurred over the span of years investigated.

For a cross-sectional sample of 40 boys each at ages 9 through 15, five somatotype categories were formed: endomorphs, mesomorphs, endo-mesomorphs, ectomorphs, and mid-types. The endomorphs had greater body bulk and lower strength and motor test means than the mesomorphs, ectomorphs, and mid-types. The endo-mesomorphs were similar to the endomorphs but exceeded them on strength and motor tests. The mesomorphs were superior to all other categories in strength and motor ability and were larger on body bulk measures than the ectomorphs and mid-types. The ectomorphs were stronger and taller and had greater hip width than the mid-types.

Considerable consistency was found between the correlations of somatotype components with measures of maturity, body size, muscular strength and endurance, and motor elements; few differences between such correlations were significant at ages 9 through 12 and 12 through 17. The inverse ponderal index had the highest correlations with somatotype component for these age spans; the ranges of these correlations for the nine years were from $-.714$ to $-.854$ for endomorphy, $-.592$ to $-.753$ for mesomorphy, and .896 to .970 for ectomorphy. For body bulk measures, the correlations were moderately high; the direction of these correlations were positive for endomorphy and mesomorphy and negative for ectomorphy. The highest body bulk correlations were between endomorphy and skinfold total, .804 to .845. Other significant correlations with somatotype components over the nine-year period were: skeletal age, positive for endomorphy and mesomorphy and negative for ectomorphy; cable-tension strength average, positive for mesomorphy; Physical Fitness Index, bar dips, and standing broad jump distance, negative for endomorphy. For the age span 12 through 17, the following correlations were significant at all ages: sitting height × chest girth, positive for endomorphy and mesomorphy and negative for ectomorphy; Rogers' arm strength score, negative for endomorphy; standing broad jump × weight, positive for mesomorphy; total-body completion time, positive (negative connotation) for endomorphy.

The relationships between somatotype components increased considerably when contrasting structural measures were held constant. The greatest increases of partial correlations over corresponding zero-order correlations were obtained between ectomorphy and linearity when body bulk measures were partialed out. For example, at the age of 12, the zero-order correlation between ectomorphy and standing height was .164; with weight held constant, the partial correlation was .926.

Multiple correlations between somatotype components as dependent variables and measures of maturity, body size, muscular strength and endurance, and motor elements were mostly high enough to warrant prediction at each age 9 through 17.

Physical Structure

The anthropometric measures included in the Medford Boys' Growth Study for all twelve years were standing height, sitting height, leg length, hip width, weight, arm girth, chest girth, calf girth, and lung capacity. Abdominal, buttocks, and thigh girths were added after the first year and skinfold measures were included starting with the fourth year. Indices based on the anthropometric tests were also utilized.

Several factor analyses studies were made in attempts to identify a general maturity factor; the matrices included tests of maturity, body size, muscular strength and endurance, and motor elements. In longitudinal factor analyses with the same boys at each age 9 through 16, the following four rotated factors related to physical structure were identified: Body Bulk-Physique, all ages, high loadings of body bulk tests and somatotype components; Body Linearity, all ages, high loadings of standing and sitting heights and leg length; Relative Sitting Height, seven ages, high loadings of sitting height/standing height; Relative Lung Capacity, five ages, high loadings of lung capacity/standing height and lung capacity.

The intercorrelations of anthropometric measures and indices were presented for the same boys ages 9 through 16 by showing the correlations with selected tests. Weight correlated mostly in the .90's with girth and in the .60's and .70's with linear measures. The correlations with skinfold total were mostly in the .70's for other bulk tests and were insignificant with linear tests. Hip width correlated largely in the .50's to .70's with body bulk and linear measures. Standing height correlated in the .90's and high .80's with the other linear measures and mostly in the .60's and .70's with body bulk tests. The highest correlations with lung capacity, largely in the .70's, were for linear measures at ages 13, 14, and 15. Correlations mostly in the .80's and .90's were obtained at all ages between chest girth × height and weight, girth measures, and standing height. Generally, correlations with arm girth, standing height, and lung capacity were lower at age 16 than at other ages.

The correlations between weight, arm girth, hip width, and chest girth × standing height and muscular strength and endurance and motor tests were comparable for the ages 7 through 18. The highest correlations were with Strength Index and cable-tension strength average, between .326 and .640; the correlations with Physical Fitness Index, pull-ups, and bar dips were mostly significant but lower; with standing broad jump, 60-yard shuttle run, and total-body reaction time, the correlations were generally insignificant. The correlations of standing height and lung capacity with the strength and motor tests were lower than for body bulk measures and more were insignificant.

Mean growth curves were described for boys from 9 to 12 and 12 to 17 years of age for the various structural measures. Brief descriptions are: weight and arm girth: nearly straightline rise from ages 7 to 11, steeper rise in concave manner to 16, and deceleration at 17. Chest girth: linear rise from ages 7 to 10, deceleration and acceleration at 11 and 12, and similar to weight from 12 to 17. Abdominal, buttocks, thigh, and calf girths: irregular from ages 8 to 12, concave from 12 to 16, and deceleration at 17. Hip width: slightly convex from ages 7 to 11, concave to 15, and deceleration to 17. Standing height: nearly straightline rise from ages 7 to 12, acceleration to 14, and convex as curve decelerates to 17. Lung capacity: irregular, starting with straightline rise from 7 to 10, slight dip at age 12, and wandering convexity during older ages.

The ranges and standard deviations of selected anthropometric tests were presented to show the extent of individual differences. The standard deviations at ages 7 and 18 respectively were: weight, 6.3 and 22.6 lbs.; arm girth, 1.4 and 2.5 cm.; hip width, 1.1 and 1.7 cm.; standing height, 2.0 and 2.5 in.; lung capacity, 11.9 and 40.6 cu. in.

In longitudinal analyses, heavy and light groups and tall and short groups were formed at ages 9 and 12; the growth patterns of these groups were followed to 12 and 17 years respectively. The differences between the means on anthropometric tests were significant at all ages in the two age spans. A similar situation existed for anthropometric indices, except sitting height/standing height in the age 12 to 17 analysis.

Inter-age correlations were obtained for anthropometric tests and indices for boys aged 7 through 12 and 12 through 17. The adjacent inter-age correlations were highest for both groups. The median correlations were in the .90's for weight, all girth and linear measures, and the indices of chest girth $\times$ height, chest girth/height, and height/$\sqrt[3]{\text{weight}}$. As the number of intervening years increased, the magnitude of the inter-age correlations declined. The highest correlations when five years intervened were between .889 and .922 for thigh girth and the linear measures for the 7–12 age group; the comparable correlations for the 12–17 age group were lower, between .746 and .755.

Three skinfold measures were made at three sites, back of upper arm, inferior angle of scapula, and lateral abdomen. With 12-year-old subjects, the intercorrelations of the three skinfold tests clustered between .797 and .810; with total skinfold, they correlated between .908 and .963. The ranges of correlations between skinfold total and other measures were: .719 to .824 for endomorphy; −.578 to −.657 for ectomorphy; .269 to .379 for mesomorphy and skeletal age; .173 to .441 for Strength Index and cable-tension strength average; −.246 and −.346 for Physical Fitness Index, bar push-ups, and standing broad jump; .182 to .268 for 60-yard shuttle run (negative connotations).

Three aspects of the Wetzel Grid, physique channels, developmental levels, and developmental ratios, were studied for boys 9 through 15 years of age. For physique channels, the highest correlations were obtained with girth measures, between .449 and .519; a multiple correlation of .901 was found with arm girth, standing height, and weight as the independent variables. Low but significant correlations were obtained with weight, Physical Fitness Index (negative), hip width, and cable-tension strength average. The highest correlation with developmental level was .984 for weight; correlations between .839 and .905 were found for Strength Index and cable-tension strength average. For developmental ratio, the highest correlations were between .480 and .522 for calf girth, chest girth, weight, and arm girth; a multiple correlation of .922 was obtained with calf girth, chronological age, and weight as independent variables.

Muscular Strength and Endurance

The strength tests included in the Medford Boys' Growth Study were those composing the Strength Index (12) and 11 cable-tension tests (24). Three battery scores derived from these tests were utilized: Strength Index and cable-tension average for gross strength and Physical Fitness Index for relative strength. The muscular endurance tests were confined to the arm-shoulder area: pull-ups, bar push-ups, and Rogers' arm strength score (12).

Studies of strength test batteries were made. By multiple correlation procedures, the number of test items to obtain the Rogers' Strength Index was reduced separately for upper elementary, junior high, and senior high school boys. Through multiple regression equations, the Strength Index can be predicted and the norms used to obtain predicted Physical Fitness Indices. A cable-tension strength battery of four tests was constructed for upper elementary school boys. Norms were developed based on age and weight in the same manner Strength Index norms were determined; a Strength Composite and a Strength Quotient were proposed, which are comparable to the Strength Index and Physical Fitness Index respectively.

In longitudinal factor analysis studies involving tests of maturity, physique type, body size, muscular strength and endurance, and motor ability elements at each age from 9 through 16, the following strength and endurance rotated factors were identified: Arm-Shoulder Endurance, all ages, high loadings of Rogers' arm strength score, pull-ups, and bar push-ups; Arm Shoulder Strength, five ages, high loadings of elbow flexion, shoulder flexion, and shoulder inward rotation strengths; Leg-Back Lift Strength, five ages, high loadings of back and leg lifts; Lower-Leg Strength, three ages, high loadings of hip flexion and extension, knee flexion and extension, and ankle plantar flexion; Grip Strength, three ages, high loadings of right and left grips; General Strength, two ages, high loadings of all strength tests.

The highest intercorrelations among the four dynamometric tests at the ages 9 through 16 were between right and left grips, .614 to .852. Generally, the highest correlations among the cable-tension strength tests were between antagonists; the highest of these correlations were between hip flexion and extension, .582 to .806. The test correlating highest at all ages with Strength Index was leg strength, .850 to .951. Nearly all correlations between cable-tension strength average and individual tests were in the .60's and .70's.

For boys at each age 7, 9, 12, 15, and 17, the highest correlations between cable-tension strength average and maturity, physique type, and motor ability tests were: .338 to .536, arm girth; .319 to .591, weight; .309 to .578, chest girth × standing height; .521 to .704, standing broad jump distance. Multiple correlations between .633 and .742 were obtained with this strength criterion; the most prevalent independent variables were standing broad jump × weight and 60-yard shuttle run. The highest correlations with Strength Index were between .504 and .713 for standing broad jump × weight. The multiple correlations ranged from .620 to .887; the most important independent variables were Rogers' arm strength score and standing broad jump × weight.

Mean connecting growth curves for muscular strength tests for boys 7 to 12 and 12 to 17 years of age are described as follows: Cable-tension strength average: straightline rise from ages 7 to 10, steeper rise to 16, and deceleration at 17 years. Shoulder flexion and shoulder inward rotation: slight increase ages 7 to 8, decrease at 9, and straightline rise to 17 years. Hip flexion: straightline rise from ages 7 to 10, dip at 11, and irregular rise to 17 years. Knee extension (most irregular): concave ages 7 to 9, plateau at 10, rise at 11, plateau at 12, additional irregularities to 16, and decline at 17 years. Ankle plantar flexion: straightline rise ages 8 to 12 and steep rise to 17 years. Left grip: straightline rise from ages 7 to 17 years, except for a plateau between 9 and 10 years. Back lift: decline from ages 8 to 9, steep rise to 11, decline at 12, and rise to 17 years.

The ranges and standard deviations of various strength tests were presented to show the extent of individual differences for boys. The standard deviations at ages 7 or 8 and 18 respectively were: cable-tension strength average, 5.2 and 27.2 pounds; ankle plantar flexion, 6.8 and 71.6 pounds; Strength Index, 117.6 and 506.9; leg lift, 81.5 and 304.8 pounds; right grip, 7.0 and 19.0 pounds.

Inter-age correlations were obtained for the strength tests for boys 7 through 12 and 12 through 17 years. Generally, these correlations were low, both for adjacent ages and when several ages intervened; the highest adjacent correlations were .725, .787, and .831 for left grip, cable-tension strength average, and Strength Index for the ages 12 to 17.

Special attention was given to the Physical Fitness Index inasmuch as it is a relative strength measure. This index correlated between .239 and .546 with gross strength tests and batteries; it had insignificant correlations with skeletal age, significant negative correlations with endomorphy and positive correlations with endomorphy, low negative correlations with body size measures, and positive correlations with motor ability test items. Multiple correlations with Physical Fitness Index ranged between .537 and .855 for the ages of 9, 12, 15, and 17; the most prevalent independent variables were Rogers' arm strength score and bar push-ups. Individual differences in Physical Fitness Index, as reflected by the standard deviation, ranged between 16.9 and 21.6 for the ages 8 through 18.

High, average, and low strength groups were formed at each age 10, 13, and 16 based separately on Strength Index, cable-tension strength average, and Physical Fitness Index. For the cable-tension strength average, the significant differences between means at the .01 level included: skeletal age at all ages for the high-average and high-low groups; all comparisons for weight, arm girth, thigh girth, and chest girth × height and most comparisons with standing height; endomorphy for all comparisons at age 10; standing broad jump and total-body reaction time for the high-low comparisons at all ages. For these comparisons, the stronger groups had highest means. By contrast, the significant differences for the Physical Fitness Index groups were confined largely to the high-low and average-low comparisons with the weaker group having highest means; the main exceptions were no significant differences for skeletal age and higher ectomorphy means for the stronger groups.

The three arm-shoulder endurance measures were given separate attention. The ranges of their intercorrelations for boys ages 9 through 16 were: .844 to .949, Rogers' arm strength score and bar push-ups; .636 to .829, Rogers' arm strength score and pull-ups; and .518 to .720, bar push-ups and pull-ups. For the same ages, the correlations of these endurance measures with endomorphy and body size measures were negative and mostly significant; low positive correlations, mostly insignificant, were obtained with maturity and gross strength measures, except between Rogers' arm strength score and Strength Index for ages 13 through 16 (.727 to .825). The growth curve for bar push-ups showed a slow rise from ages 8 to 12, followed by a steep rise to 17 years. The standard deviations at ages 8 and 18 respectively were 2.5 and 7.0 for bar push-ups, 3.0 and 3.5 for pull-ups, and 27.5 and 219.5 for Rogers' arm strength score.

Motor and Athletic Abilities

The motor ability test items included in the Medford Boys' Growth Study were standing broad jump, 60-yard shuttle run, and total-body and arm-hand reaction, movement, and completion times. The athletic abilities of the subjects participating in interscholastic athletics were judged as outstanding, regular players, and substitutes at the upper elementary, junior high, and senior high school levels.

Four methods of scoring the standing broad jump were investigated. The following multiple correlations obtained with 12-year-old boys contrast their merits in reflecting independent variables. (a) Distance × weight, .902: weight, Strength Index, and skinfold total. (b) Weight/distance, .908: abdominal girth, Physical Fitness Index, and skinfold total. (c) Leg length/distance, .717: Physical Fitness Index, leg length, 10-foot run, and skinfold total. (d) Distance jumped, .690: Physical Fitness Index, 10-foot run, sitting height, skinfold total, and cable-tension strength average. At ages 12 and 15, distance jumped correlated highest with Rogers' arm strength score (.557 and .638), 60-yard shuttle run (−.574 and −.616), and total-body reaction time (−.469 and −.525). A mean growth curve and the extent of individual differences for distance jumped were presented for boys from 7 to 18 years.

A multiple correlation of .650 was obtained for 14-year-old boys with 60-yard shuttle run; the independent variables were standing broad jump, Physical Fitness Index, and total-body reaction time. A mean growth curve and the extent of individual differences were given for this event.

For 13-year-old boys, total-body and arm-hand reaction times correlated .44. Neither of these reaction measures correlated significantly at the .05 level with 26 tests of maturity, body size, strength, and motor ability elements. Significant correlations were obtained for movement and completion times, especially with 60-yard shuttle run (.40 to .58) and standing broad jump (−.26 to −.49) for both tests and with Physical Fitness Index (−.58 and −.48) for total-body movement and completion times. Athletes had significantly faster reaction times than nonparticipants at all ages in junior high school.

The study of athletes is a unique phase of the Medford Boys' Growth Study, since interscholastic athletics are conducted in upper elementary, junior high, and senior high schools. In this monograph, data were assembled in support of basic conclusions regarding the characteristics of athletes. These conclusions follow.

1. Boys who make and are successful on athletic teams are definitely superior to their peers in maturity, physique, body size, muscular strength, endurance, and power, and motor ability. Thus, the decision as to whether boys are physically

ready for such participation, commonly made in elementary and junior high schools, should be determined by factors other than chronological age.

2. Some fundamental characteristics of 12-year-old elementary school, 15-year-old junior high school, and 17-year-old senior high school athletes are clearly evident at younger ages, although differences in characteristics exist at the three school levels.

3. The longitudinal significance of the physical characteristics of athletes may be extended to specific sports and some variations in these characteristics exist for the various sports and at different school levels.

4. The general physical fitness of all boys, as reflected in their relative strength, is an indirect contributing factor to a higher physical fitness level of athletes, especially in elementary and junior high schools.

5. The gross strength of athletes participating in all interscholastic sports is consistently high at all school levels.

6. The explosive muscular power of athletes participating in all interscholastic sports is consistently high at all school levels.

7. Although successful athletes generally have common characteristics, the pattern of these characteristics varies from athlete to athlete; where a successful athlete is low in an important trait, he compensates in another.

8. Outstanding elementary school athletes may not be outstanding in junior high school, and outstanding junior high school athletes may not have been outstanding in elementary school. Longitudinal test profiles reveal distinguishing differences between athletes in these categories.

Differences between boys who elected and who did not elect physical education in the eleventh grade were studied; for each category, differentiation was made between those who participated and who did not participate in interscholastic athletics. Although the differences were not always significant, those boys who did not elect physical education and did not participate in interscholastic athletics were inferior to all other groups on 22 tests of maturity, physique, body size, muscular strength and endurance, motor performances, and scholastic achievement. The tests showing generally significant differences were 60-yard shuttle run, Rogers' arm strength score, bar push-ups, total-body reaction time, and amount of participation in out-of-school physical education activities at the time of physical education election. One year later, these same boys had not gained as much as physical education electees in tests of muscular strength and endurance.

Implications for Physical Education

This section presents some major implications of results from the Medford Boys' Growth Study for physical education. No doubt, the reader will observe others from a critical review of the monograph.

Tests

A number of tests have been examined and evaluated; others have been modified or simplified; and new test batteries have been constructed. The application of these tests to physical education are indicated below.

SKELETAL AGE. Skeletal age (49) is not a test that can be given routinely in physical education, since it requires X-ray equipment and darkroom facilities. However, for those physical educators who wish to use it as a maturational test in research studies, the reduction of bones for the assessment of skeletal age from around 30 to four is a time-saving advantage; the four bones are the capitate, metacarpal III, proximal phalanx III, and middle phalanx III. The modification of the X-ray equipment to restrict X-ray exposure may also be noted.

PUBESCENT ASSESSMENT. Once boys enter adolescence, pubescent assessment may be used to evaluate their physical maturation. In the Medford study, pubescent status was assessed in accordance with the five categories described by Greulich and associates (50) as representing successive stages in the development of the genitals and the pubic hair. Of three ages, 10, 13, and 16, maturation was differentiated most effectively at 13 years, although this method was not as sensitive as was skeletal age; at 16 years, maturational differentiation was more limited; at 10 years, little or no value could be attributed to this method. Considerable overlapping in skeletal age occurred for the pubescent categories at single ages. With few exceptions, the 13- and 16-year-old boys who were advanced in pubescent development had higher mean scores on body size, strength, and motor tests.

SOMATOTYPE. Multiple correlations between each of the somato-type components (92) and various anthropometric tests and indices were high enough to warrant prediction of the individual components. Regression equations were computed for high multiple correlations for each age 9 through 17. These equations appear in Chapter 3.

STRENGTH INDEX. Multiple correlations between .977 and .998 were obtained between the Strength Index (12) and various items composing the SI battery separately for boys in upper elementary, junior high, and senior high schools. At each school level, the number of test items was reduced from the original seven composing the battery. Regression equations for each of the multiple correlations were computed; these equations appear in Chapter 5. By use of the appropriate equation, the physical educator can approximate each boy's SI; then, the regular SI norms can be used to estimate Physical Fitness Indices.

CABLE-TENSION STRENGTH BATTERY. For boys in the upper elementary school, grades four, five, and six, a multiple correlation of .98 was obtained between the average of 18 cable-tension strength tests (24) and the four tests of shoulder extension, trunk extension, knee extension, and ankle plantar flexion. From these four tests, two battery scores were formed, as follows: Strength Composite: a gross strength score, obtained by adding the strength scores achieved on the four cable-tension tests. Strength Quotient: a strength score relative to age and weight, derived by dividing the normal Strength Composite into the achieved Strength Composite and multiplying by 100. These battery scores are comparable in nature to the Strength Index and Physical Index respectively.

ARM-SHOULDER ENDURANCE SCORES. The so-called "arm strength scores" in common use are actually not strength scores of the arm and shoulder muscles; while strength is necessary to perform pull-ups and bar push-ups, the basic items in such scores reflect the endurance of these muscles. In the Medford study, two arm strength scores were utilized, those by McCloy (73) and by Rogers (12, 84). McCloy's arm strength score correlated around .95 with weight, thus is primarily a function of weight rather than muscular endurance. An attempt was made to improve the function of Rogers' arm strength score, but without success. This arm strength score was found to be the best score available in its relationship to motor ability performances.

STANDING BROAD JUMP. The common method of scoring standing broad jump performance (12) is by distance jumped. Distance jumped should be considered a relative power test, since the amount of weight projected is not considered in the score. In the Medford series, several methods of scoring performance in this jump were investigated. The following are mentioned with their multiple correlation relationships (the figures in parentheses are the multiple correlations for the respective methods): (a) Distance jumped (.690): Physical Fitness Index, 10-foot run, sitting height, skinfold total, and cable-tension strength average. (b) Distance × weight (.902): weight, Strength Index, and skinfold total. (c) Weight/distance (.908): abdominal girth, Physical Fitness Index, and skinfold total. (d) Leg Length/distance (.717): Physical Fitness Index, leg length, 10-foot run, and skinfold total. When comparing athletes and nonparticipants, only distance jumped and distance × weight produced significant mean differences.

Curriculum Implications

While analyses pertaining to the mental and the personal-social aspects of the Medford Boys' Growth Study were not presented in this monograph, some reference will be made to these results in drawing curriculum implications. The supporting data will not be presented. Suffice it to say that the interrelationships between physical-motor, academic achievement, and personal-social adjustment were low and frequently significant.

Perhaps, too, it should be stated that, as a group, Medford boys are superior both physically and scholastically. An indication of physical superiority is the achievement of consistently high averages at all ages on the Physical Fitness Index test. The annual PFI's of the boys at each age from 8 through 18 years of age ranged from 105 to 118 (when, according to normal expectations, the mean is 100 and the third quartile is 115). The superior athletic records of Medford High School athletic teams are well-known in Oregon; Medford teams have consistently been in contention for state championships and have frequently won them. Academically, the school district has recorded average performances well above national norms on standard tests; between 55 and 60 percent of its graduates go on to college or university. In the Medford project, the effects of these superiorities are not known. It can be said that, generally speaking, the relationships obtained were for subjects at higher than normal levels of physical status and academic achievements; this fact in itself may imply a positive relationship between the two. However, the effects on relationships introduced by the normal number of physically underdeveloped boys were not adequately examined.

With these considerations in mind, curriculum applications for physical education are made below, based in results of the Medford Boys' Growth Study.

1. The analyses of growth data through factor analyses, correlations, and mean differences between discrete groups formed on various tests presented in this monograph have implications for physical education, as follows:

   a. Positive loadings were found on most tests at ages 9, 10, and 14, which may infer that these ages are especially favorable for physical education. Negative loadings, indicating growth lags, were general at age 11 especially, but also at ages 12, 13, 15, and 16, which may suggest a special need for developmental activities during these years.
   b. The factoring of muscular strength tests revealed considerable specificity at ages 9 to 14 inclusive; at ages 15 and 16, a single general strength factor occurred. The need to direct strengthening exercises at individual muscle groups seems desirable during the younger ages; these exercises can be more general to the total musculature at the older ages.
   c. Differences in the physical maturity of boys have greater implications for effective participation in physical activities between the ages of 9 and 15 inclusive, especially at age 15. At age 17, maturity has less significance. As far as is known,

participation in vigorous physical activity does not affect skeletal age. However, differences in the maturity of boys needs to be considered in planning physical education programs.

d. Body size and gross strength are well related, but small boys can compensate for strength differences through developmental exercise. On the other hand, little relationship exists between body size and relative strength, obviously, since strength norms are typically based on age and weight.

e. As has been known, but shown again in this monograph, an excess amount of adipose tissue is a hindrance to motor activity. Every effort should be made in physical education to secure weight reduction for obese boys through medical consultation, diet, and exercise.

2. Orientation of boys and girls to the need for exercise as a way of life should be stressed in order to attain and maintain total effectiveness. Studies have shown that lack of exercise invites the early onslaught of degenerative diseases, the ready tendency toward obesity, a physically unfit existence, and generally inept motor performances. In addition, it affects mental accomplishments and personal-social relations.

3. Some of the physical traits underlying the individual's total effectiveness are not subject to appreciable improvement through exercise; these traits include maturity, physique type, and body size and proportion. However, such traits need to be considered in forming judgments of each child's capabilities. Due to phenotype changes in somatotype components, it may be inferred, however, that endomorphy may be reduced through diet and exercise, that mesomorphy may be increased through muscular development, and that extreme ectomorphy effects may be alleviated through increased mesomorphy.

4. Other physical traits related to the boy's effectiveness as a total being are improvable through proper utilization of exercise. These traits include muscular strength, muscular endurance, muscular power, and circulatory endurance. Tests of these traits should be included in the physical education program; and appropriate activities should be selected and presented so that boys and girls can reach and maintain proper standards on such tests.

5. Medford and other research shows that boys performing low on tests of muscular strength, muscular endurance, and circu-

latory endurance, three fundamental physical fitness components, are especially handicapped in many ways. These individuals are prone to degenerative diseases and obesity, have greater difficulty in scholastic achievement, and do not maintain personal-social relationships readily. Provisions should be made in physical education to identify such physically unfit individuals and to provide effective programs for their improvement.

6. The physical educator should apply appropriate tests and other evaluative procedures, so that he may determine, ideally, the maturity, physique, structural, strength, and motor characteristics of his pupils. Where choices must be made for practical considerations, tests of gross and relative muscular strength, endurance, and muscular power should have priority.

7. The motor performance expectations, including performances on strength and endurance tests, should be judged, in part at least, from a realization of the individual's strengths and weaknesses, especially as they apply to maturity, physique, and body size characteristics. Boys with a high degree of endomorphy are definitely limited in physical activities; on the other hand, the mesomorph is well adapted to motor performances. The small, immature, and weak boy is definitely handicapped in physical education when in competition with the large, mature, and strong boy. In general, mature, mesomorphic, and large boys have great muscular strength and power. However, compensations for deficiencies in certain of these traits may be made by strengths in others; for example, the small boy with high relative strength, speed, and agility may perform well in many types of motor skills.

8. The usual system of scheduling physical education by free periods after all academic classes are formed should be abandoned. At times, physical education classes are scheduled by random assignments within a given grade; at other times, boys from a complete school level, such as junior high school, are assigned to the same class. This whole presentation on individual differences cries out that these practices are wrong. Means must be found for effective grouping for and/or within physical education classes in order to insure reasonable homogeneity of motor potentialities and to provide an adequate opportunity for meeting individual physical fitness needs.

9. The physical educator should consider boys as total, integrated beings. Each child brings more than his body to the gymnasium, the playground, and the athletic field; he also brings his mind, his emotions, and his unique personal and social traits. Those physical educators who have been privileged to conduct case studies of physically unfit individuals have inevitably been forced to consider their total integrity. Physical educators should take the initiative in presenting such evidence to administrators, classroom teachers, parents, and the public. Their action should be reciprocated, since each child brings to the classroom not only his mind, but also his body, his emotions, and his personal-social traits.

References

1. Bailey, Don C., "Longitudinal Analyses of Strength and Motor Development of Boys Ages Twelve through Seventeen Years," Microcard Doctoral Dissertation, University of Oregon, 1968.
2. Bayley, Nancy, and Samuel R. Pinneau, "Tables for Predicting Adult Height from Skeletal Age," as contained in W. W. Greulich and S. I. Pyle, *Radiographic Atlas of Skeletal Development of the Hand and Wrist*, 2nd ed. Stanford, Calif.: Stanford University Press, 1959.
3. Bell, Richard Q., "An Accelerated Longitudinal Approach," *Child Development*, 24, No. 2 (June, 1953), pp. 144–152.
4. ———, "An Experimental Test of the Accelerated Longitudinal Approach," *Child Development*, 25, No. 2 (December, 1954), pp. 281–286.
5. Borms, Jan, "Relationships Between Selected Maturity, Physique, Body Size, and Motor Factors and the Gross and Relative Strength of Ten, Thirteen, and Sixteen-Year-Old Boys," Microcard Master's Thesis, University of Oregon, 1965.
6. Brozek, Josef, "Body Dimensions and the Estimation of Men's Reference Weight," *Science*, 124, No. 3224 (October, 1956), p. 685.
7. ———, *Body Measurement and Nutrition*. Detroit: Wayne University Press, 1956.
8. ———, "To Be or Not to Be Fat," *Journal of American Dietetic Association*, 29, (May, 1953), p. 344.
9. Bruch, Hilde, "The Grid for Evaluating Physical Fitness (Wetzel),"

Journal of American Medical Association, 118, No. 15 (April 11, 1942), p. 1289.

10. Burt, John J., "Factor Analysis of Potential Maturity Indicators of Thirteen-Year-Old Boys," Microcard Doctoral Dissertation, University of Oregon, 1962.

11. Carter, Gavin H., "Reconstruction of the Rogers Strength and Physical Fitness Indices for Upper Elementary, Junior High, and Senior High School Boys," Microcard Doctoral Dissertation, University of Oregon, 1957.

12. Clarke, H. Harrison, *Application of Measurement to Health and Physical Education,* 4th ed. Englewood Cliffs, N.J.: Prentice-Hall, Inc., 1967.

13. ———, "Characteristics of the Young Athlete: A Longitudinal Look," *AMA Proceedings of the Eighth Annual Conference on the Medical Aspects of Sports,* November 27, 1966, p. 49.

14. ———, "Characteristics of the Young Athlete: A Longitudinal Look," *Kinesiology Review 1968,* Washington, D. C.: American Association for Health, Physical Education, and Recreation, 1968.

15. ———, "Improvement of Objective Strength Tests of Muscle Groups by Cable-Tension Methods," *Research Quarterly,* 21, No. 4 (December, 1950), p. 399.

16. ———, *Muscular Strength and Endurance in Man.* Englewood Cliffs, N.J.: Prentice-Hall, Inc., 1966.

17. ———, "Nature and Extent of Individual Differences and Their Significance for Physical Education and Athletics," *Oregon School Study Council Bulletin,* 10, No. 10 (April, 1967), pp. 1–35.

18. ———, "Objective Strength Tests of Affected Muscle Groups Involved in Orthopedic Disabilities, *Research Quarterly,* 19, No. 2 (May, 1948), p. 118.

19. ———, "Relation of Physical Structure to Motor Performance of Males," *American Academy of Physical Education, Professional Contributions No. 6,* November, 1958, p. 71.

20. ———, Theodore L. Bailey, and Clayton T. Shay, "New Objective Strength Tests of Muscle Groups by Cable-Tension Methods," *Research Quarterly,* 23, No. 2 (May, 1952), p. 136.

21. ———, and Jan Borms, "Differences in Maturity, Physical, and Motor Traits for Boys of High, Average, and Low Gross and Relative Strength," *Journal of Sports Medicine and Physical Fitness,* 8, No. 3 (September, 1968), p. 3.

22. ———, and Gavin H. Carter, "Oregon Simplifications of the Strength and Physical Fitness Indices," *Research Quarterly,* 30, No. 1 (March, 1959), p. 3.

23. ———, and David H. Clarke, *Advanced Statistics.* Englewood Cliffs, N.J.: Prentice-Hall, Inc., 1972.

24. ———, and David H. Clarke, *Developmental and Adapted Physical Education.* Englewood Cliffs, N.J.: Prentice-Hall, Inc., 1963.

25. ———, and Ernest W. Degutis, "Comparison of Skeletal Age and Various Physical and Motor Factors with the Pubescent Development of 10, 13, and 16-Year-Old Boys," *Research Quarterly,* 33, No. 3 (October, 1962), pp. 356–368.

26. ———, and Ernest W. Degutis, "Relationships Between Standing Broad Jump and Various Anthropometric and Strength Tests of 12-Year-Old Boys," *Research Quarterly,* 35, No. 3 (October, 1964), p. 258.

27. ———, L. Richard Geser, and Stanley B. Hunsdon, "Comparison of Upper Arm Measurements by Use of Roentgenogram and Anthropometric Techniques," *Research Quarterly,* 27, No. 4 (December, 1956), p. 379.

28. ———, and Don Glines, "Relationships of Reaction, Movement, and Completion Times to Motor, Strength, Anthropometric, and Maturity Measures of 13-Year-Old Boys," *Research Quarterly,* 33, No. 2 (May, 1962), p. 194.

29. ———, and James C. E. Harrison, "Differences in Physical and Motor Traits Between Boys of Advanced, Normal, and Retarded Maturity," *Research Quarterly,* 33, No. 1 (March, 1962), pp. 13–25.

30. ———, and Noel R. Hayman, "Reduction of Bone Assessments for the Skeletal Age Determinations of Boys," *Research Quarterly,* 33, No. 2 (May, 1962), pp. 202–207.

31. ———, Robert N. Irving, and Barbara Honeyman Heath, "Relation of Maturity, Structural, and Strength Measures to the Somatotypes of Boys 9 Through 15 Years of Age," *Research Quarterly,* 32, No. 4 (December, 1961), pp. 449–460.

32. ———, and Richard A. Munroe, *Test Manual: Oregon Cable-Tension Strength Test Batteries for Boys and Girls from Fourth Grade Through College.* Eugene, Ore.: Microcard Publications in Health, Physical Education, and Recreation, 1970.

33. ———, and Arne L. Olson, "Characteristics of 15-Year-Old Boys Who Demonstrate Various Accomplishments and Difficulties," *Child Development,* 38, No. 2 (June, 1965), p. 559.

34. ———, and Kay H. Peterson, "Contrast of Maturational, Structural, and Strength Characteristics of Athletes and Nonathletes 10 to 15 Years of Age," *Research Quarterly,* 32, No. 3 (October, 1961), p. 163.

35. ———, and Theodore G. Schopf, "Construction of a Muscular Strength Test for Boys in Grades 4, 5, and 6," *Research Quarterly,* 33, No. 4 (December, 1962), p. 515.

36. ———, and Morgan E. Shelley, "Maturity, Structure, Strength, Motor Ability and Intelligence Test Profiles of Outstanding Elementary and Junior High School Athletes," *Physical Educator*, 18, No. 4 (December, 1961), p. 132.

37. ———, and J. Stuart Wickens, "Maturity, Structural, Strength, and Motor Ability Growth Curves of Boys 9 Through 17 Years of Age," *Research Quarterly*, 33, No. 1 (March, 1962), p. 26.

38. Cureton, Thomas K., "Vital Capacity as a Test of Condition for High School Boys," *Research Quarterly*, 7, No. 4 (December, 1936), p. 80.

39. Day, James A. P., "Longitudinal Analyses of Maturity and Physical Growth of Boys Ages Seven Through Twelve Years," Microcard Doctoral Dissertation, University of Oregon, 1967.

40. Degutis, Ernest W., "Relationships Between the Standing Broad Jump and Various Maturity, Structural, and Strength Measures of Twelve-Year-Old Boys," Microcard Master's Thesis, University of Oregon, 1959.

41. ———, "Relationship Between Selected Physical and Motor Factors and the Pubescent Development of Ten, Thirteen, and Sixteen-Year-Old Boys," Microcard Doctoral Dissertation, University of Oregon, 1960.

42. Flynn, Kenneth W., "Relationship Between Various Standing Broad Jump Measures and Strength, Speed, Body Size, and Physique Measures of Twelve-Year-Old Boys," Microcard Master's Research Paper, University of Oregon, 1966.

43. Franzen, Raymond, *Physical Measures of Growth and Nutrition*. New York: American Child Health Association, 1929, p. 48.

44. Garn, S. M., and E. L. Gorman, "Comparison of Pinch-Caliper and Teleoroentgenogrammetric Measurements of Subcutaneous Fat," *Human Biology*, 28, No. 4 (December, 1956), p. 407.

45. Gates, Donald D., and R. P. Sheffield, "Tests of Change of Direction as Measurement of Different Kinds of Motor Ability in Boys of the Seventh, Eighth, and Ninth Grades," *Research Quarterly*, 11, No. 3 (October, 1940), p. 136.

46. Geser, L. Richard, "Skinfold Measures of Potential Maturity Indicators of Nine-Year-Old Boys," Microcard Doctoral Dissertation, University of Oregon, 1965.

47. Glines, Don, "Relationships of Reaction, Movement, and Completion Times to Certain Motor, Strength, Anthropometric, and Maturity Measures," Microcard Doctoral Dissertation, University of Oregon, 1960.

48. Gray, Robin K., K. B. Start, and D. J. Glencross, "A Test of Leg Power," *Research Quarterly*, 33, No. 1 (March, 1964), p. 44.

49. Greulich, W. W., and S. I. Pyle, *Radiographic Atlas of Skeletal*

Development of the Hand and Wrist. Stanford, Calif.: Stanford University Press, 1959.

50. ———, and others, "Somatic and Endocrine Studies of Puberal and Adolescent Boys," *Monograph of the Society for Research in Child Development,* 7, No. 3, Serial No. 33 (1942).

51. Harman, Harry, *Modern Factor Analysis,* 2nd ed. Chicago: The University of Chicago Press, 1967.

52. Harrison, James C. E., "The Relationships Between Selected Physical and Motor Factors and the Skeletal Maturity of Nine, Twelve, and Fifteen-Year-Old Boys," Microcard Doctoral Dissertation, University of Oregon, 1959.

53. Hayman, Noel R., "Reduction of the Number of Bone Assessments Necessary for Skeletal Age Determination of Adolescent Boys," Microcard Doctoral Dissertation, University of Oregon, 1959.

54. Heath, Barbara Honeyman, "Need for Modification of Somatotype Methodology," *American Journal of Physical Anthropology,* 24, No. 1 (January, 1966), p. 87.

55. Hotelling, H., "The Selection of Variates for Use in Prediction, with Some Comments on the General Problem of Nuisance Parameters," *Annals of Mathematical Statistics,* 11 (1940), pp. 271–283.

56. Howe, Bruce L., "Test Profiles of Outstanding Twelve-Year-Old Elementary School Athletes at None, Twelve, and Fifteen Years of Age," Microcard Master's Thesis, University of Oregon, 1966.

57. Hunsicker, Paul A., and Richard L. Donnelly, "Instruments to Measure Strength," *Research Quarterly,* 26, No. 4 (December, 1955), p. 408.

58. Hunt, Edward E., and William H. Barton, "The Inconsistency of Physique in Adolescent Boys and Other Limitations of Somatotyping," *American Journal of Physical Anthropology,* 3, No. 1 (March, 1959), pp. 323–341.

59. Irving, Robert N., "Comparison of Maturity, Structural, and Muscular Strength Measures for Five Somatotype Categories of Boys Nine Through Fifteen Years of Age," Microcard Doctoral Dissertation, University of Oregon, 1959.

60. Jones, Harold E., *Motor Performance and Growth.* Berkeley: University of California Press, 1949.

61. Jordan, David B., "Longitudinal Analysis of Strength and Motor Development of Boys Ages Seven Through Twelve Years," Microcard Doctoral Dissertation, University of Oregon, 1966.

62. Kaiser, H. F., "The Varimax Criterion for Analytic Rotation in Factor Analysis," *Psychometrika,* 23, No. 3 (September, 1958), pp. 187–200.

63. Kelly, Brian J., "Single-Year and Longitudinal Comparisons of

Maturity, Physique, Structural, Strength, and Motor Characteristics of Seventeen- and Eighteen-Year-Old Athletes and Nonparticipants," Microcard Doctoral Dissertation, University of Oregon, 1969.

64. Kretschmer, E., *Physique and Character*, trans. W. J. H. Sprott. New York: Harcourt, Brace and Co., Inc., 1925.

65. Krogman, Wilton M., "Constitutional Types," *Ciba Symposia*, 3, No. 9 (December, 1941), pp. 1058–1087.

66. Kurimoto, Etsuo, "Longitudinal Analysis of Maturity, Structural, Strength, and Motor Development of Boys Fifteen Through Eighteen Years of Age,," Microcard Doctoral Dissertation, University of Oregon, 1963.

67. Lasker, Gabriel W., "The Effects of Partial Starvation on Somatotype," *American Journal of Physical Anthropology*, 3, No. 3 (September, 1947), pp. 323–341.

68. Lawson, Patricia A., "An Analysis of a Group of Motor Fitness Tests Which Purport to Measure Agility as They Apply to Elementary School Girls," Microcard Master's Thesis, University of Oregon, 1959.

69. McCloy, Charles H., "An Analysis for Multiple Factors of Physical Growth at Different Age Levels," *Child Development*, 11, No. 4 (December, 1940), pp. 249–277.

70. ———, "A New Method of Scoring Chinning and Dipping," *Research Quarterly*, 2, No. 4 (December, 1931), p. 132.

71. ———, *Appraising Physical Status: Methods and Norms*, Iowa City: University of Iowa Studies in Child Welfare, No. 15, June, 1938.

72. ———, *Appraising Physical Status: The Selection of Measurements*, Iowa City: University of Iowa Studies in Child Welfare, No. 12, March, 1936.

73. ———, "Recent Studies in the Sargent Jump," *Research Quarterly*, 3, No. 2 (May, 1932), p. 235.

74. Mayer, Jean, *Overweight: Causes, Cost, and Control*. Englewood Cliffs, N.J.: Prentice-Hall, Inc., 1968, p. 31.

75. Mitchell, Reid J., "Single-Year and Longitudinal Comparisons of Maturity, Physique, Structural, Motor, and Strength Characteristics of Fifteen-Year-Old Junior High School Athletes and Nonparticipants," Microcard Doctoral Dissertation, University of Oregon, 1968.

76. Morton, Alan R., "Comparison of Sheldon's Trunk-Index and Anthroposcopic Methods of Somatotyping in Their Relationships to the Maturity, Structure, and Motor Ability of the Same Boys Nine Through Sixteen Years of Age," Microcard Doctoral Dissertation, University of Oregon, 1967.

77. Munroe, Richard A., "Relationships Between Somatotype Components and Maturity, Structural, Strength, Muscular Endurance, and Motor Ability Measures of Twelve-Year-Old Boys," Microcard Doctoral Dissertation, University of Oregon, 1964.

78. ———, H. Harrison Clarke, and Barbara Honeyman Heath, "A Somatotype Method for Young Boys," *American Journal of Physical Anthropology*, n.s. 30, No. 2 (March, 1969), p. 195.

79. Petersen, Kay H., "Contrast of Maturity, Structural, and Strength Measures Between Nonparticipants and Athletic Groups of Boys Ten to Fifteen Years of Age," Microcard Doctoral Dissertation, University of Oregon, 1959.

80. Phillips, D. Allen, "Annual Factor Analysis of Potential Maturity Indicators of the Same Boys from Nine Through Sixteen Years of Age," Microcard Doctoral Dissertation, University of Oregon, 1968.

81. Pryor, J. W., "Development of the Bones as Shown by the X-ray Method," *Bulletin of the State College of Kentucky*, Series 2, No. 5, 1905.

82. Radcliff, Robert A., "Relationships Between the Sixty-Yard Shuttle Run and Various Maturity, Physique, Structural, Strength, and Motor Characteristics of Fourteen-Year-Old Boys," Microcard Master's Thesis, University of Oregon, 1963.

83. Ragsdale, Lee V., "Contrast of Maturity, Physical, and Scholastic Measures Between Boys Who Elect and Who Do Not Elect Physical Education in Grade Eleven," Microcard Doctoral Dissertation, University of Oregon, 1966.

84. Rogers, Frederick Rand, *Physical Capacity Tests in the Administration of Physical Education*. New York: Bureau of Publications, Teachers College, Columbia University, 1926.

85. Sandstrom, E. Roy, "Longitudinal Analyses of Total-Body Reaction Time and Movement Time of Junior High School Boys," Microcard Master's Thesis, University of Oregon, 1967.

86. Santa Maria, D. Lainé, "Longitudinal Analysis of Maturity and Physical Growth for Boys Ages Twelve Through Seventeen Years," Microcard Doctoral Dissertation, University of Oregon, August, 1968.

87. ———, "The Relationship of Rogers' Arm Strength to Various Other Types of Strength Measures," Microcard Master's Research Paper, University of Oregon, 1968.

88. Sargent, Dudley A., "Intercollegiate Strength Tests," *American Physical Education Review*, 2, No. 4 (December, 1897), p. 108.

89. Schopf, Theodore G., "Construction of a Muscular Strength Test for Boys in Grades Four, Five, and Six," Microcard Doctoral Dissertation, University of Oregon, 1961.

90. Sekeres, David J., "Relationships Between Selected Physical, Motor, Scholastic, and Psycho-Personal Factors and the Skeletal Maturity of Nine, Twelve, Fifteen, and Seventeen-Year-Old Boys," Microcard Doctoral Dissertation, University of Oregon, 1969.

91. Sheldon, William H., "Brief Communication on Somatotyping, Psychiatyping and Other Sheldonian Delinquencies, 1965," Paper presented to the Royal Society of Medicine, London, England, May 13, 1965.

92. ———, C. Wesley Dupertuis, and Eugene McDermott, *Atlas of Men.* New York: Harper & Brothers, 1954.

93. ———, Nolan, D. C. Lewis, and Ashton M. Tenney, "Psychiatric Patterns and Physical Constitution," in *Schizophrenia: Current Concepts and Research*, D. V. Sira Sankar, ed. Hicksville, N.Y.: PJD Publications, Ltd., 1968, pp. 838–912.

94. ———, S. S. Stevens, and W. B. Tucker, *The Varieties of Human Physique.* New York: Harper and Brothers, 1940.

95. Shelley, Morgan E., "Maturity, Structure, Strength, Motor Ability, and Intelligence Test Profiles of Outstanding Elementary School and Junior High School Athletes," Microcard Master's Thesis, University of Oregon, 1960.

96. Sinclair, Gary D., "Stability of Physique Types of Boys Nine Through Twelve Years of Age," Microcard Master's Thesis, University of Oregon, 1966.

97. ———, "Stability of Somatotype Components of Boys Twelve Through Seventeen Years of Age and Their Relationships to Selected Physical and Motor Factors," Microcard Doctoral Dissertation, University of Oregon, 1969.

98. Smith, Peter E., "Investigation of Total-Body and Arm Measures of Reaction Time, Movement Time, and Completion Time for Twelve, Fourteen, and Seventeen-Year-Old Athletes and Nonparticipants," Microcard Master's Thesis, University of Oregon, 1968.

99. Smith, Richard J., "Relationships Between Gross and Relative Strength and the Maturity, Physique Type, Body Size, and Motor Ability Elements of Boys Seven, Nine, Twelve, Fifteen, and Seventeen Years of Age," Microcard Doctoral Dissertation, University of Oregon, 1968.

100. Tanner, James M., "Reliability of Anthroposcopic Somatotyping," *American Journal of Physical Anthropology*, 12, No. 2 (June, 1954), pp. 257–265.

101. ———, and J. S. Weiner, "The Reliability of the Photogrammetric Method of Anthropometry," *American Journal of Physical Anthropology*, 7, No. 2 (June, 1949), p. 145.

102. Todd, T. Wingate, *Atlas of Skeletal Maturation: Part I: The Hand.* St. Louis, Mo.: The C. V. Mosby Company, 1937.

103. Tomaras, William A., "The Relationship of Anthropometric and Strength Measures of Junior High School Boys to Various Arm Strength Criteria," Microcard Doctoral Dissertation, University of Oregon, 1958.

104. Torpey, James E., "Factor Analysis of Potential Maturity Indicators of Sixteen-Year-Old Boys," Microcard Doctoral Dissertation, University of Oregon, 1965.

105. Tucker, William B., and William A. Lessa, "Man: A Constitutional Investigation," *Quarterly Review of Biology*, 15, No. 3 (September, 1940), pp. 265–289.

106. Ward, I. Barrymore, "Relationships Between Standing Broad Jump and Selected Physical Variables and Comparison of these Criteria for Twelve and Fifteen-Year-Old Athletes and Non-Athletes," Microcard Master's Thesis, University of Oregon, 1967.

107. Watt, Norman S., "Maturity, Structural, and Motor Convergence Growth Analysis of Boys Seven Through Seventeen Years of Age," Microcard Doctoral Dissertation, University of Oregon, 1963.

108. Weinberg, Herbert A., "Structural, Strength, and Maturity Characteristics as Related to Aspects of the Wetzel Grid for Boys Nine Through Fifteen Years of Age," Microcard Doctoral Dissertation, University of Oregon, 1964.

109. Wetzel, Norman C., *The Treatment of Growth Failures in Children.* Cleveland: NEA Service, Inc., 1948.

110. Whittle, H. Douglas, "Effects of Elementary School Physical Education Upon Some Aspects of Physical, Motor, and Personality Development of Boys Twelve Years of Age," Microcard Doctoral Dissertation, University of Oregon, 1956.

111. Wickens, J. Stuart, "Maturity, Structural, Muscular Strength, and Motor Ability Growth Curves of Boys Nine to Fifteen Years of Age," Microcard Doctoral Dissertation, University of Oregon, 1958.

112. Wiley, Roger C., "Single-Year and Longitudinal Comparisons of Maturity, Physique, Structural, Strength, and Motor Characteristics of Twelve-Year-Old Elementary School Athletes and Nonparticipants," Microcard Doctoral Dissertation, University of Oregon, 1963.

113. Willee, Albert W., "Factor Analysis of Potential Maturity Indices of Nine-Year-Old Boys," Microcard Doctoral Dissertation, University of Oregon, 1964.

Other Medford Theses

(To April 15, 1970)

Other theses in the Medford Boys' Growth Study by graduate students at the University of Oregon are listed below. All of these studies are on Microcards.

Anderson, Robert B., "A Study of Personal Adjustment and Social Status Measures of Nonparticipants and Athletic Groups of Boys Ten to Fifteen Years of Age," Doctoral Dissertation, 1965.

Becker, Charles J., "The Construction of Maturity and Anthropometric Test Norms for Boys Nine Through Fourteen Years of Age," Master's Thesis, 1960.

Broekhoff, Jan, "Relationships Between Physical, Socio-Psychological, and Mental Characteristics of Thirteen-Year-Old Boys," Doctoral Dissertation, 1966.

Buhrmann, Hans G., "Longitudinal Study of the Relationship Between Athletic Participation, Various Social-Psychological Variables, and Academic Achievement of Junior High School Boys," Doctoral Dissertation, 1968.

Clarke, David H., "Social Status and Mental Health of Boys as Related to Their Maturity, Structural Characteristics, and Muscular Strength," Doctoral Dissertation, 1959.

Clayton, Robert D., "Construction of Norms for Strength Tests Composing Rogers' Strength Index Battery for Boys Nine Through Fourteen Years of Age," Master's Thesis, 1960.

Coefield, John R., "Relationship Between Academic Achievement and

Maturity, Physical, and Personality Measures of Twelve-Year-Old Boys," Doctoral Dissertation, 1965.

Cross, John A., "Relationships Between Physical Characteristics of Boys at Twelve and Fifteen Years of Age and Their Personality Characteristics at Eighteen Years of Age," Doctoral Dissertation, 1968.

Day, James A. P., "Relationships Between Intelligence and Selected Physical, Motor, and Strength Characteristics of Boys Nine, Thirteen, and Seventeen Years of Age," Master's Thesis, 1965.

Devine, Barry M., "Analysis of Responses on a Sociometric Questionnaire and the Re-Examination of Structural and Strength Relationships for Nine and Eleven-Year-Old Boys," Master's Thesis, 1960.

DiNucci, James M., "Longitudinal Analysis of the Academic Achievement of Boys Nine to Seventeen Years of Age as Related to Selected Physical Variables," Doctoral Dissertation, 1968.

Docherty, David, "Longitudinal Analysis of the Rate and Pattern of Growth of Selected Maturity, Structural, Strength, and Motor Ability Measures of Boys Ten to Sixteen Years of Age," Master's Thesis, 1967.

Drowatzky, John W., "Mental, Social, Maturity, and Physical Characteristics of Boys Underaged and Normal-Aged in Elementary School Grades," Doctoral Dissertation, 1965.

Flynn, Kenneth W., "Responses on the Davidson Adjective Check List as Related to Maturity, Physical, and Motor Ability Characteristics of Sixteen-Year-Old Boys," Doctoral Dissertation, 1967.

Greene, Walter H., "Interrelationships between Measures of Personal-Social Status and the Relationships of These Measures to Selected Physical Factors of Ten-Year-Old Boys," Master's Thesis, 1961.

———, "Peer Status and Level of Aspiration of Boys as Related to Their Maturity, Physique, Structural, and Motor Ability Characteristics," Doctoral Dissertation, 1964.

Harrison, James C. E., "The Construction of Cable-Tension Strength Test Norms for Boys Seven, Nine, Twelve, and Fifteen Years of Age," Master's Thesis, 1958.

Hindmarch, Robert G., "Significance of Physique, Maturational, Body Size, Strength, Motor Ability, and Reaction Time Characteristics of Eight-Year-Old Boys," Doctoral Dissertation, 1962.

Jarman, Boyd O., "Academic Achievement of Boys, Nine, Twelve, and Fifteen Years of Age as Related to Various Strength and Growth Measures," Master's Thesis, 1958.

———, "Interrelationships Between Academic Achievement and Selected Maturity, Physique, and Motor Measures of Fifteen-Year-Old Boys," Doctoral Dissertation, 1965.

Jordan, David B., "A Longitudinal Analysis of the Mental Health of Boys Age Fifteen to Seventeen Years," Master's Thesis, 1964.

Kozacioghi, Guney, "A Study of the Relationship Between Interests and Physical Traits of Seven and Eight-Year-Old Boys," Master's Thesis, 1960.

Lynde, Robert E., "Longitudinal Analysis of Interest Scores of Boys Ten to Twelve Years of Age as Related to Selected Physical Variables," Master's Thesis, 1968.

———, "Longitudinal Analysis of Occupational Interest Scores of Boys Fifteen Through Seventeen Years of Age as Related to Various Physical Characteristics," Doctoral Dissertation, 1969.

McNally, Eugene W., "Relationships of General Interests to Maturity, Structure, and Strength of Nine Through Fourteen-Year-Old Boys," Doctoral Dissertation, 1960.

Miller, Jeffrey O., "Longitudinal Analysis of the Relationship Between Measures of Self-Determination and Social Interaction and Selected Physical Variables in Boys Twelve to Seventeen Years of Age," Doctoral Dissertation, 1967.

Moutis, Nicholas P., "Longitudinal Analysis of Academic Achievement Related to Selected Maturational, Structural, Strength and Motor Characteristics of Boys Ten Through Twelve Years of Age," Dissertation, 1967.

Olson, Arne L., "Characteristics of Fifteen-Year-Old Boys Classified as Athletes, Scientists, Fine Artists, Leaders, Scholars, or as Poor Students or Delinquents," Doctoral Dissertation, 1961.

Page, Joseph T., "Comparison of the Academic Achievement of Boys Ten, Thirteen, and Sixteen Years of Age as Related to Selected Non-Academic Variables," Doctoral Dissertation, 1965

Reynolds, Robert M., "Responses on the Davidson Adjective Check List as Related to Maturity, Physical, and Mental Characteristics of Thirteen-Year-Old Boys," Doctoral Dissertation, 1965.

Stafford, Elba G., "Single-Year and Longitudinal Comparisons of Intelligence and Academic Achievement of Elementary and Junior High School Athletes and Nonparticipants," Doctoral Dissertation, 1968.

Stolsig, Charles A., "The Construction of Cable-Tension Strength Test Norms for Boys Eight, Ten, Thirteen, and Sixteen years of Age." Master's Thesis, 1960.

Stratton, Stephen T., "Methods of Grouping Boys Nine Years of Age According to Their Level of Aspiration Based on Grip Strength Efforts," Master's Thesis, 1960.

———, "The Reliability of Level of Aspiration Scores and Their Relationship to Measures of Growth and Development of Eleven-Year-Old Boys," Doctoral Dissertation, 1964.